WHEN ROCK MET HIP-HOP

ALSO BY STEVEN BLUSH

American Hardcore: A Tribal History (2001)
.45 Dangerous Minds: The Most Intense Interviews From Seconds Magazine
American Hair Metal (2007)
American Hardcore: A Tribal History (Second Edition) (2010)
Lost Rockers: Broken Dreams and Crashed Careers (2016)
New York Rock: From the Rise of the Velvet Underground to the Fall of CBGB (2017)
Bustin' Balls: World Team Tennis 1974-1978, Pro Sports, Pop Culture and Progressive Politics (2020)
American Hair Metal: Can't Get Enough (Second Edition) (2023)
When Rock Met Disco: The Story of How The Rolling Stones, Rod Stewart, KISS, Queen, Blondie, and More Got Their Groove on in the Me Generation (2023)
When Rock Met Reggae: How the Cultural Crossover of Bob Marley, The Clash, The Specials and More Changed the Face of Rock Music (2024)

WHEN ROCK MET HIP-HOP

HOW RUN-DMC, AEROSMITH, ANTHRAX, THE BEASTIE BOYS, AND MORE CROSSED CULTURAL AND MUSICAL BOUNDARIES

STEVEN BLUSH

Backbeat Books

BACKBEAT BOOKS
Bloomsbury Publishing Inc, 1359 Broadway, 12th Floor, New York, NY 10018, USA
Bloomsbury Publishing Plc, 50 Bedford Square, London, WC1B 3DP, UK
Bloomsbury Publishing Ireland, 29 Earlsfort Terrace, Dublin 2, D02 AY28, Ireland
BLOOMSBURY, BACKBEAT BOOKS and the Diana logo are trademarks of Bloomsbury Publishing Plc
First published in the United States of America 2026

Copyright © Steven Blush, 2026
Cover design: Sally Rineheart

Cover images (top to bottom): © Niels Van Iperen / Hulton Archive / Getty Images; © Ron Wolfson / Rock Negatives / MediaPunch / Alamy; © Mick Hutson / Getty Images; © Raymond Boyd / Michael Ochs Archives / Getty Images

All rights reserved. No part of this publication may be: i) reproduced or transmitted in any form, electronic or mechanical, including photocopying, recording or by means of any information storage or retrieval system without prior permission in writing from the publishers; or ii) used or reproduced in any way for the training, development or operation of artificial intelligence (AI) technologies, including generative AI technologies. The rights holders expressly reserve this publication from the text and data mining exception as per Article 4(3) of the Digital Single Market Directive (EU) 2019/790.

Bloomsbury Publishing Inc does not have any control over, or responsibility for, any third-party websites referred to or in this book. All internet addresses given in this book were correct at the time of going to press. The author and publisher regret any inconvenience caused if addresses have changed or sites have ceased to exist, but can accept no responsibility for any such changes.

Library of Congress Cataloging-in-Publication Data

Names: Blush, Steven author
Title: When rock met hip-hop : how Run-DMC, Aerosmith, Anthrax, the Beastie
  Boys, and more crossed cultural and musical boundaries / Steven Blush.
Description: New York : Backbeat Books / Bloomsbury Publishing Inc, 2025. |
  Includes bibliographical references and index.
Identifiers: LCCN 2025030940 (print) | LCCN 2025030941 (ebook) | ISBN
  9781493078028 trade paperback | ISBN 9781493078035 epub | ISBN
  9798765161647 pdf
Subjects: LCSH: Rap (Music)--History and criticism | Rock
  music--1981-1990--History and criticism
Classification: LCC ML3531 .B58 2025 (print) | LCC ML3531 (ebook) | DDC
  782.421649--dc23/eng/20250730
LC record available at https://lccn.loc.gov/2025030940
LC ebook record available at https://lccn.loc.gov/2025030941

ISBN:
PB: **978-1-4930-7802-8**
ePDF: **979-8-7651-6164-7**
eBook: **978-1-4930-7803-5**

Typeset by Deanta Global Publishing Services, Chennai, India
Printed and bound in the United States of America

For product safety related questions contact productsafety@bloomsbury.com.

To find out more about our authors and books visit www.bloomsbury.com and sign up for our newsletters.

Dedicated to my homegirls, Alyssa Fisher and Jackie Fisher Blush

CONTENTS

FOREWORD BY BILL ADLER	IX
CAST OF CHARACTERS	XII
AUTHOR'S NOTES	XX
PROLOGUE	XXV
INTRODUCTION	1
EARLY HIP-HOP	7
NEW WAVE RAP	23
CROSSOVER	39
BILLY SQUIER	47
RUN-DMC	51
WALK THIS WAY	59
DEF JAM	69
PAUL'S BOUTIQUE AND BEYOND	97
PUBLIC ENEMY	107
BRING THE NOISE	115

CONTENTS

NEW YORK	123
WEST COAST	139
JUDGMENT NIGHT	173
DETROIT	187
TRIP-HOP	193
ALTERNATIVE RAP	199
ALT-ROCK RAP	205
NU-METAL	215
LOUD ROCKS	225
CONCLUSION	235
APPENDIX: LOST GEMS	241
BIBLIOGRAPHY	256
INDEX	279
ABOUT THE AUTHOR	291

FOREWORD
BY BILL ADLER

When considering the career of Mr. Steven Blush, it seems pretty clear that the child was the father of the man, or at least that young man was the father of today's middle-aged gent.

Steven is the author of *When Rock Met Hip-Hop*, a collection of question-and-answer interviews with the people who, song-by-song, made the musical marriage described in the title happen. The exact format was defined by *Seconds* Magazine, which was founded, edited, and independently published by Blush. *Seconds*'s debut issue first saw the light of day in 1986. Promoting interviews within its pages, the cover featured the first cover story of the Beastie Boys, a New York hardcore punk band whose members had already been transformed by hip-hop and whose debut album, *Licensed to Ill*, was at that very moment making it the face of rock music lovers all over the world to experience the same revolutionary transformation.

For its part, *Seconds* was the magazine where rock and hip-hop met. Blush was a relative newcomer to hip-hop, but he had been—and remained—a devoted adherent of punk, hardcore, and heavy metal for years. (The author, in 2001's *American Hardcore: A Tribal History*, asserted that hardcore "was a dirty little secret that nobody talked about when it came to music.") That is why, the Beasties aside, the other band

FOREWORD

names spelled out on the cover—and interviewed at length inside—were Metallica, Butthole Surfers, the Damned, Circle Jerks, Radiators, Volcano Suns, the Sound, and Culturcide. Rock and rap aside, the debut issue of *Seconds* was also where and when rock met R&B (in an interview devoted to Big Joe Turner), and rock met Go-Go (in a story about the red-hot funk then radiating out of Washington, DC).

Of course, even in the early years, this hardcore/hip-hop affinity was never confined to the Beasties or *Seconds*. Blush's taste has always been broad. In *Details*, his account of Anthrax's decision to cut a cover version of Public Enemy's "Bring the Noise"—and Chuck D and Flavor Flav's decision to join the thrash metal crew on wax—Blush quotes Chuck shrugging off the notion that this partnership was somehow unlikely: "We said, 'Why not do something that will show both audiences that it is the same thing? It is attitude, speed, and still being hard without being soft.'"

This book tracks the evolving rock-rap synthesis starting with the emergence of the very first rap records in 1979 through detailed accounts of two decades' worth of boundary-crossers, including Onyx, Red Hot Chili Peppers, Body Count, Rage Against the Machine, Eminem, Kid Rock, De La Soul, Beck, Luscious Jackson, Limp Bizkit, and System of a Down—as well as such one-time-only novelty hookups as the Fat Boys/Beach Boys' rap-juvenation of "Wipeout."

All of Steven's outstanding research and analysis aside, it is worth noting that hip-hop met rock well before rock met hip-hop. Hip-hop music at the start—during the half-dozen years (1973–79) before the advent of rap records—was primarily a DJ's art form. These mixmasters listened to all kinds of records in search of funky tidbits that they could play over and over again, cutting seamlessly from one turntable to a second turntable holding another copy of the same record, to create a hard-rocking bed for the rhymes spit by the rappers at the front of the stage.

In 1986, a pair of Bronx DJs, "Breakbeat Lenny" Roberts and "Breakbeat Lou" Flores, compiled and released the introductory volume

FOREWORD

of *Ultimate Breaks and Beats* (Street Beat Records), a game-changing series that would grow to comprise twenty-five volumes over the next five years. Much of it was soul and funk, and a considerable slice was jazz. However, there was also plenty of rock, including the Rolling Stones' "Honky Tonk Women," Billy Squier's "The Big Beat," Aerosmith's "Walk This Way," Thin Lizzy's "Johnny the Fox," Steve Miller Band's "Take the Money and Run," John Cougar's "Jack & Diane," ESG's "U.F.O.," Liquid Liquid's "Cavern," and Gary Numan's "Films." The series' first volume even included "Mary, Mary" by the Monkees (TV's G-rated version of the Beatles)—a recording that never charted on *Billboard*'s Hot 100, let alone its Hot Black Singles chart—but was nonetheless sampled by Run-DMC for their 1988 hit of the same name.

Apart from its intrinsic appeal, one of the primary reasons hip-hop music succeeded so quickly and powerfully is that the pop music of the 1980s was comparatively weak. It was not only that mainstream rock had curdled into little more than big hair and spandex by then. Funk was likewise beginning to parody itself; the golden era of soul was a decade prior, and disco was splintering into a dozen subgenres of lesser impact. In short, the moment was ripe for disruption and regeneration. It was the moment when rock and hip-hop collided.

Ultimately, hip-hop's crossover appeal went far beyond its effect on rock music. Consider the chemistry that occurred when R&B and hip-hop intersected. And jazz. And then country music. Am I dreaming, or might all of this savory tumult justify a whole new separate series of books?

Meanwhile, let us salute Mr. Blush for his deep dive into rock's various romances. The excellent *When Rock Met Hip-Hop* happens to be the third volume in a trilogy of its own. The first, published in 2023, was *When Rock Met Disco*. The second, published in 2024, was *When Rock Met Reggae*. I believe the moment Steven Blush met rock has become a blessing to music lovers everywhere.

CAST OF CHARACTERS

AARON FUCHS: Tuff City Records

AD-ROCK: Beastie Boys

ADAM DUBIN: video director

ADAM YAUCH: Beastie Boys

AFRIKA BAMBAATAA: Soul Sonic Force

ALI SHAHEED MUHAMMAD: A Tribe Called Quest

ANTHONY KIEDIS: Red Hot Chili Peppers

ARTHUR BAKER: producer

BARRINGTON HENDRICKS: jpegmafia

BART LEWIS: Smashed Gladys

BECK: pop star

BIG DADDY KANE: rapper

BILL ADLER: Def Jam historian

BILL GOULD: Faith No More

BILL LASWELL: producer

BILL STEPHNEY: Def Jam

CAST OF CHARACTERS

BILLY GRAZIADEI: Biohazard

BILLY SQUIRE: guitarist, vocalist

BOBBY CHOUINARD: Billy Squire

BOBBY HAMBEL: Biohazard

BOBBY MARZ: Marz

BOBBY SIMMONS: Stetsasonic

BRAD WILK: Rage Against the Machine

BRAD XAVIER: Kottonmouth Kings

B-REAL: Cypress Hill

CARLO McCORMICK: culture critic

CHARLIE AHEARN: filmmaker

CHARLIE BENANTE: Anthrax

CHESTER BENNINGTON: Linkin Park

CHIP LOVE: Hesher

CHRIS CORNELL: Audioslave (RIP)

CHRIS STEIN: Blondie

CHUCK D: Public Enemy

CHUCK MOSELEY: Faith No More (RIP)

CLEM BURKE: Blondie

CL SMOOTH: Pete Rock & CL Smooth

CORY ROBBINS: Profile Records

CRAZY LEGS: breakdancer

DADDY G: Massive Attack

DADDY X: Kottonmouth Kings

DALE THOMPSON: Bride

DANNY BOY: House of Pain

DANNY SCHULER: Biohazard

DANTE ROSS: producer

CAST OF CHARACTERS

DAVE MUSTAINE: Megadeth
DARYL JENIFER: Bad Brains
DEBORAH HARRY: Blondie
DEL THA FUNKEE HOMOSAPIEN: rapper
DJ LETHAL: House of Pain, Limp Bizkit
DJ MUGGS: Cypress Hill
DJ SHADOW: mixologist
DR. DRE: NWA
DMC: Run-DMC
DONDI: graffiti artist
DONNIE IRIS: pop star
DONNY RADELJIC: Shootyz Groove
DOUG POMEROY: engineer
DRAKE: rapper
DREW STONE: NYHC scene
D.X. FERRIS: author
EAZY E: NWA
EDDIE MARTINEZ: "Rock Box" guitarist
EL-P: Run the Jewels
ERIC HOFFERT: The Speedies
EVAN SEINFELD: Biohazard
EVERLAST: House of Pain
FAB 5 FREDDY: *Yo! MTV Raps*
FERNANDO ROSARIO: Smashed Gladys
FIRSTBORN: Young Black Teenagers
FLEA: Red Hot Chili Peppers
FRED DURST: Limp Bizkit
FREDRO STARR: Onyx

CAST OF CHARACTERS

FUTURA 2000: graffiti artist
GABBY GLASER: Luscious Jackson
GEOFF BARROW: Portishead
GERARD LOVE: Teenage Fanclub
GIL BITTON: Endo
GLENN DANZIG: The Misfits, Danzig
GLENN O'BRIEN: *Interview* Magazine
GODFATHER: Boo-Yaa T.R.I.B.E.
GRANDMASTER FLASH: Grandmaster Flash and the Furious Five
GREG GUTFELD: Fox News
HANK SHOCKLEE: Bomb Squad production team
HAPPY WALTERS: Immortal Records
HARRY ALLEN: Public Enemy publicist
HAVOC: Mobb Deep
HUEY MORGAN: Fun Lovin' Criminals
IAN ASTBURY: The Cult
ICE CUBE: NWA
ICE-T: Body Count
ILL BILL: rapper
J MASCIS: Dinosaur Jr.
JALIL: Whodini
JAM MASTER JAY: Run-DMC
JERRY HELLER: NWA manager
JILL CUNNIFF: Luscious Jackson
JIM MARTIN: Faith No More
JIMI HAZEL: 24-7 Spyz
JIMMY DESTRI: Blondie
JIMMY G: Murphy's Law

CAST OF CHARACTERS

JIMMY POP: Bloodhound Gang

JOE PERRY: Aerosmith

JOEY BELLADONNA: Anthrax

JOHN CONNOR: Dog Eat Dog

JOHN KING: Chung King House of Metal

JOHN KING: Dust Brothers

JOHN KOLODNER: Geffen Records

JOHN LYDON: Public Image Ltd.

JOHN McCREA: Cake

JONATHAN DAVIS: Korn

JONNY Z: Megaforce Records

KAMRON: Young Black Teenagers

KANGOL KID: UTFO

KATE SCHELLENBACH: Beastie Boys

KEITH SHOCKLEE: Bomb Squad production team

KERRY KING: Slayer

KID ROCK: rapper

KILLER MIKE: Run the Jewels

KIM GORDON: Sonic Youth

KOOL HERC: DJ

KOOL MOE DEE: rapper

KURTIS BLOW: rapper

LAJON WITHERSPOON: Sevendust

LARRY SMITH: Run-DMC producer

LL COOL J: rapper

LOU KOLLER: Sick of It All

MACHINE GUN KELLY: rapper

MALCOLM McLAREN: rapper, entrepreneur (RIP)

CAST OF CHARACTERS

MARK ARM: Mudhoney

MARK McGRATH: Sugar Ray

MARIA FERRERO: publicist

MARIO CALDATO, JR: engineer

MC SERCH: 3rd Bass

MELLE MEL: Grandmaster Flash and the Furious Five

METHOD MAN: rapper

MICHAEL FRANTI: The Disposable Heroes of Hiphoprisy

MICHAEL HOLMAN: artist, filmmaker

MICHAEL McKEEGAN: Therapy?

MIKE BORDIN: Faith No More

MIKE D: Beastie Boys

MIKE DOUGHTY: Soul Coughing

MIKE SCHNAPP: industry insider, celebrity DJ

MIKE SHINODA: Linkin Park

MIKE SIMPSON: Dust Brothers

MONEY MARK: keyboardist

MONICA LYNCH: Tommy Boy Records

MUNKY SHAFFER: Korn

NECRO: Non Phixion

NITEBOB: Aerosmith soundman

PAGE HAMILTON: Helmet

PETE NICE: 3rd Bass

PETER FLUID: 24-7 Spyz

POSDNUOS: De La Soul

PRINCE MARKIE DEE: Fat Boys

Q-TIP: A Tribe Called Quest

RAEKWON: Wu-Tang Clan

CAST OF CHARACTERS

REY OROPEZA: Downset

RICK RUBIN: Def Jam, American Recordings

ROBERT DEL NAJA: Massive Attack

RODDY BOTTUM: Faith No More

RUN: Run-DMC

RUSSELL SIMMONS: Def Jam, Rush Management

SAGE FRANCIS: rapper

SCARFACE: Geto Boys

SCHOOLLY D: rapper

SCOTT IAN: Anthrax

SCOTT KOENIG: Rush Management (RIP)

SEBASTIAN STEINBERG: Soul Coughing

SE'DIVINE THE MASTER MIND: World Famous Supreme Team

SEN DOG: Cypress Hill

SENSATIONAL: rapper

SERJ TANKIAN: System of a Down

SHAVO ODADJIAN: System of a Down

SHIFTY SHELLSHOCK: Crazy Town

SIR MIX-A-LOT: rapper

SPIKE XAVIER: Kottonmouth Kings

STEVEN TYLER: Aerosmith

STICKY FINGAZ: Onyx

TED NUGENT: rock star

THE PRINCIPLE: Caveman

T LA ROCK: rapper (RIP)

TOM ARAYA: Slayer

TOM MORELLO: Rage Against the Machine

TOMMY SILVERMAN: Tommy Boy Records

CAST OF CHARACTERS

TREVOR HORN: producer

TRICKY: rapper, musician

TRUGOY: De La Soul

VERNON REID: Living Color

VINCE NEIL: Motley Crue

VIOLENT J: Insane Clown Posse

WAYNE STATIC: Static-X

WES BORLAND: Limp Bizkit

WONDER MIKE: The Sugarhill Gang

ZACK DE LA ROCHA: Rage Against the Machine

AUTHOR'S NOTES

WHEN ROCK MET HIP-HOP: Beastie Boys and Run-DMC, modern music revolutionaries, 1987. Trinity Mirror / Mirrorpix / Alamy Stock Photo.

> *I dress to kill, I love the style*
> *I'm an MC, you know, who's versatile*
> —Run-DMC, "Sucker MCs"

Welcome to *When Rock Met Hip-Hop*, the third book in a trilogy that encompasses 2003's *When Rock Met Disco* and 2024's *When Rock Met*

AUTHOR'S NOTES

Reggae. In the first two books, I researched the histories of music movements that merged with rock to create some of the most incredible music of our time. I was a club DJ and a dedicated collector of the disco and reggae eras. However, I was a few years too young to participate in those lifestyles.

The 1980s and 1990s were among the most significant periods in music history. New styles emerged, including hip-hop, new wave, hardcore punk, and the rise of thrash metal. A critical development was the varying degrees of crossover between these genres, which led to new variations that have shaped today's music. Combining rock and hip-hop cultures was pivotal, as it infused fresh energy into the music and had a profound impact on global culture.

As a participant in the early days of New York hip-hop, I can offer insights based on my firsthand experiences. I cannot hold back with facts because I was actively involved in the scene. This tome is not my first book. I am not thirty-five, but I am attempting to understand a culture that emerged forty to fifty years ago; I lived through it. More importantly, my life felt enriched by it.

As someone with broad taste, not just writing about rap, I related to the rebel attitude and supported it. Throughout my career, I have reviewed and interviewed numerous prominent figures in rock and hip-hop, contributing to major publications such as *Spin, Interview, Details, High Times,* and *The Times of London.* I served as the music editor for *Paper* Magazine and publisher of *Seconds* Magazine. Additionally, I DJed at legendary clubs and parties, digging through crates to bring rock and rap together at the hottest NYC nightspots. I also promoted or managed several notable Downtown nightclubs.

I attended classic shows and private showcases, where I mingled with noteworthy figures in the hip-hop world. The gold and platinum records on my wall serve as evidence of these experiences. This background gives

AUTHOR'S NOTES

ROCK MEETS RAP, Seconds Magazine #1 foresaw the future, photo: Josh Cheuse; art direction Bob Piersanti; publisher: Steven Blush/¾1986. Author's Collection.

AUTHOR'S NOTES

me a unique perspective as a historian, and you, the reader, will benefit from my firsthand experiences living on the front lines.

This history of rock and hip-hop is not a story of intersecting genres but a narrative about cultural cross-collisions. It marks the point at which Black hip-hop kids connected with punk and rock subcultures, evolving into an increasingly interracial phenomenon. The earliest rap records mimicked or sampled disco music—like "Rapper's Delight" based on "Good Times" by Chic.

When Rock Met Hip-Hop explores the origins and evolution of the diverse rap movement, highlighting pivotal moments in the crossover between rock and hip-hop. It begins with urban DJs discovering the breakbeats of Billy Squier and AC/DC. Milestones include Rick Rubin and the Beastie Boys collaborating with Slayer guitarist Kerry King on "No Sleep Till Brooklyn," and Run-DMC's Jam Master Jay blending his turntables with Aerosmith's Joe Perry's guitar solos in "Walk This Way."

This work also highlights Anthrax's heavy metal remix of Public Enemy's "Bring the Noise," as well as grunge producer Butch Vig's Sub Pop label reinvention of House of Pain's "Shamrocks & Shenanigans." Additionally, it showcases the intense energy of the Onyx-Biohazard collaboration "Slam" and the pivotal rock-rap soundtrack of *Judgment Night*. The narrative culminates with the groundbreaking first album by Rage Against the Machine, Aesop Rock's "Kill 'Em All" deconstructing King Crimson's "20th Century Schizoid Man," and the '00s emergence of "nu-metal," which signaled the decline in critical acclaim for this alliance of rock and hip-hop.

The interviewees provided leads for further research, often suggesting that I speak with other individuals involved in the scene. I want to extend my heartfelt thanks to everyone involved with this labor of love: Tony Mann, George Petros, Michael Holman, Carlo McCormick,

AUTHOR'S NOTES

Pete Nice, Bill Adler, Drew Stone, Danny Boy O'Connor, Evan Seinfeld, Michael J. Schnapp, DX Ferris, Fernando Rosario, and Bob "Nitebob" Czaykowski.

Special thanks to my agent, Lee Sobel, for his support and encouragement in launching this trilogy. Profound gratitude to Chris Chappell, Barbara Claire, Emily Burr, Peter Perez, Carey Cameron, Karthik Manickam, Jessica Thwaite, and the entire Backbeat-Bloomsbury team. Extra special thanks to powerhouse publicists Leyla Turkkan, Jamie Roberts, and Maria Ferrero, as well as to the entire Blush, Radick, Fisher, and Goldstein families.

When Rock Met Hip-Hop is one of pop music's most remarkable stories; although the genre came and went, it changed the course of music history. My involvement with rock and hip-hop has made me love this story even more.

Steven Blush
NYC 2026

PROLOGUE

The richest, fuck around, you won't fix it
Toke, heavy metal, settle shit, rebel shit
—Ice-T, "The 7th"

DANNY BOY: We all grew up in the 70s listening to Led Zeppelin, AC/DC, and Rush. Being a regular white kid back then, that's what we were into. There was no hip-hop at the time, but we understood what a breakbeat was. I hear a hip-hop beat when I hear the monster drum sound of "Black In Black." When I listen to classic Zeppelin, I hear a dope rhyming pattern. (2024)

ICE-T: I've always been into metal. I can reflect on listening to records by Sabbath, T. Rex, Mott The Hoople, and Traffic. All of my records have interesting samples like that. I've always had a rock and roll state of mind. Now, I think that rock and roll is any time that you rock and roll the system. If you rock the system, you're doin' rock and roll, meaning rap is rock and roll. (1991)

SEN DOG: Metal bands were everywhere we grew up. When you went to parties, it might be a DJ party or a rock and roll party with guys playing their instruments in the backyard. The music levels were incredible

PROLOGUE

at that point because you had metalheads, hard rock dudes, b-boys breakdancing and pop-locking, and some people just barely starting to rap. I went to these metal parties to get drunk or smoke, but I started paying close attention to the music. As the years progressed, I became more of a metalhead. (2022)

CHUCK D: Metal has two things I love: attitude and speed. Metal shows were a learning experience for me. I watched sound and lighting technicians enhance metal groups. Seeing metal shows, I realized that rap groups are missing out on a lot. One thing I know about metal is that there is a genuine attitude behind it, so I give a lot to my audience. I also know that other rap groups can learn from metal when kicking it out to their audience. (1988)

SCARFACE: I was in a heavy metal band in junior high: High Energy. The kids in school called me Jimi. Judas Priest was the best; I love Rob Halford. "Freewheel Burning" was the shit. I'm a big fan of Southern rock, too. Billy Gibbons and Dusty Hill from ZZ Top visited us in the studio for our last record. That was unbelievable. (1994)

DMC: Rob Halford is incredible. I don't know if he knows it, but he is fucking amazing. He's like James Brown, Michael Jackson, Freddie Mercury, Frank Sinatra, Sammy Davis Jr., and Chuck D all rolled into one! (2018)

EL-P: I've always had an attraction to heavy music, from heavy rock and metal to heavy rap and everything. I enjoy anything that gets to music's more emotional and dark side. I also grew up listening to the Gang of Four, Suicide, the Melvins, the Clash, and all the hip-hop music that influenced me. EPMD was heavy. Public Enemy was heavy. Ice Cube was heavy. I've always gone toward that realm. What got me moving was stuff that punched you in the gut. (2018)

PROLOGUE

KILLER MIKE: I'm lucky to have grown up when you could see Run-DMC and Metallica the same summer, like 1983–84—whether it was *Kill 'Em All* or *Run-DMC*. My mom and my sisters were into the light and airy stuff. But I was into rage. Early rap and metal provided an outlet, so you didn't have to be angry. You get it all out and play the music as loud as possible. Even before then, the rock I gravitated toward was heavy, so it was Zeppelin, Sabbath, and Southern rock. It always had darkness to it. And it had to feel cinematic. (2018)

NECRO: We loved extreme music and started developing this sick style. It took three years to transform into it fully. I was never influenced by the metal-rap shit done previous to my shit. Some of that stuff is legendary, like Run-DMC and Aerosmith, but it didn't make me want to do it. I knew it was time to create a fusion for my goals, and I did that. (2007)

MACHINE GUN KELLY: Before I started listening to rap music, I was really into metal and punk. I listened to that whole era of heavy music. I got picked on as a kid because of how I dressed. Metal and punk music got me through that tough time. I know many people don't understand it, but I love metal. I think being on the Warped Tour helped many people know where I was coming from musically. I also learned that many of the metal dudes on the tour loved rap so much. They'd say, "Come check out these beats I made!" It was incredible to see that! (2013)

SCHOOLLY D: I've shared stages with the Red Hot Chili Peppers and Firehose. But when you go back to the roots of rock, it's Black. When you say "rock" now, the first eighty artists you're gonna think about are white. Now, I'm not a racist. But what I'm sayin' is, "If we started this shit, how come we can't play it or take it back and do what we want with it without people sayin', 'It's not that way,' to 'This is token,' or 'You're copying REO Speedwagon or Cinderella?' What the fuck do you mean

PROLOGUE

I'm fuckin' copying Cinderella?" What are people saying to us? I can't use a guitar! It's fucked up when you think about it. (1988)

ICE CUBE: Rock and roll is not an instrument; it's not even a style of music. Rock and roll is a spirit that has evolved since the emergence of blues, jazz, bebop, soul, R&B, rock, heavy metal, punk rock, and hip-hop. What connects us all is that spirit. Rock and roll is not conforming to the people who came before you and creating your path in music and life. Rock and roll is outside the box. And rock and roll is what we do because all we ever wanted was to tell the world, "Damn, that shit was dope." (2016)

SENSATIONAL: I had never heard rock and roll before I discovered hip-hop. I love loud music and enjoy partying. But I never listened to that raw rock and roll sound before Run-DMC, Public Enemy, and all that crazy stuff with the Beastie Boys. Now, it's all part of the same flavor. (2000)

B-REAL: I was always a rock fan before I even knew what hip-hop was. Ironically, I became a hip-hop fan because I started out as a metal fan. It took a while to get comfortable with live instrumentation because it's easier to perform hip-hop with turntables because the sound isn't overwhelming. Live instrumentation is more complicated. There's more energy because the onstage sound is so powerful that it's overwhelming in a good way. (2018)

EAZY-E: I've given my life to hip-hop, and rapping is where it's at. But rock and roll is the shit, and heavy metal is the ultimate form of rock. When I see these rock dawgs onstage, I see how hard they're bringin' it. Rap needs to rock that hard. The future of rap is when it rocks like heavy metal. (1994)

INTRODUCTION

> *You want to be a rock superstar in the biz*
> *And take shit from people who don't know what it is*
> —Cypress Hill, "(Rock) Superstar"

Rock music was the most significant white sound of the late twentieth century, and hip-hop emerged as the fresh new Black sound for the 1980s. The creative fusion of genres breathed new life into rock, energized hip-hop, and sparked a surge in the music world. Cultures with more similarities than differences found common ground in a crossover sound. Welcome to *When Rock Met Hip-Hop*.

EVERLAST: Hip-hop is about freedom, speaking your mind, and expressing yourself. That's how we live. Rock music has been the ultimate expression of freedom since the white people got their shit from the Black man. When you mix rock and hip-hop, the total energy of the guitars and beats is off the hook. It's natural and electric. (1993)

Segregation defined the music of the 1970s and 1980s. Black radio wheezed with jazz fusion, urban contemporary, "Quiet Storm" soul, and orchestral disco. White rockers hated "black music," but the sounds they espoused were rooted in Black music. Rock critics dismissed any African American guitarist not named Jimi. So-called open-minded punk rockers paid lip service to rock against racism but buried their heads in a "Disco Sucks" mindset. Every pop formula had seemingly gone stale.

DMC: When I was a kid growing up in Hollis, Queens, New York, early 1970s rock radio was incredible. It was Sly & The Family Stone. It was also Neil Young with Crosby, Stills, Nash & Young. It was the Jackson Five with Led Zeppelin, the Rolling Stones, and the Beatles. It was Janis Joplin and Diana Ross. So you had this whole world that talked about, outside of love and living the rock star life, the real issues that affected people. But things quickly changed. (2022)

In the early days of hip-hop, mainstream radio hesitated to play rap music. However, advertisers had no qualms about spending money on rappers. Fat Boys' Prince Markie Dee appeared in the first Swatch watch ads. Sprite began its decades-long connection to hip-hop by featuring Kurtis Blow in some of its first national advertisements. Run-DMC's "My Adidas" caught the attention of the head of Adidas, striking the first formal endorsement deal with a non-athlete, giving $1M in 1986 to start a long-term relationship.

RUN: When Run-DMC and Adidas hooked up, it changed music, changed product endorsement, and changed business. It was more than just Run-DMC being the first to get a sneaker product endorsement with an athletic company. We brought people together; we brought business together; we brought genres together. We have impacted all the generations up until now. (2013)

The melding of rock and hip-hop could have been a smoother transition. The artists and their fans were slow to accept change from their

INTRODUCTION

favorite musicians, whether from rap crews or heavy metal rock groups. But what almost every one of these seminal ensembles blending different styles had in common was that they originated in New York—back when NYC was the most tolerant, anything-goes artistic apex in the world.

MIKE SCHNAPP: The rockers wanted to rap, and the rappers wanted to rock. The rappers talked about being rock stars because they wanted that identity. Anytime you hear guitar in rap, you're intrigued. Rock and rap originated in a collaborative New York melting pot, as the city has always been a proudly multicultural hub. However, many metal bands around the world have never incorporated rap into their music. (2024)

Before the astounding ascent of Def Jam Recordings, Rick Rubin and Russell Simmons co-produced Run-DMC's third album, 1986's *Raising Hell*, for Profile Records. Punk guitarist Rubin loved underground hip-hop but understood that rap had a perception problem with being "real music." That was the thinking behind his pursuit of Aerosmith for the "Walk This Way" collaboration with Run-DMC, which paved the way for the rap-rock movement that reverberated in music for years. Rick had some experience in this matter, having achieved a modicum of success bridging rock and hip-hop on a 1985 indie 12" with the punky Beastie Boys rapping over AC/DC's "Back in Black."

CHUCK D: Rock is, and will always be, in a world of its own. Rock has its rules; they have rock radio if they can't get on pop radio. Rap radio can grow, but all other aspects of rap and hip-hop must grow as well. But when you bring together rock and hip-hop, it's easier to get the hip-hop across to the rock crowd. (1996)

"Walk This Way" had a profound impact on rock and hip-hop audiences. It is now widely considered one of music history's most important and influential records. Rubin's 1986 rock-rap opus *Licensed to Ill* by the Beastie Boys sounded like his simultaneous production of Slayer's *Reign in Blood*. Scott Ian of Anthrax turned up the volume on his band's 1991 deconstruction of Public Enemy's "Bring the Noise." Rap began as a bunch of singles; the rock-rap crossover elevated hip-hop to album status.

HANK SHOCKLEE: Hip-hop and rock and roll are almost the same. In hip-hop and rock and roll, you can get that same kind of energy from using different instruments. Rock and roll is primarily associated with the use of guitars. If you weren't playing a guitar, you'd be considered that you weren't doing rock and roll. I wanted to do rock and roll, but I was also deeply into hip-hop, so I tried to combine breakdancing and rock and roll to see how you could blend those two styles together. (2005)

The West Coast took over in 1992 with the *Rage Against the Machine* album and 1993's *Judgment Night* soundtrack featuring musical pairings ranging from Helmet and House of Pain to Pearl Jam and Cypress Hill. That development opened doors for a new generation of California "nu-metal," from Korn to System of a Down to Linkin Park.

TOM MORELLO: I was excited by the prospect of playing hip-hop music within the context of a punk rock band, and I wasn't going to make any excuses for not being a DJ. At that time, my chief influences were Terminator X and Jam Master Jay, and I was determined to recreate the record scratching and DJ elements—those rich, bizarre textures—on my guitar. (2022)

INTRODUCTION

Merging rock and hip-hop was difficult for most hardcore rappers, who instinctively understood white audience crossover was not "true to the game." Crossing over requires a multicultural mindset, confidence, and tolerance.

CL SMOOTH: If you add on with the rock audience to what you have, it's not a matter of, "Yo, because you have a white audience, you lose your black audience." It's that you have the gift of having both. Me going into an arena full of white people is not selling out. My spiritual vibe is never gonna change. It will make me know that more people are listening to me besides my boys on the corner. (1994)

RAEKWON: You gotta work hard in this business. You gotta get out to your fans and kick it to them like regular niggas. That's hard for me because I'm coming from the streets. It's hard for me to put on that superstar status. That's what I like about all these grunge rock bands. I'm not saying they come from the streets because they don't. But I like how there's no superstar shit going on. (1995)

EARLY HIP-HOP

*Now, what you hear is not a test, I'm rappin' to the beat
And me, the groove, and my friends are gonna try to
move your feet*
—The Sugarhill Gang, "Rapper's Delight" (1979)

To understand the rise of hip-hop, it's crucial to know how it started. Hip-hop's early days can be traced back to the 1970s underground culture that emerged within a three-mile radius of Harlem and the South Bronx. At that time, New York City was facing severe socioeconomic challenges, particularly affecting minority communities. The city was on the brink of bankruptcy, crime rates were soaring, and widespread social and financial instability prevailed. This low-income environment gave rise to the rapid growth of hip-hop as a form of expression and entertainment, reflecting the urban struggle of the time. Hip-hop originated in the parks during the summer and in community centers at other times of the year, where DJs played a mix of disco, funk, and soul.

KEITH SHOCKLEE: Hip-hop started down at the parks in the summertime. It was a sound system culture, which then evolved into a DJ culture, marking the beginning of the sound system era. Well, we didn't have a term for records. We just played whatever was hot. Disco, funk, soul—whatever was hot and funky—was what you played in the park. (2023)

MICHAEL HOLMAN: More than any other musical movement, disco is the mother of hip-hop. There are different musical progenitors—rock in some ways, and obviously, funk and soul were a big part of it. However, disco was more immediate; it was going strong while hip-hop was being born before it even had a name. You had people putting on park jams outdoors in the summer and in community centers in the winter. These were places where kids who were too young to go to the discos downtown in Manhattan, like Studio 54, which they probably could have never gotten into because they didn't know the right people. It was the petri dish that gave rise to hip-hop. (2024)

These park events laid the foundation for what became known as hip-hop. Inspired by his native Jamaican "soundsystems," DJ Kool Herc (Clive Campbell) played a pivotal polyrhythmic role in the early days of hip-hop by introducing his "breakbeat" technique, which debuted at the "Back to School Jam" in 1973. Herc also developed the rhyming spoken wordplay that future MCs would later perform.

KOOL HERC: Hip-hop started when my father brought a PA system and didn't know how to hook it up. I played with the music and bought a few records to play at my house. When I was doing that, I saw a lot of kids playing outside in the backyard. One day, my sister asked me to throw a party. She wanted me to play at a party at 1520 Sedgwick Avenue, so I got around twenty records that I felt were good enough. We had a party, charged twenty-five cents to come in, and made 300 dollars.

Meanwhile, Afrika Bambaataa (Lance Taylor) formed the Universal Zulu Nation to promote unity, peace, and justice through hip-hop culture. Bambaataa organized Harlem block parties, introducing DJing, rapping, breakdancing, and graffiti to misguided youth, redirecting their energy away from gang-related activities.

AFRIKA BAMBAATAA: In the earliest days, we'd have parties in the community center, and I'd bring my house system down, and someone else would bring theirs to the other side of the room. We'd hand out flashlights, and you'd have the lights off, and you'd have your flashlight, choosing which records you wanted. So when you put on one record—you might put on, say, "Dance to the Music" by Sly and the Family Stone—then, when you know that it's finished, somebody might put on James Brown's "It's a New Day" on the other side. (1986)

Grandmaster Flash (Joseph Sadler) revolutionized DJing by making the turntable a musical instrument, incorporating techniques like scratching to create rhythmic feedback. His novel approach and lightning-fast mixing—manipulating the vinyl with his fingers, toes, elbows, and foreign objects—set a new standard for the hip-hop community.

HANK SHOCKLEE: My cousin in the Bronx used to tell me like, Yo man, we got this guy named Flash because he mixes so fast. He said, "Yo, he's got like 13 turntables." I was like, "Ain't nobody mixing with 13 turntables!" But his excitement at how Flash was going back and forth with records made it seem like he had thirteen turntables because you're going from one record to the next so quickly. He was the inventor of the quick mix. (2023)

GRANDMASTER FLASH: Placing my fingertips on the vinyl was a blast. I'd watched music aficionados and people who spun records. 99.9 percent of the time, they'd use the tone arm to select the desired track. But for me, rule number one—how I broke it—was that I took duplicate copies and shoved them into a record jacket. I had to control the particular music segment that I had to play. The only way I could do that was by placing my fingertips on the record so that I could go forward, backward, or counterclockwise. So, my style was not agreeable to most, but it was the only way I'd have absolute control over the vinyl. (2022)

The Sugarhill Gang's "Rapper's Delight" inspired the global rise of rap music. Sugar Hill Records, the famous label of soul star Sylvia Robinson (known for 1972's "Pillow Talk") and backed by her enterprising husband Joe, produced and released the smash hit on September 16, 1979. Sylvia witnessed Lovebug Starski's performance in a club performing the new rap style, which had yet to receive radio play. Sylvia took some lyrics from Grandmaster Caz's notebook, and the musical break was "Good Times" by Chic. The upbeat lyrics offered a lively escape from the dark days of 1970s life, with charismatic rappers delivering smooth lines filled with female-friendly innuendo. The fifteen-minute track became the best-selling 12-inch single of all time, selling fourteen million units and transforming Sugar Hill into a multi-million-dollar operation.

BILL ADLER: Sylvia Robinson was an unrecognized genius; she built a label like Motown. She created the ideas behind those earlier rap hits in a pre-rap idiom—produced with pricey equipment in a home studio with a house band. That was old-school compared to what was being made in the streets and the community. (2024)

On March 25, 1979, a record titled "King Tim III (Personality Jock)" was released by the legendary NYC funk group Fatback Band. This record, starring guest rapper Tim Washington, came out months before "Rapper's Delight." It was a 12" single from their disco-style album *Fatback XII*. The song barely made an impact on the R&B charts and was not initially referred to as "rap," and was quickly usurped by "Rapper's Delight" to become the standard for the genre.

WONDER MIKE: I knew hip-hop would be big in New York, and I thought it'd be big in the States, but I did not think it'd have global appeal. I remember thinking fifteen years later about The Sugarhill Gang, "Wow, we made it this far!" (1999)

DJ MUGGS: I got turned on to hip-hop about 1979. The Treacherous Three, all that. But when I heard "Rapper's Delight," it was over, dawg. I caught the fucking fever. That was one of those songs where you would immediately be cool if you knew all the words. So in school, we'd memorize the whole damn ten minutes and clown on each other if someone got a lyric wrong. We never heard anything like that before. Every generation wants its heroes and its music. When I heard rap, I knew this was my shit right here. (2018)

The next step in the cultural crossover was the brilliance of "The Message" by Grandmaster Flash and the Furious Five. The group consisted of DJ Flash and five rappers, led by Melle Mel, who initially did not want to write a socially conscious song about the realities of ghetto life. Their significant hit on Sugar Hill Records introduced a unique new style, with the rappers taking turns to deliver lyrics and integrating their voices with Flash's wild turntablism. "The Message" was not a party record; its nihilism resonated with the cynical punk and new wave explosion.

MELLE MEL: Our group, Flash and the Furious Five, did not want to do "The Message" because we were used to doing party raps, you know, boasting about how good we are and all that. And when the record company brought the record to us to do, I just caved. I said, "Listen. If this is the record we need to make, I'll do it." It was certainly not a big thing, but I never thought it would be so pivotal. (2023)

The incredible success of Sylvia's Sugar Hill Records, based in New Jersey, paved the way for the next generation of independent rap labels in New York City. This scene involved Aaron Fuchs' Tuff City Records, founded in Queens, which promoted artists like Spoonie Gee, Cold Crush Brothers, and Marley Marl, and Manhattan labels like Cory Robbins' Profile Records (famous for Run-DMC) and Tommy Boy Records, begun by New Music Seminar cofounder Tommy Silverman, known for Soul Sonic Force, De La Soul, and House of Pain.

AARON FUCHS: When I told Bambaataa I wanted to sign an MC crew, I didn't know he'd bring me the greatest of all, the Cold Crush Brothers. When I befriended Barry Michael Cooper, a fellow music critic for the *Village Voice*, I had no idea he had cultivated a friendship with Spoonie Gee, one of the most influential hip-hop artists of the old-school era. (2015)

TOMMY SILVERMAN: I went to hear Bambaataa after learning about the breakbeat phenomenon and the b-boy concept in 1980 and wanted to know more about it. I called up Bambaataa and went to see him at T-Connection in the Bronx, and that's how I first heard him and Red Alert and Jazzy Jay spinning an incredible variety of music in a way I'd never heard before. I just asked him if he wanted to make a record, and that was the beginning of Tommy Boy's career when he said yes. The real revelation was to hear Kraftwerk, Billy Squier, Bob James, Cerrone, and the Monkees mixed in with James Brown and Sly Stone and all of this funk music. (2015)

EARLY HIP-HOP

> *It's like a jungle sometimes*
> *It makes me wonder how I keep from goin' under*
> —Grandmaster Flash and the Furious Five,
> "The Message" (1982)

Rap traces back to fast-talking Southern radio hosts, bawdy Black comedians, and Jamaican "toasters" who would talk over instrumental "versions." In the 1950s, white radio hosts like Alan Freed and Wolfman Jack rhymed on the radio. By the 1960s, DJs at a small New York AM soul station called WWRL, such as Frankie Crocker, Eddie O'Jay, and Gary Byrd, spoke in syncopated rhythm. In the 1970s, New York disco DJs would repeat breaks and encourage dancers to get down and boogie.

"Rappers" were emcees who spoke in rhymes, usually over the instrumental breaks on DJ-scratched records. Rapping involved a singer improvising over a funky break in a poetic manner. The "rap cadence" originated with boastful, comic, sexy, or relevant rhyming to popular disco and funk records.

"MC" comes from Master of Ceremonies, like at an old-school awards show. Rap MCs grabbed the mic, promoted the DJ, and energized the crowd. It is difficult to identify the first MC, but by the mid-1970s, people began calling themselves MCs at parties; notable figures like Cowboy, Lovebug Starski, and DJ Hollywood rocked parties at the Apollo. Early MC rap groups included the Treacherous Three, Cold Crush Brothers, and the Funky 4 + 1.

Rap music emerged as a minimalist street form of vocal delivery that commingled rhymes, rhythm, chatter, and salty street lingo. It stood in stark contrast to the more orchestrated music at "classy" discotheques and nightclubs. Initially, major record labels, buoyed by the wealth from the disco era, dismissed rap as a passing trend not worth investing in.

WHEN ROCK MET HIP-HOP

DMC: We had to find records with beats. Rock records always had a break in them where the drums would play, and maybe a bassline would play with the drums, or perhaps a rock guitar would play with the drums because we couldn't rap over the vocals. So rock—not just for Run-DMC, but for every rapper before us—was a big part of our repertoire. You had to have rock records inside your record case to give a good show because not only did they have the break that you needed, but they were also hard, and rap, back in the day, was considered heavy music. (1998)

> *South Bronx, New York that's where I dwell*
> *To a lot of people, it's a living hell*
> —Grandmaster Caz (featuring Chris Stein),
> "Wild Style Subway Rap" (1983)

"Hip-hop" encompassed the rap music lifestyle. In simple terms, rap is the music, while hip-hop is the culture. Hip-hop incorporated turntablism (MCs rapping, DJs scratching), breakdancing (b-boy breaking), and graffiti art. Urban fashion emerged as a new form of expression, and street slang gained mainstream acceptance. Cardboard sheets served as dance floors for breaking, and brick walls became canvases for graffiti. When the Uptown scene moved Downtown, hip-hop got presented in a way new-wave starving artists could understand. Artist/journalist Michael Holman coined the term "hip-hop" in the January 1982 edition of Leonard Abrams' *East Village Eye*. This multifaceted movement changed culture.

CARLO MCCORMICK: Most people I knew never thought hip-hop would take over the world. We understood it as a New York thing. However, it evolved into a language of youth, with kids around the globe engaging in graffiti and then rapping. I'm unsure how much we saw that, but we all knew this was special. (2024)

HARRY ALLEN: Hip-hop is young people talking about what they see and want to do about it. It comes from how Black people live—a slightly charged-up version, faster and more intense. It's like Black life squared. (1992)

Breaking (not to be called "breakdancing") was highly innovative at the time, with fantastic body flips, footwork, glides, and spins on various body parts in energetic displays. Notable NYC b-boys have roots dating back to the 1970s with Afrika Bambaataa's Zulu Kings from Harlem. The fashion of the time was 1970s Uptown streetwear, characterized by items such as tracksuits, bomber jackets, and oversized shoelaces. There were rivalries between breaking crews, with one of the most personal being that between Rock Steady Crew, the famous South Bronx team led by Richard "Crazy Legs" Colon, and the New York City Breakers, a team formed by Michael Holman in 1981, starring some of the best b-boys in the city.

CRAZY LEGS: I was inventing moves. I was creating moves that no one had ever done before. I transformed dance into something more acrobatic and dynamic by incorporating spins on the back and windmills. I had what we call "b-boy fever." That's when all you want to do is go out and find people to battle and battle and battle. (2024)

MICHAEL HOLMAN: I did a lot of work with Rock Steady Crew. I told Crazy Legs I wanted to show my friends Downtown real b-boy battling. I knew a Bronx crew, the Floor Masters, who were faster, harder, and made more athletic moves. I saw an opportunity there, so Phase2 and I approached them about this idea. We had to create a new breaking crew by raiding other b-boy crews for the most powerful breakers, which we called New York City Breakers. Then we cut to the chase and kicked out most of the original Floor Masters and got guys from all the five boroughs. We formed this all-star team, which became the first to appear on national TV on *Merv Griffin*. Then, there was no looking back. We had whole crew routines that told total narratives: beginning, middle, and end. The performances were beyond. (2024)

In 1984, the hip-hop film *Beat Street* depicted the real-life rivalry between the Rock Steady Crew and the New York City Breakers. The movie portrayed South Bronx high school students embracing hip-hop culture. It starred Rae Dawn Chong, Harry Belafonte, and Holman produced it, and *High Times* editor Steve Hagar wrote it. The film featured cameos by Kool Herc, Grandmaster Flash, Afrika Bambaataa, and Doug E. Fresh. That same year, the New York City Breakers released the genre's first instructional b-boy video covering popping, locking, and electric boogaloo.

Wild Style was the first hip-hop film, documenting the roots of street art as a form of pop culture. Charlie Ahearn's 1983 low-budget classic got shot in the South Bronx, the Lower East Side, and various MTA subway yards. It provided the first visual evidence of MC/DJ battles, breakdancing, aerosol art, and urban fashion. The film skillfully contextualized underground hip-hop for a sophisticated white audience as the next step in the creative process. The *Wild Style* soundtrack album, with Grandmaster Caz, Grand Wizzard Theodore, and Rammellzee, was released on Chris Stein of Blondie's Animal imprint through Chrysalis Records.

CHARLIE AHEARN: When I made *Wild Style*, I thought I was making an art film. It came from things I'd been doing for years, which involved creating a film that connected to a community. I thought that was the way an art movie should be done. It's like creating a shared vision for a film and then using it to unite and organize this group. In other words, things were happening naturally for many different people. We were all caught up in the movements happening around us. I wasn't a film producer; I was more like an artist. However, that was great because everyone assumed I knew what I was doing from that moment on! (2023)

FUTURA 2000: Our crew had angst and rebellion. We were not happy, and we wanted change. That's how our graffiti scene happened. We wanted to express ourselves. We were willing to break the law to do that. (2020)

DONDI: Writing on subways was an excellent way to communicate my ideas. Moving into the gallery, I had a whole new audience to communicate with, which was beneficial because it prompted my work to evolve. (2010)

FAB 5 FREDDY: I looked at it as a pioneer for being involved in making the first hip-hop film, *Wild Style*, and for having exhibited my paintings along with Lee Quiñones at big galleries in Italy. I was representing the subway school, but I was also aware of the art world, how it worked, and why. (1997)

Jean-Michel Basquiat and Michael Holman, both men of color, created minimalist music in the Downtown clubs that connected to hip-hop culture, but their focus was on something other than rap music. Their band, Gray, was a noise group with elements of Harlem free jazz. Basquiat used to walk around Alphabet City with a boombox, blasting Einstürzende Neubauten. This scenario created a high level of cultural hybridization.

CARLO McCORMICK: Punk and hip-hop shared a set of sonic strategies that were so interesting then. I used to love seeing the work of

Christian Marclay, who is now very famous. Back then, he was mixing and using those big industrial school turntables. It was similar to Fluxus music, which was concurrent with the emergence of hip-hop. So, if you think about how post-punk was cut and paste, you know, tear it up and start all over again: that Jamie Reid Sex Pistols album cover, in a ransom-note style. That was the essential mindset of hip-hop DJs and sample culture. There was a natural affinity between the two DIYs, as they met, and both, by not following the rules, came up with new ways around the dead ends of rock and disco music at the time. (2024)

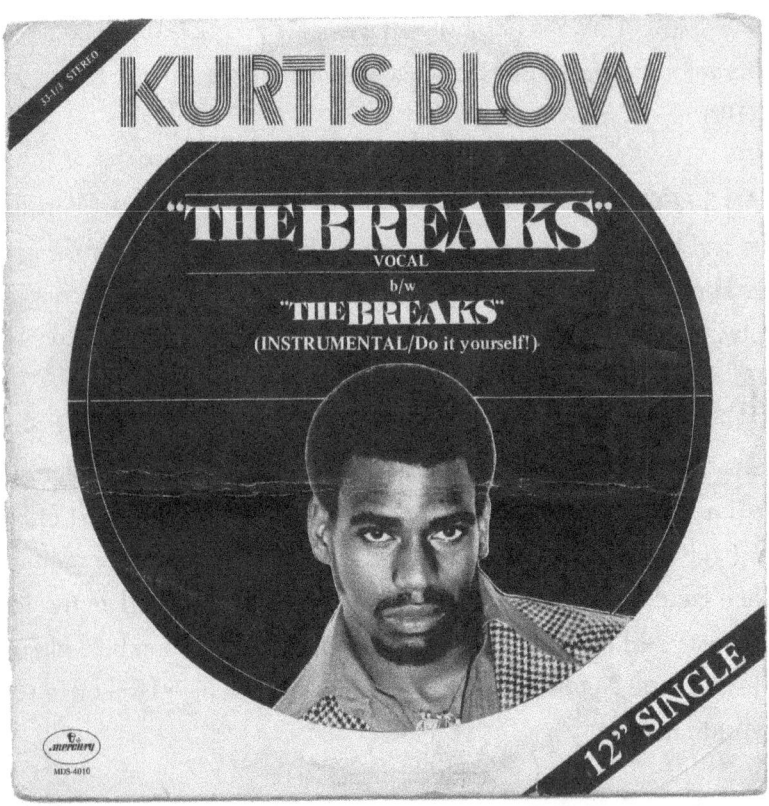

THESE ARE THE BREAKS: Kurtis Blow, "The Breaks," was the first rap hit to crossover at new wave rock clubs, 1980. Records / Alamy Stock Photo.

EARLY HIP-HOP

*Clap your hands, everybody, if you got what it takes
'Cause I'm Kurtis Blow, and I want you to know that
these are the breaks*
—Kurtis Blow, "The Breaks" (1980)

Kurtis Blow played a significant role in the rise of hip-hop as the first global rap star and Russell Simmons' first management client. His 1979 hit, "Christmas Rapping," was the first and only Christmas song to receive airplay into early spring. In 1980, "The Breaks," a James Brown-meets-Chic jam that arguably, the sexiest song of the era, became the most prominent rap song on pop radio and the second Gold-certified rap single, following "Rapper's Delight." His shows in 1981–82 opening for the Clash included their famed 17-concert run at Bond's International at Times Square. [This writer remembers hostile anti-rap audiences hurling vulgar invectives and n-bombs].

Curtis Walker was a Harlem breakdancer and aspiring star. He befriended fellow City College of New York (CCNY) freshman Simmons, and the two started throwing parties at CCNY and the Night Fever Disco on Jerome Avenue in the Bronx. Their promotions made Rush Productions the main force at midtown college parties and concerts at the Hotel Diplomat. When Simmons became manager, he wanted Curtis to project a star image, so he rebranded his partner as "Kurtis Blow." When Kurtis began touring the metropolitan area, his DJ was Russell's twelve-year-old brother Joseph Simmons, billed as "The Son of Kurtis Blow."

KURTIS BLOW: I taught Rev how to rap and DJ. This was around 1978. He used to practice in the attic because their dad bought him a turntable for him to practice on. He was five or seven years younger than Russell and I. He was running around the park jams in Queens and stuff. And at the time, calling someone your "son" was a compliment, similar to calling someone your protégé. So the "Son of Bambaataa" was Afrika Islam. And Run, at one point, was the "Son of Kurtis Blow"! Right after I got signed, he was my DJ for a while as well. Rev Run was my disco son; we would play music and have fun! (2018)

Joe Simmons and Darryl McDaniels have been best friends since first grade at St. Pascal's Catholic in St. Albans, Queens. Darryl got into hip-hop after seeing Joe spin for Blow. McDaniels briefly studied business administration at St. John's University, while Simmons started his degree in mortuary science at LaGuardia College. However, their passion for hip-hop led the nineteen-year-olds to launch Run-DMC in Darryl's parents' basement, joined by Joe's old friend DJ Jason Mizell. They practiced the call-and-response style that made them masters of the playground.

Russell paired Kurtis with music journalists-turned-producers J.B. Moore and Robert "Rocky" Ford. The pair convinced Mercury Records to sign Kurtis as the first rapper on a major label. In late 1979, Mercury released "Christmas Rappin," a cool twist on "Twas the Night Before Christmas" that sold over 400,000 copies, becoming one of the first successful rap singles and a timeless X-mas classic. Kurtis' self-titled 1980 album, with cover art of a bare-chested Blow dripping in gold, included a head-scratching soul/rock remake of Bachman Turner Overdrive's "Takin' Care of Business." It was the first time rock and hip-hop met, even though it was a throwaway track.

KURTIS BLOW: To be rap's first celebrity was so rewarding, especially from 1979 to 1985—the best times of my life. I was the first rapper signed to a major label, meaning they had offices in every major city. So, every time I made a record, they would fly me out to Paris, Belgium, or Berlin. I was the first rapper to perform in Paris. Sometimes, it was for a tour. But other times, they'd send me places. And when I got there, they'd have all kinds of press setups: radio, print, and television, one interview after the next. Everybody at the time was so curious about this thing called hip-hop. I was trailblazing the path and barely twenty years old. I discovered while in Europe that my record hit number one! And I was no older than twenty-one at the time. It was amazing. (2018)

> *When freaks get dressed to go out at night*
> *They like to wear leather jackets, chains and spikes*
> —Whodini, "The Freaks Come Out At Night" (1983)

Whodini, a client of Russell Simmons, was the first rap group to have consecutive Top 40 chart hits with "Five Minutes of Funk," "The Haunted House of Rock," "Friends," and "Freaks Come Out at Night." They epitomized the era's "fly" style, sporting anti-pimp sportswear, Kangol berets, high school letterman sweaters, noticeable bling, and creative songs with a positive vibe. Their extensive 1982 tour helped pave the way for hip-hop's broader acceptance.

JALIL: We had a lot of "road stories" from those days—stuff that happened to us while spreading this new rap music around the world. There was a lot of sex. There was a lot of partying. There was a lot of theft. There was also considerable confusion. I guess it's just like life—anything can happen. (2013)

Kool Moe Dee of the Treacherous Three faced the challenge of rapping after Busy Bee's live routine at a Christmas party in 1981. Moe Dee responded by delivering an impromptu diss, unleashing a rapid-fire cadence that was unheard of at the time. He verbally attacked sixteen-year-old LL Cool J three years later for allegedly copying his rhymes. Their early onstage "battles" became iconic in New York, with Moe Dee outperforming LL Cool J at the Apollo Theater. However, he overplayed his hand and ultimately lost the culture war.

KOOL MOE DEE: I'm the most articulate. I utilize more vocabulary than the average rapper. I stick to themes. I don't make a record called *The Wall* and then start talking about the cars on the street. I stay focused. I use innovative rhythms. I syncopate a lot. I know that I utilize more speaking tools than other rappers. (1988)

NEW WAVE RAP

*Down in the Village, you might think I'm silly,
but you can't tell the women from the men sometimes*
—Grandmaster Flash and the Furious Five,
"New York, New York"

New York was the epicenter of the cultural universe. Over the past century, every art, music, fashion, culture, and political movement has its roots in the Five Boroughs. Global sounds like jazz, folk, disco, punk, and rap originated on the city's streets. Downtown Manhattan became a hub of creativity. Andy Warhol, a prominent figure in New York City's cultural scene, operated his Factory by Union Square, where he launched the first significant modern cultural publication, *Interview* Magazine.

Hip-hop began in Uptown but gained momentum in the "punk discos" or "new wave discos." This surge of popularity in trendsetting circles put rap on the map. The effect was mutual: rap inspired fresh new sounds and styles, while punk and new wave injected hip-hop with instant artistic credibility, be it "Rapture" by Blondie or "Buffalo Gals" by Malcolm McLaren.

WHEN ROCK MET HIP-HOP

CHRIS STEIN: It was so exciting to see this whole other world that was going on at the same time as what was happening Downtown in New York, even though we were only vaguely aware of it. It took a while for all that stuff to start coming together later. I was very excited because, on a sociopolitical level, these marginalized kids were finally finding their voice. It was so inspiring. (2020)

From 1978 to 1982, Glenn O'Brien, the music editor of *Interview* Magazine, hosted the Manhattan Cable TV show *TV Party*. The show, known as the meeting place for people from Uptown and Downtown, was hailed by David Letterman as "the greatest TV show ever." Chris Stein of Blondie was the cohost, and the guests included Deborah Harry, David Bowie, Iggy Pop, Robert Fripp, David Byrne, Nile Rodgers, George Clinton, John Lurie, and Robert Mapplethorpe. Jean-Michel Basquiat painted canvases, and Fab Five Freddy (Fred Braithwaite) was also part of the scene. It was common for everyone to smoke weed on camera.

GLENN O'BRIEN: The show ran on Channel D and Channel J and was quite popular with the kids. We lucked into following *The Robin Byrd Show* for a while and so inherited an audience of horny guys. We also got a big high school following, thanks to smoking a bunch of pot and talking shit. The show never *officially* ended—Chris got sick and almost died, I got married and decided I needed to make some money, some people went to rehab, some left town, and some died of AIDS, which had just appeared. It seemed like everything was suddenly changing, and it had been getting longer and longer since the last show. We had a good run fucking up television, though: cursing, getting high, advocating subversion, and being party desperados. (2014)

FAB 5 FREDDY: *TV Party* was a magnet for the coolest and most exciting culture-makers on the Downtown scene, and of course, Chris Stein and Debbie Harry were critical to the underground. I was able to discuss my plans and ideas with many of these folks and receive great advice on how to execute my assault on pop culture. Glenn was like a mentor, and I drew up my plans and executed them: painting, exhibiting my work Downtown, collaborating with Charlie Ahearn, and helping to make the film *Wild Style*. Our concept of using the actual artists and practitioners portraying themselves in the movie, such as graffiti artists, rappers, DJs, and break dancers, helped put those pioneers on the map. Ending up in a starring role was a last-minute idea that thrust me to the forefront of the culture. (2020)

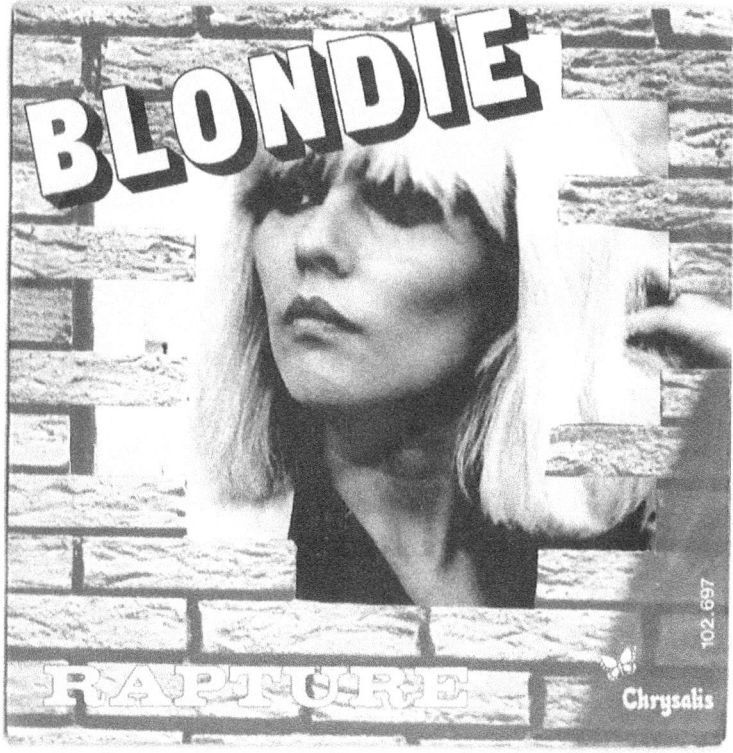

AND YOU DON'T STOP: Blondie crossed punk and pop with disco, reggae, and hip-hop—with "Rapture," 1980. Records / Alamy Stock Photo.

WHEN ROCK MET HIP-HOP

*You try to run, but he's got a gun
And he shoots you dead, and he eats your head*
—Blondie, "Rapture" (1980)

Blondie, a New York punk band with new wave appeal, became legendary for their versatility. The hip group defined when rock met disco with "Heart of Glass," when rock met reggae with "The Tide is High," and when rock met hip-hop with the 1980 release of "Rapture," which opened doors for the rap revolution. "Rapture," the first rap single to hit #1 on the charts, was unique in using original music rather than sampling other artists.

DEBORAH HARRY: We had the first number-one—I put quotes around "rap" because it's not strictly a rap song. It's an homage. We loved what was going on. We were at a street level at the time, and we saw the kids doing what they did and what it meant, and I felt like, "This is important stuff." It was a gamble; we had no idea it would top the charts. I'm proud that we created the first rap song with its accompanying music. At that time, rapping was often done over loops; they would take loops from Chic and others and create scratches with the turntables. It was a different animal. They called it hip-hop. (2012)

"Rapture" came out of Glenn O'Brien's *TV Party* when Fab 5 Freddy invited Debbie Harry and Chris Stein to the South Bronx to see the Funky 4 + 1 rapping and scratching. Chris and Debbie loved the experience so much that they name-checked Fab 5 Freddy and DJ Grandmaster Flash.

CHRIS STEIN: Fab Five Freddy brought us to this event Uptown in 1977, and it was an exciting moment. It was me, Debbie, him, Glenn O'Brien, and Patti Astor. I'd never seen rap in person before. The energy level was phenomenal. It was located in a Police Athletic League facility, similar to a civic center. It was parallel to what was happening Downtown, but they were completely separated. So it was a no-brainer to do something with a rap. It seemed the obvious way to go. (2023)

The song's lively mix highlighted unique elements, such as Debbie Harry's fresh vocals with an edgy presentation and the variation in tempos while maintaining a freestyle feel. The saxophone, double-tracked and blaring over Stein's energetic guitar, was performed by renowned session musician Tom Scott (famous for the *Taxi Driver* theme).

DEBORAH HARRY: I only did one vocal take for "Rapture." That was fine for the melody, but I would have preferred more time on the rap. What was new about "Rapture" is that we approached it like a standard piece of music at a time when rap relied on beats and samples. The exciting aspect is that it goes alongside a particular era and state of mind. If I hear something that could be improved on? Well, that's all shoulda, woulda, coulda, right? I mean, "Rapture" did pretty well anyway. (2022)

The name-check helped Fred get the job as *Yo! MTV Raps* cohost. Grandmaster Flash and his crew didn't understand it, so his manager didn't allow him in the video. When Flash didn't show up, Jean-Michel Basquiat stepped in, although he needed direction to make it look like he was cutting and scratching. The "Rapture" video, shot in the East Village in 1980 by director Keith Macmillan, featured cameos by Lee Quiñones and Fab 5 Freddy, spray-painting aerosol art.

Autoamerican, Blondie's fifth album, successfully combined the new hip-hop with a punk/new wave attitude, creating a bold new sound on

"Rapture." The hit album also contained their reggae update of The Paragons' "The Tide is High."

JIMMY DESTRI: When we did *Autoamerican*, the label said, "Go in and make just like *Eat to the Beat*, a great pop record." So we made *Autoamerican*, and we loved "Rapture." They thought it was insane, but it reached number one in two weeks. (2003)

CHRIS STEIN: Both "Rapture" and "The Tide is High" helped bring certain kinds of Black music to masses of white kids—the white rock audience—that may never have heard otherwise. I think that's great because it served a larger purpose. (1982)

CLEM BURKE: Not to get too self-righteous, but Blondie, along with a handful of other bands in the mid-1970s, changed music for the better. And about "Rapture"—it is not a rap song, but a song with rap in it. Rap was a beat. We created a song with a strong melody that incorporated rap. We always combine genres, which is a significant legacy of the Blondie sound. (2018)

> *I guess I must admire*
> *the need to set things on fire*
> —Futura 2000, "The Escapades Of Futura 2000" (1982)

Futura 2000 (Lenny McGurr) is a renowned New York City graffiti artist known for his abstract approach to subway art. He was close friends with Jean-Michel Basquiat and was a part of the *TV Party* scene. He befriended the Clash, taught them about hip-hop culture, and worshipped Joe Strummer as a father figure. During their year-plus of *Combat Rock* touring, the Clash would have Futura on stage with his spray-paint cans and ladders, creating large graffiti backdrops as the band performed. Futura's combination of art and music further united the emerging punk and hip-hop subcultures.

FUTURA 2000: I felt what was happening with rap music then, and I got inspired while on the road with the Clash, so I wrote this rap about graffiti. Joe heard it and got the boys together, laid down a rhythm track, and I dropped the lyrics. I did it to have a cassette to play for my New York friends. I wasn't trying to become a rapper. I saw it as an homage to New York graffiti. (2020)

The Clash's Mick Jones offered to produce Futura and contributed by making beats and playing bass. In 1982, a two-song 12" 45-rpm Maxi-Single of "The Escapades Rap" b/w "The Escapades Dub" was recorded at Electric Lady Studios with engineer Joe Blaney. The record had a sticker stating "Music Composed and Performed by THE CLASH." Futura added rhymes and references to his cool friends and old scenes, with vocal input by Fab Five Freddie and Dondi, creating a mesmerizing rock-rap-dub-art integration that connected to the Clash's mission to bring white punks on dope to Black culture. Futura also painted the back cover and declared his battle cry: "From Brooklyn to Brixton."

FAB 5 FREDDY: The Clash reached out to Futura to get a better sense of the New York urban experience, and he obliged by taking them to graffiti hangouts in the Bronx, the amphitheater on the Lower East Side where the final concert scene in *Wild Style* was filmed, and our studio in Alphabet City. Blondie's "Rapture" had hit number one, and the members of the Clash were impressed and curious. They were already interested in reggae and wanted to learn more about hip-hop. They asked Futura to accompany them to Europe to paint graffiti live during their concerts. (2020)

BUFFALO GALS: Malcolm McLaren introduced Europe to hip-hop culture and fashion, 1981. Victor Watts / Alamy Stock Photo.

> *Wooh, girl, it's a pity that you're so dirty*
> *You're only dancin' just to be friendly*
> —Malcolm McLaren, "Buffalo Gals" (1982)

Malcolm McLaren was a British fashion designer who managed the Sex Pistols and provided career advice to Adam Ant and Bow Wow Wow during his visit to New York in 1981. McLaren's life changed when he got introduced to hip-hop by Downtown critic Michael Holman, who brought McLaren to a Zulu Nation party in the South Bronx. Malcolm was so immersed in the scene's energy that he became involved in the nascent New York hip-hop scene and put his unique spin on the art form.

MALCOLM McLAREN: Michael and I made our way through the crowd, pushing and shoving until I got to where the music was coming from, in front of these two decks, and shook hands with this substantial fat guy who later became known to me as Afrika Bambaataa. I witnessed young kids popping in and out among the decks and messing with the records. It was extraordinary. As far as I could see, the sound coming out was inarticulate, a jumble of rough noises that sounded a little like a guitar but more like a concrete chisel. And I realized the sound came from how they manipulated their hands on the decks, moving records backward and forward between the two. It was making music out of other people's music. The crowd grew increasingly volatile as time passed, sometimes erupting into pitched battles. At one point, the crowd moved to the sides, and a group of kids did incredible gymnastic dancing. I can speak with authority when I say no music embodies the original spirit of rock and roll more than today's rap music. (1984)

"Buffalo Gals" and "Double Dutch" were hit singles from his 1983 album *Duck Rock*. "Buffalo Gals" introduced British crowds to hip-hop culture with rapping, turntablism, breakdancing, and graffiti. The song starred the scratching technique of the World Famous Supreme Team, discovered by McLaren at a Bronx street party. "Double Dutch" referenced the urban skipping-jump-roping game, with Malcolm name-checking double-dutch groups in the chorus. The music video showcased American Double Dutch League crews competing in a school gym.

Duck Rock was an eclectic mix of global styles, akin to a Smithsonian field recording, incorporating folk music from diverse cultures. McLaren's goal was to unite diverse musical forces, similar to the Pistols' vision of a white riot in 1977. The eighteen-minute "mini-LP" party mix *D'Ya Like Scratchin'* introduced dance floor re-edits/remixes of five *Duck Rock* tracks, highlighting McLaren's innovative use of sound manipulation techniques, from digital delay to *musique concrète*. Malcolm collaborated with studio wizard Trevor Horn, noted for his work with Yes and The Art Of Noise.

TREVOR HORN: When Malcolm rapped "Buffalo Gals," I had to stand there and punch him in the chest in time with the track because he'd sing too fast. I'd have to say, "No, Malcolm," and thump his chest so he'd sing in time until he said, "Right, I get it." So after about four takes, I got tired. I stopped doing it, and he said, "You've gotta keep hitting me. Come on, what's your problem?" And I'd say, "I'm exhausted, Malcolm." So that's how we got the vocal. (2013)

The Beastie Boys' "B-Boy Bouillabaisse" off *Paul's Boutique* sampled the scratching, big beats, and sparse vocals of "Buffalo Gals." Ironically, the Beasties had sued British Airways over the unlicensed use of their beats from "Beastie Revolution," the B-side to "Cooky Puss." Malcolm was masterfully savvy and knew how to create a total package.

SE'DIVINE THE MASTER MIND: We didn't have a relationship with Malcolm. Malcolm was a player, and I know a player when I see one. We didn't do anything but sit down and chat. The most money I have ever made was having somebody down with me like that. The best way to get money, depending on who you are, is to put somebody down like that. He put us down, and it didn't bother me that he was white or he was considered a devil. Man, we were trying to get money. I wasn't trying to have sex with white women. It didn't change me at all. But some of the best players I could get the most money with were because of their complexion. (2010)

> *Up out your seats, make your body sway*
> *Socialize, get down, let your soul lead the way*
> —Afrika Bambaataa & Soul Sonic Force, "Planet Rock" (1982)

Soul Sonic Force starred Afrika Bambaataa, who conceived "Planet Rock," the most essential dance hit of the early 1980s. With its spartan

ROCK ROCK DON'T STOP: Afrika Bambaataa and Soul Sonic Force united rap, electro, funk, and NYC punk, 1982. Pictorial Press Ltd / Alamy Stock Photo.

beats, percussive polyrhythms, and electro mindset, "Planet Rock" was one of the most significant hip-hop records to cross over between Black and white clubs.

In the 1970s, Afrika led a violent Harlem street gang called The Black Spades. When his boys began to die off and the violence ceased working, he launched the positivity of the Zulu Nation. Afrika became famous in New York nightlife when he started DJing at decadent Downtown nightclubs like Danceteria, Negril, and an old roller rink called The Roxy, where Afrika displayed his techno-bling, imperially attired in ornate costume, shades, and headdress.

"The Godfather of Hip-Hop" formed Soul Sonic Force with New York's top dance music producer, Arthur Baker, and synthesizer player/co-producer John Robie. DJ John "Jellybean" Benitez set the industry on its ear when he reconfigured the song's sonic frequencies for the dance floor. With the aural intercourse of Bam and three anonymous rappers, "the first Black electronic group" sounded like a late-night runaway freight train of rump-shaking ecstasy. The raps and beats appealed to all music fans, geared and primed to party together.

ARTHUR BAKER: When we entered the studio, I wanted to make something "Uptown" and "Downtown." From the very beginning, that was the idea. It differs from how we lucked into that; we were going for that. We wanted a record that people into Talking Heads and Sugarhill Gang would play. That had much to do with Bam because Bam was open to that. If he had said "no," we wouldn't have done it for that record. He was open to that because he was DJing Downtown and Uptown. He was the first guy to be able to cross those boundaries. (2013)

AFRIKA BAMBAATAA: I wanted to make something funky with a hard electronic bass and beat. I have to credit Yellow Magic Orchestra, Kraftwerk, and Gary Numan. Numan was doing that thing with "Bombers." That was one of the early records we used to play when rappers were rapping. I'm not sure if Gary knows how many Black and Latino youth jammed to his music. It was fun. It got wild when we started performing. It was bugged out—an exciting scene. (2014)

The twelve-inch single "Planet Rock" (Tommy Boy), recorded at NYC's Intergalactic Studios, achieved gold status and popularized the genre of "robo-funk" or "electro-funk." The track incorporated a Fairlight machine for claps, orchestral blasts, a Prophet-5 synth, a MicroMoog, an 808 drum machine, and vocoder vocals. The call-and-response style of party-rocking got called "MC poppin."

ARTHUR BAKER: There was very little equipment, and that was it. It was like two synths, a drum machine, and the Fairlight for effects. And we had one delay to give that metallic sound a bit around his vocals. So we had that, and it got cut through in a fucking great Neve board. That's why it sounded so fat! (2021)

"Planet Rock" was an edgy hip-hop hit, but it was more of a dance record than a rap record. But it was a crucial crossover smash. Bam, the provocative street philosopher with a bold vision of hip-hop, created a song with transformative powers. "Planet Rock" heavily sampled from the cold synth rhythms of Kraftwerk (over which the German trio later sued him) and Ryuichi Sakamoto's Yellow Magic Orchestra. The success of "Planet Rock" elevated Baker's status in the dance world. Months later, he produced the dance-rock masterpiece "Confusion" by New Order.

AFRIKA BAMBAATAA: You've got to be musically inclined and love music and not get caught up in the fact that this person is from that race or that nationality. All that shit is irrelevant. If it's good, it's good. And as my audience became more international, I'd keep playing things, and people would say, "I don't like metal" or "I don't like funk." So, I'd take them on a musical journey and say, "Well, you just danced to some." (2008)

> *Fascist, chauvinistic government fools*
> *People, Muslims, Christians and Hindus*
> —Time Zone, "World Destruction" (1984)

Time Zone was a groundbreaking 1980s rock-rap hybrid, a one-off collaboration between Bambaataa and John Lydon (Sex Pistols/Public Image Ltd). Bill Laswell, known for his work with the eclectic funk-jazz collective Material, produced the session, giving it a sharp electronic edge. Afrika Bambaataa rapped about global conspiracies, while John Lydon expressed his disdain for the human race.

AFRIKA BAMBAATAA: Nostradamus said there would be a war between Islam and Russia with America, and you can see that happening. There wouldn't have been any Cold War conflicts because the Russians and Americans were cooling off, and the Islamic nations were rising. That's why I wrote "World Destruction." (2010)

JOHN LYDON: Bambaataa is like me. He loves all music. As a DJ, he'd do fantastic crossovers between Parliament or the Ohio Players and mix it with Kraftwerk. That was exciting to listen to. The audience's eyes would be wide open. I'd always be there in the middle of the dance floor, having a great time. We got together in the studio, where I met Bill Laswell, the bloke who produced Bam's album. We put "Time Zone" together, and that's how rap kicked out! (2017)

The 1984 election-year recording opened with snippets of Democratic candidate Walter Mondale's plea for nuclear disarmament. The song criticized Reagan and Mondale for supporting large military budgets. Despite Johnny's unusual musical style, his political views, a mix of left- and right-wing, perfectly fit the lyrics. He highlighted the threat of Mutually Assured Destruction in a Cold War nuclear battle between the United States and USSR.

AFRIKA BAMBAATAA: I was talking to Bill Laswell, saying I needed somebody crazy, and he thought of John Lydon. I knew he was perfect because I'd seen the movie he'd made (*Copkiller*) and knew about all the Sex Pistols and Public Image stuff. So we got together and created a smashing, crazy version, as well as a version where he cursed the Queen something terrible, which never got released. (2022)

BILL LASWELL: That record was a very natural thing at the time. I received a call from Afrika Bambaataa, who wanted to incorporate the elements he had used in heavy metal to create "World Destruction." He asked me, "Do you know Def Leppard?" And I laughed, "No, I don't know Def Leppard." At that time, I didn't know many metal people. I would later on, but not then. So I told him I'd just gotten to know John Lydon. I told him that he was Johnny Rotten, who had been in the Sex Pistols, saying, "It's not what I'd call metal, but you might think it is!" And he thought that sounded good. So, we recorded this very quickly, which seemed natural to me. (2009)

The single and video released by Celluloid Records, associated with Laswell, was a marriage of punk and funk. It employed electronic instruments played by Downtown stars like Bernie Worrell on keyboards, Nicky Skopelitis on guitar, and Laswell on bass. This record came out two years before Aerosmith and Run-DMC's "Walk This Way."

JOHN LYDON: It was a perfect rap song but didn't have a hook or chorus. So, I came up with the "Time Zone" refrain. It was a fabulous juxtaposition of voices, with Bambaataa's heavy delivery, which we now know is a hallmark of rap ideology in presentation. I'm squeaking up there like an angry young man. You put the two together, and it made a beautiful record. But it was not liked when it first came out. The label I was on said the same thing: "There's no place for this kind of music. You won't get on any playlists." Well, the story of my life is that whenever I've done anything musically, it's never been on any playlists. It takes them years to catch up, and then they play it. I think we spent $22 on the video. It involved lots of ketchup. That was the budget: McDonald's Heinz Ketchup for the blood smears. And it worked! (2015)

CROSSOVER

*I rock mad styles, I hop turnstiles
I rock all mics, I last all night*
—House of Pain, "Shamrocks & Shenanigans"

The crossover of punk, rock, and rap changed music for the better. This desegregation was a slow transition that ultimately benefited everyone. It was multiculturalism before anyone spoke in those terms. The era's zeitgeist embodied the "crossover" within the punk and metal scenes, whether it was the underground hardcore bands that had "gone metal," such as Agnostic Front and SSD, the thrash metal explosion led by Slayer and Anthrax, or the rock-rap crossover of Run-DMC, Beastie Boys, and Public Enemy.

AFRIKA BAMBAATAA: Punk rockers were the first white artists to accept hip-hop and started collaborating with us. We looked at each other crazy at first, but after a while, everybody was cool with each other and hangin' together. People thought there were gonna be race wars, but we shut them the fuck up. You had everyone dancing under one roof, whether it went Downtown or up in the South Bronx. You'd see punk rockers come to our neighborhood and join the line with everyone else, blending in with the people. (1995)

WHEN ROCK MET HIP-HOP

KEITH SHOCKLEE: In the early 1980s, we regularly went back and forth to Manhattan because we went to Danceteria and hung out with the punk rock bands. It was a point where punk and hip-hop were like the bastard children of music. We had that deep connection, and that's where it all started. (2023)

Hip-hop DJs first crossed over in their search for the ultimate breakbeats, finding Led Zeppelin and Billy Squier.

AFRIKA BAMBAATAA: To all the people at the clubs who said, "I ain't into heavy metal," I'd play Led Zeppelin or Foghat and then move into that. Like Led Zeppelin, I'd play "Whole Lotta Love" and "Black Dog." Foghat's "Slow Ride," Rush's "Tom Sawyer," "Honky Tonk Woman," "Miss You," "Hot Stuff," Billy Squier's "The Big Beat," and Eddie Money's "Baby Hold Onto Me." I united people by playing all sorts of shit. (2017)

PETE NICE: If you listen to the early tapes by Kool Herc and all these guys—a good seven years before Run-DMC—was this deliberate attempt to bring music together. The percussion was the foundation of the rock-rap relationship. The original hip-hop was about heavy-bottomed hard rock with breakbeats: Aerosmiths *Toys in the Attic*, Led Zeppelin's "When the Levee Breaks," Rare Earth's "Get Ready," the Monkees' "Mary Mary," and Steppenwolf's "Magic Carpet Ride." I knew most of those songs from high school, but I learned them from watching the great DJs rework them. Then I started diggin' in the crates. When we were at Columbia, Bobby Colomby, the drummer for Blood, Sweat & Tears, became a big A&R man and producer there. He heard our sample of his music blasting out of another room and bugged out. We also had a run-in with the lawyers from Gary Wright's estate when we hadn't cleared the "Dream Weaver" and "Love Is Alive" samples. So, the rap-meets-hip-hop story goes way deeper than most people think. (2024)

DMC: We used to rap over rock records before we made our own records because we had to find records with beats. And rock records, James Brown records, always had a break where the drums would play, and maybe a bassline would play with the drum, or perhaps a rock guitar would play with the drum because we couldn't rap over the vocals. So rock was a big part of our repertoire, not just for Run-DMC but for every rapper before us. You had to have rock records inside your record case to give a good performance because not only did they have the break that you needed, but they were also hard, and rap, in the beginning, was a hard music genre. (1998)

Punk rock and hip-hop emerged as underground New York music, inner-city siblings who impacted and earned each other's respect. Hip-hop's lyrical messages picked up where punk rock left off.

DANTE ROSS: Hip-hop was Black punk rock. It was dangerous, rebel music and seemed like a natural evolution. (2011)

RICK RUBIN: I was a fan of hardcore punk music. I looked at Black rap music as the equivalent of white hardcore. It took music out of Madison Square Garden and down to street level. (1985)

BILL ADLER: Adam Horovitz discusses how, if you lived in Downtown New York back then, you could hear punk rock and rap records being played together. The club DJs had that kind of range. They could program that kind of music simultaneously. It wasn't discomforting, it wasn't disconcerting, it wasn't disjunctive; it made sense. Horowitz was just a teenager attending parties, underage, and listening to them, absorbing the experience. It didn't seem remarkable to him because it was just part of the mix. (2015)

WHEN ROCK MET HIP-HOP

PETE NICE: I see people romanticize it, but the punk and hip-hop crowds did not coexist. The Furious Five opened for the Clash, and people in the crowd booed and hated the Black shit. Chuck Valle of Murphy's Law engineered my first album, and I was like, "Who the fuck is Murphy's Law?" I knew who Henry Rollins was, but he was only in our video because Bob Dylan's son was our video director, and he wanted him to be in it. We were not big fans of rock—Living Colour, we knew from the studios and hanging out at the clubs—but we were the Latin Quarter crew. We were 100 percent hip-hop. Classic rock or 1970s rock breaks; I knew every Doors lyric from growing up. But there was no love between the punk and hip-hop crowds; let's be real. (2024)

DANNY BOY: There were cultural clashes between rap and rock music. Punk rockers hated jocks and rockers. Then, a schism emerged when hip-hop arrived, especially for us white guys in the hip-hop scene. But that's why we put our foot down: "We're Irish, you don't like us doing hip-hop? Fuck you, blow me." (2011)

Punk and hardcore underwent its heavy metal crossover, and the natural merger of punk, metal, rock, and hip-hop marked the subsequent phases of musical integration.

MARIA FERRERO: When you ask me about "when rock met hip-hop," I think about the late 1980s crossover. It sounds like a natural concept for us today, but the music was very separate back then. Even just within metal, there was East Coast, West Coast, and New Wave Of British Heavy Metal, and they were all their own thing. The hardcore scene despised the metal scene, yet after a few years, a punk-metal crossover scene emerged, featuring bands from the hardcore side, such as the Cro-Mags and Suicidal Tendencies, alongside bands like S.O.D. from the metal side. Then you had Kerry King of Slayer collaborating with the

Beastie Boys, Run-DMC with Aerosmith, and Anthrax teaming up with Public Enemy. Then came Rage Against the Machine, followed by the emergence of nu-metal. It was such an exciting time. (2024)

DANNY BOY: By 1984, I was breakdancing, doing graffiti, and completely into hip-hop culture. And I could count on one hand the number of credible white guys in suburbia who were not only into hip-hop but were willing to take an ass beating or give an ass beating to be down with that. We had problems with that. That same year was the first Suicidal [Tendencies] record. That was the first punk record I related to, mainly because they came from the West Coast. It was transformative for me. Suicidal started as a two-tone gang, and we had our punk gang in the Valley connected to FFF. They got into fights with people, which was how we lived. So, from the start, it was an amalgamation of cultures. We had a clique, and we would run around. We were a ragtag bunch. We had a few Black dudes, a few white dudes, and a few Mexican dudes. (2024)

EVAN SEINFELD: Back in the 1980s, music was segregated to the point that in my neighborhood of Canarsie, Brooklyn, there was a giant mural on the wall across from my high school, next to the bagel store called The Nosher, of Eddie from Iron Maiden killing Eddie, the Funhouse Clown. The name of the mural was "Eddie Killed The Clown." It was rock versus disco. But coming from Canarsie, I also loved disco and roller disco, dancing on my skates, and that form of expression. I didn't understand the hatred. Even in the early Biohazard days, when we were one of the big metal bands at L'Amour, I was also there every Wednesday for techno nights with DJ Frankie Bones and DJ Lenny Dee—which my rock friends could not relate to. It was always met with, "What the fuck is wrong with you, man?" At around the same time, in the late 1980s, hip-hop was exploding, emerging from house music and freestyle. Rappers like Run-DMC, NWA, LL Cool J, Eric B. and Rakim, Big Daddy Kane, and Grand Poobah, I was relating to because of all the similarly crazy shit I grew up with in Brooklyn and on the subway. The lyrics were far more relatable than the fantasy lyrics in heavy metal music, which spoke to my soul. I had not yet seen the future. (2024)

DREW STONE: Growing up in New York, being a city kid, and going to public school, there was a time in the early 1980s when hardcore punk, heavy metal, and what we know as hip-hop were all running head to head. They were all underground movements; they weren't high profile then. There was a lot of overlap. You would go to a hardcore show, and kids would do graffiti outside. You'd go to a street party or house party when there were rappers, graffiti, and some hardcore kids. Breakdancing was a big part of it, too. And you can't separate breakdancing and slam dancing. It was all coming from the same melting pot of New York City. And none of these small communities were that far in front of the others. There were no superstars in hip-hop or hardcore yet. There was still this us-against-them mentality. There was no unreachable, unattainable that any of this stuff would be viable, commercially, or monetized. It was almost incomprehensible. Nobody was doing graffiti to get wealthy. Nobody was doing hardcore to get rich. I must also say that none of these musical terms existed at that time. It wasn't known as hardcore. It was known as hip-hop back then. So I think that added to the flavor; you couldn't put your finger on it. These were youth movements. You know, "If the kids are united, they will never be divided." I mean, that's what it was. We didn't have beef with hip-hop kids or graffiti artists. I know the graffiti scene is often driven by beef. But we were all part of this urban community and culture. Early on, it was a head-to-head competition. It was much later that things were assimilated into the commercial lexicon. That turned into pasteurized processed cheese food. Get it? (2024)

CROSSOVER

DARYL JENIFER: It crossed over at all angles. Eddie from Leeway was like a b-boy in rock. Jimmy of Murphy's Law was a rock b-boy as well. He was one of the illest MCs back then, but he was in a hardcore band. Run-DMC's records even featured rock guitars back then. And then we kicked off the band Brooklyn after Yauch got off the road. We were sort of ahead of our time, kicking shit like that. (2016)

DMC: Hip-hop and punk rock are brother and sister. We don't give a fuck; we say what we wanna say, and we dress how we wanna dress. Some people think "old-school" refers to a specific period, but it is also a way of presenting oneself through one's sound, look, style, and personality. (2020)

AD-ROCK: Rap is no huge thing—it's like punk rock or something. (1985)

BILLY SQUIER

Spread your ear pollution, both far and wide
Keep your contributions by your side
—Billy Squier, "The Stroke"

Billy Squier blasted some of the most incredible guitar riffs in rock history. His crisp sound made for some of the most famous samples in rap history. Billy's clean, sanitized, sustained chords elevated his rock legacy from a mildly successful AOR mainstay to a wildly wealthy and predominant hip-hop pioneer.

BILLY SQUIER: People have sometimes written that I am the king of hip-hop. But honestly, I didn't even know what hip-hop was back then. And I don't think I can claim all that much credit; after all, I just gave them a beat. In the end, if they're happy, I'm happy. (2005)

DMC: Shout-out to Billy Squier. He's the godfather of hip-hop. You can't say George Clinton or James Brown without putting Billy Squier in there. That's the diversity of the music. (2018)

Squier started his career as one of New England's biggest 1970s rock stars, alongside Aerosmith's Steven Tyler and Boston's Brad Delp. He was the lead singer of Piper (also billed as "Piper featuring Billy Squier"), an iconic band known for its Led Zeppelin-style sound. Despite releasing two solid albums over two years and touring America with Kiss, Piper never achieved national success. Piper and Kiss shared manager Bill Aucoin, who chose to work with Piper instead of Van Halen. In 1975, *Circus* Magazine hailed Piper's debut as "the greatest debut album ever by an American rock band."

In 1980, Aucoin went bankrupt, and Piper disbanded. Billy Squier pursued a solo career, which exploded with his first album, 1980's *Tale of the Tape*, with the anthemic "The Big Beat." Billy made the record at the Band's Levon Helm's barn/studio in Woodstock with producer Eddy Offord, known for his work with Yes and Emerson, Lake & Palmer. Squier's second and most successful album, 1981's self-produced *Don't Say No*, remained on the charts for two years with hits like "The Stroke," "Lonely is the Night," "In the Dark," and "My Kinda Lover." *Don't Say No* has sold nearly four million copies to fans of rock music and rock breakbeats.

Bobby Chouinard, the former drummer of Piper, was primarily responsible for that signature Squier sound, thanks to his punchy 4/4 rhythms. "The Big Beat" showcased Chouinard's powerful drum beats, with additional percussion by Squier smacking his hand against a snare case. The hip-hop impact of "The Big Beat" was immediate, as the Cold Crush Brothers started using the song in their live performances by 1981.

BOBBY CHOUINARD: "The Big Beat" has this huge bass drum sound. I didn't know what a breakbeat was. But how could you not appreciate the universal interest? I got that sound in the studio by using my kit and hitting as hard as possible. My studio setup only consists of two floor toms, one rack drum, a snare, and a bass drum. I use five drums because that's all I require. I'm too lazy to play any more drums than that! (1985)

Squier distanced himself from the rock world after facing a vicious backlash over the homoerotic choreography of director Kenny Ortega in his "Rock Me Tonite" video. Then came a successful second wind as the most-sampled musician in hip-hop history, with his guitar and vocals sampled over 300 times. Squier's breakbeats became integral to the rap sound, particularly with "The Stroke," one of the most sampled songs ever.

BILLY SQUIER: I was living the life with some pretty successful records. But when hip-hop artists started using "The Stroke" and "The Big Beat," I was shocked. I didn't even get it at first. But at this point, I'd be a fool not to understand the influence. (1993)

In 1983, Run-DMC first sampled "The Big Beat" in their song "Here We Go." The following year, UTFO used the same sample in "Roxanne, Roxanne," which spawned its use in over a dozen "response songs." The emergence of the new sampling phenomenon helped create a new genre that combined rock and hip-hop. "The Big Beat" was also used in rap classics like Big Daddy Kane's 1988 "The Big Beat," A Tribe Called Quest's 1993 "We Can Get Down," Jay-Z's 2004 "99 Problems," Nas featuring will.i.am's "Hip Hop is Dead," A$AP Rocky's 2011 "Out of this World," Alicia Keys' 2012 "Girl on Fire," and Eminem's 2013 "Berzerk," produced by Rick Rubin.

BIG DADDY KANE: I think he has millions of fans who love his body of work, but probably thousands of fans who love him. He's someone who helped mold and shape hip-hop with his music. I would categorize him with James Brown, the Honeydrippers, and Chic. He gave the b-boys and b-girls a track to dance to, but it would only be a DJ or an MC who knew who Billy Squier was. (2013)

BILLY SQUIRE: The sampling of my music has been unexpected and mind-blowing. I had no idea what lay in store when I recorded "The Big Beat" in 1979, but it has taken on a cult-like personality, and I'm like the Robert Johnson of hip-hop! It's very cool. (2005)

RUN-DMC

BLACK AND WHITE: Run-DMC on *American Bandstand*, 1986. Ron Wolfson / MediaPunch / Alamy Stock Photo.

> *The rhymes I say, sharp as a nail*
> *Witty as can be and not for sale*
> —Run-DMC, "Rock Box"

Run-DMC—rap's original superstars—best defined the rock-met-hip-hop crossover. Run-DMC didn't invent hardcore hip-hop, but they reinvented it live and on vinyl like no act had done before. Darryl "DMC" McDaniels, Joseph "Run" Simmons, and Jason "Jam Master Jay" Mizell were barely twenty years old, boyhood friends still living with their parents in the middle-class neighborhood of Hollis, Queens. That's where they gained popularity by hosting parties in the hardscrabble Black suburbia bordering Long Island. The group wasn't doing Harlem raps about drug dealing or sexual proclivities; they came from God-fearing families, attended Catholic schools, and commuted to local colleges before fame beckoned. Their earliest music focused on community outreach, featuring pep-talk-like affirmations and danceable beats designed to boost positivity. After Run's DJ career as "The Son of Kurtis Blow," the original plan was to launch a solo career for Run as "Run The MC." Fortunately, Darryl's initials were "DMC," so the name made sense.

EVERLAST: What made me love hip-hop was Run-DMC. They had a song called "Rock Box" that was all heavy metal guitars and a beat, and it was incredible. It was the greatest thing I'd ever heard. (1999)

PETE NICE: I grew up on Run-DMC. Run-DMC changed the game. Between 1983 and 1984, they were so strong. The records had such a strong image, such a strong fashion look, and such lyrically solid themes—and that's before mentioning the power of the music! They rocked so much harder than every rock band back in the day. (2024)

RUN: The only thing we did was make dope rap records. (2024)

Run-DMC created a b-boy style—characterized by unlaced Adidas, Lee jeans, leather jackets, gold chains, and black fedoras—that transcended crowds and transformed popular culture. They broke down hip-hop's barriers and became living legends. Run-DMC achieved this not by watering down their music and sweetening their sound but by remaining true to their street-corner ethos and, most importantly, by being themselves.

JAM MASTER JAY: Before us, rap was corny. Everything was soft. Nobody made hard beats on records. Everybody just wanted to sing but didn't know *how* to sing. There was no real meaning to a rapper. Bambaataa and Flash, and all of them were getting weak. Everybody was saying that rap was a fad. And before Run-DMC came along, rap music could have been a fad. None of them were making hard-hitting street jams. We came and got ill. There it is. (1986)

RUN: When we came in, we dressed as we wanted and did our thing. We were street. We were hard. When people saw us, they saw that we were regular people. We didn't go around with no braids in our hair, flicking them around. People tend to like what's real. And we were real. (1986)

BILL ADLER: Run-DMC boiled everything down to beats and rhymes. They were so locked in that they weren't just matching rhymes but finishing each other's sentences. So, even if they didn't know the lyrics or the name of the group, like with Aerosmith, they were deeply immersed in the origins of the breakbeats. It wasn't a giant step for Run-DMC to make the records they did. It was Black guys playing rock and roll and calling it rap. And it turned out to be rock and roll. (2024)

After Run graduated high school, his older brother reluctantly agreed to manage the fledgling group. Russell got Run-DMC signed to a long-term deal with Profile Records. Their first 12" of 1983, "It's Like That" b/w "Sucker MCs," shot to the Top 20 hits on the R&B charts with heavier beats than any previous rap record. The two MCs were so locked in, while Jam Master Jay mixed torrential turntablism and crushing beats with the wallop of the heaviest metal of its day.

CORY ROBBINS (Profile Records): All the Sugar Hill label records were very well produced, very slick, and much like funk records. They were great, but they were a specific type. So when Run-DMC came around, it was a new sound. And it didn't take to the market instantly. (2016)

Run-DMC with "Rock Box" (Profile Records, 1984) became an instant b-boy classic. The gold-selling album presented a fresh hip-hop vision, highlighted by cleverly clipped, back-and-forth staccato verses over spare, funky, programmed beats with Jimi Hendrix-esque and Ernest Isley-inspired metal-funk guitar solos. They made the album at Greene Street Studios in SoHo, where the legendary New York cult metal band Riot was in the studio recording simultaneously. This experience was eye-opening for the young Queens b-boys, who were soon on their way to becoming the first rap act on rock radio rotation and MTV airplay with their heavy-handed urban style. What Run-DMC songs shared was an organic, authentic, and original approach. They were rough, rugged, harsher, sparser, and rougher-sounding than their competitors.

RUSSELL SIMMONS: The radio played funk and disco songs. I had a complete disdain for the mainstream; I was rebelling against it. I didn't want to hear anything that sounded like it was on the radio. I wanted to do something new. There was a rebellion in the streets, and kids played funky records, whether it was jazz, blues, heavy rock, or funky R&B, like James Brown. They'd rap over them and create their music, something that was a better soundtrack for what they were living. That was the start of hip-hop as an expression for people who felt left out of the mainstream. (2011)

Larry Smith, the producer and writer of "Rock Box," was a bass player from Queens. He gained experience touring with chitlin-circuit soul star Jerry Washington. A significant connection to Russell Simmons was that he was friends with Russell's older brother, Danny Simmons, at Andrew Jackson High School. Smith had previously played in a band with session guitarist Eddie Martinez, who played guitar on "Rock Box." Known for producing hits for Kurtis Blow and Whodini, Smith simplified the arrangements and balanced the music to make it more accessible to listeners. While many credit Run-DMC's "Walk This Way" with Rick Rubin as rock-rap's start, the story began with "Rock Box" and Larry Smith. Sadly, Larry's story ended tragically. After suffering a massive stroke in 2007, he was left paralyzed and unable to speak. He spent the remainder of his life in a nursing home as "a ward of the state" until his passing in 2014.

BOBBY SIMMONS: Larry Smith was the king of that big beat sound. He used heavy snare and kick. One thing I learned from Larry was that he excelled with melodies and basslines. I wish I were in the studio when they did "Rock Box" and "King of Rock." That was a pivotal moment for hip-hop. (2014)

LARRY SMITH: I had to fight to get that song recorded. They didn't want to do it with the guitar in there. But they started seeing it once I brought my friend Eddie Martinez in and showed them. (2006)

EDDIE MARTINEZ: I knew Larry and Russell dug it; I dug the shit out of it. We were all on board. But Run and DMC came in, and they didn't get it. They didn't understand this enormous rock guitar thing that was weaving in between their raps. (2023)

RUN: We tamed the guitar. We didn't like it too wild. So that's how we kept it. We want to make it raw, though, because we like our music to be loud! (1985)

WHEN ROCK MET HIP-HOP

EDDIE MARTINEZ: At first, the guitar wasn't a primary instrument in hip-hop. It was beats, bottom, and DJs doing their thing, spinning and scratching. But "Rock Box" changed that with a new flavor that made the guitarist crank up on some beats. The first big guitar was on "Rock Box." Larry Smith asked me to put a big rock guitar on it, and I went to work. When I first heard "Rock Box," it was sparse. It was a DMX drum machine, a bass guitar, the tinkling synth motif, Run-DMC rap, and Jam Master J's vibe. I reinforced the bass line with massive-sounding guitars, built on my riffs, harmonized them, and then soloed over the whole track. It was a guitar orchestra. (2023)

LARRY SMITH: I played in rock and roll bands. I was down with the speed metal—hard and dirty—that's where that came from. An engineer named Rod Hui from Greene Street was the first to put a reverb effect on the drums on those Run-DMC songs, and it became a signature sound for hip-hop. (2014)

"Rock Box" was the first rap hit on MTV. The song's performance video spotlighted Eddie Martinez's guitar skills and marked the beginning of rap merging with rock. This crossover set the stage for the success of "King of Rock" and their collaboration with Aerosmith on "Walk This Way," as well as many other similar crossovers.

RUN: "Rock Box" was the first rock-rap record. It sounds so normal today, but when we first heard it, that shit was like psychedelic drugs. Larry Smith was putting us over metal guitars. It's not an acid-rock guitar but a funky guitar to get you moving. That's our claim to fame. It wasn't a remake. Using guitars over hip-hop beats had never been done like that before. (2019)

DMC: When we did "Rock Box," I wanted to do Billy Squier's "The Big Beat" over it. So Larry pulled out the DMX drum machine and said, "D, play the beat." I created my own beat because I didn't want to bite a sample. I made it sound different. I laid the beat down. Run and I dropped our rhyme routine over it and left the studio. When we came back, it had the bells, guitar, and bassline on it, and Larry turned it into "Rock Box," the phenomenon. The song got us on MTV and on our way to superstardom. It captures our look and the swagger we brought to the scene. It was a great time in New York because it *was* the grunge. It's all in the "Rock Box" vibe—punk, disco, hip-hop, CBGB, Lou Reed, Ramones, Madonna. We didn't have to try to be something we weren't. Run-DMC fits in as Run-DMC. (2014)

CORY ROBBINS: We intentionally cast a little white boy in the video in a white rock club with a predominantly white crowd so that MTV would play it—and it worked. (2023)

DMC: We didn't invent hip-hop. But we reinvented it. We'd do "Rock Box" at every show, no matter what. We opened the doors to blend rock and rap, creating the dopest rap and rock records. We rock hard, and we rock the box. Every single time. (1993)

> *I'm the king of rock—there is none higher*
> *Sucker MCs should call me Sire*
> —Run-DMC, "King of Rock"

King of Rock, Run-DMC's second album, released in early 1985, was hip-hop's first platinum album. "King of Rock," the album's groundbreaking single, propelled the group beyond cult status. The song was a pioneering amalgam, uniting musical genres and pushing the boundaries of rock and hip-hop, leaving an indelible mark on the cultural landscape. While Run-DMC had added a rock edge to early hip-hop with "Rock Box," "King of Rock" unleashed a new level of rock in rap, presenting in-your-face vocals, pounding drums, monster riffs, and searing solos.

Putting out a rap album called *King of Rock* was a bold declaration. The new kings of hip-hop brought rap to rock without samples or disco tracks. Larry Smith and guitarist Eddie Martinez produced the record, but the group parted ways with Smith due to his unsuccessful attempts at adding musicality. Although *King of Rock* didn't make it to the *Billboard* Top 100, it sold nearly 500,000 copies upon release and eventually went platinum. The music video, which starred David Letterman's sidekick Larry "Bud" Melman, became a classic with frequent airplay on MTV.

DMC: When I said I was the "King of Rock," it was because that music truly appealed to me. Seventies rock radio created me, and it's one of the major factors that contributed to my success in hip-hop. (2020)

WALK THIS WAY

DON'T CALL IT A COMEBACK: Aerosmith (Joe Perry, Joey Kramer, Steven Tyler, Tom Hamilton, Brad Whitford), 1988. Photofest.

> *It was three young ladies in the school gym locker*
> *And they found they were lookin' at D*
> —Run-DMC and Aerosmith, "Walk This Way"

"Walk This Way" is historically significant due to Run-DMC's collaboration with Aerosmith. The song appeared on Run-DMC's third album for Profile, *Raising Hell*, a cultural milestone for hip-hop. It was the first multi-platinum rap album and contained three other hits: "It's Tricky," "My Adidas," and "You Be Illin'." With production credits to Russell Simmons and Rick Rubin, *Raising Hell* solidified Run-DMC's position as rap royalty and kick-started hip-hop's Golden Age. Their hard rock revamp helped bridge the cultural gap between white suburban rock fans and the Black hip-hop community.

DMC: It was so cool that we did the song with Aerosmith. We could have remade it alone, but it wouldn't have had the same impact. Their fans asked, "Why are they with the rap guys!?" Our fans didn't know any better and thought, "Why are they doing a record with The Rolling Stones!?" When Steven Tyler smashed the mic stand through the wall, that's what happened. Rock and rap broke barriers and came together. (2018)

After the "moderate" sales of "Rock Box" and "King of Rock" (neither of which became Top Ten singles), the rappers began to reconsider their rock music direction. At the same time, Aerosmith was struggling with the damaging effects of hard drugs. Steven Tyler was in poor condition, struggling with addiction and crashing on people's couches after the release of 1982's *Rock in a Hard Place*, which was the only Aerosmith record without guitarist Joe Perry. Perry returned for 1986's *Done with Mirrors*, named for their cocaine use. When Aerosmith soundman Robert "Nitebob" Czaykowski connected Rick Rubin with their manager Tim Collins, the band had no idea what they were getting into. Collins agreed to Rubin's offer of $8,000 for a day's work at Magic Ventures Studios.

RICK RUBIN: We finished the album—and I listened to it and felt like something was missing. That came simultaneously with this conversation about how rap was not real music. To people who were not already fans, the gap was so significant that not only did they not understand it, but they also did not see it as music. I was looking for a way to bridge that gap, finding a piece of music that was familiar and already hip-hop-friendly so that on the hip-hop side, it would make sense, and on the non-hip-hop side, you'd see it wasn't so far away. (2016)

NITEBOB: There was a great rock and roll shop on 8th Street in Greenwich Village called It's Only Rock and Roll. That's where you could get your British books, magazines, and memorabilia. I used to stop there to see Scott Koenig, who ran the record section. Scott later worked with the Beastie Boys. One time, I went, and Rick Rubin was there. We were sitting there hanging out, and Rubin says he has been working on something and asks me if I know what rap is. I told him I did because in the early 1980s, when I was working with Evelyn "Champagne" King, we did a lot of West Coast shows with five rappers dressed like gladiators. Rick told me he was working with this rap act and had the idea of putting Aerosmith and Run-DMC together. He had been reaching out to their management but was not getting anywhere. I was working with Aerosmith again for the first time in years. So I said, "Oh okay, I can help you . . . " I called Joe Perry and asked if he knew what rap music was. You gotta give points to Joe Perry for picking up and saying, "I'd love to hear this!" Then Rick sent him some records. Next thing you know, they went to New York. A chance meeting in a record store sparked a cultural shift. It wasn't as if there was some global plot to merge these things. (2024)

DMC: When Rick Rubin suggested we redo the song, me and Run were like, "You're taking this rock-rap shit too far—you're going to ruin us. That's gonna be fake; nobody in hip-hop will like it." But he persuaded me and Jay to listen to the lyrics, so we put the needle on the record. When Steven Tyler opened his mouth, we got on the phone: "Y'all motherfuckers. We're gonna be ruined!" We had this big argument. (2023)

WHEN ROCK MET HIP-HOP

NITEBOB: This is the story Rick Rubin told me: Run-DMC carried their records around in milk crates, and the spines of those records would get worn, so they didn't know the names of the bands. Their cover got beat up, so they only saw "Toys in the Attic." They thought it was "Walk This Way" by Toys in the Attic. (2024)

JOHN KOLODNER: Rick Rubin came to me and said, "I have this great idea." I didn't think about it as a watershed moment. I felt in my head, "Good luck to you working with two people who are higher than a kite." (2016)

After overcoming cultural issues, they transformed a 1975 hard rock classic into a fantastic hip-hop track. When Run-DMC got hold of Aerosmith's funky little number, they did more than a good cover; it was a societal breakthrough. The song's significance was its heavy airplay on white rock radio, introducing a new sound to a new audience. "Walk This Way" single-handedly rejuvenated Aerosmith's fading career and re-established the 1970s act as a household name. Yet Aerosmith never attempted another rock-rap fusion.

STEVEN TYLER: I loved rap. I used to go looking for drugs on Ninth Avenue, and I would go over to Midtown or Downtown, and there would be guys on the corner selling cassettes of their music. I'd give them a buck or two, which was the beginning of my noticing what was happening in New York at the time. (2016)

JOE PERRY: We had reservations about it. Our fans might not like it. However, our love for music and our willingness to try new things far surpassed that. I heard a direct connection between what they were doing and the blues. All you had to do was have a boombox and some wit and talent. And a way to express yourself, which is what they were doing on the street corner—which is what blues was. To me, it was like a direct connection. The only thing that was missing was my guitar. (2019)

The "Walk This Way" video, a pinnacle of rock video history, brought together Black and white people, as well as rock and rap cultures. The video's concept was developed around Steven Tyler and Joe Perry playing the song loudly in a practice space next to Run-DMC. The rappers didn't like the music and yelled for the rockers to turn it down. Run-DMC retaliated by increasing the volume on their turntables and drum machine as they began their hip-hop version of the song. Aerosmith was upset by the intrusion. Steven Tyler broke down the walls with his mic stand as they cut to a concert sequence in an old run-down theater in Union City, NJ, in front of a wild, mainly white audience. Producer Jon Small shot the video with a modest budget of $67,000. In a cost-saving move, instead of flying in Tom Hamilton, Brad Whitford, and Joey Kramer, the rest of Aerosmith were impersonated by three members of the New York glam-metal band Smashed Gladys.

FERNANDO ROSARIO: Steven Tyler is very cool and funny. He told a lot of jokes. Joe Perry kept to himself, although I still managed to get a few autographs from him. But Steve is like Mr. Friendly and gregarious. He wants to make everybody laugh. He's just a fun, sweet guy. At least, that's the impression I got from him. (2024)

BART LEWIS: Steven Tyler went out of his way not to be involved with Run-DMC. It was weird that he spent as much time talking to me as he did ignoring them. It could be a music business thing. Somebody's riding somebody's coattails, and each of them thinks it's the other. Aerosmith believes, "This song is going to make you guys huger stars than you are." Run-DMC thinks, "They're going to have a comeback based on doing this with us." However, the ice did seem to break as the hours passed. (2019)

WHEN ROCK MET HIP-HOP

FERNANDO ROSARIO: Sally Cato, the lead singer of Smashed Gladys, taught me everything about rock and roll. She got us the video gig because she was the makeup artist, hairstylist, clothing designer, and set designer; she had done a lot of videos. I was a kid, like twenty years old; I didn't know anything. So I'm working at a clothing store then, and I get a phone call from Sally, saying, "Are you available? We have to do a video with Steven Tyler, Joe Perry, and Run DMC." I was surprised, as one would be. But that's how we got the gig. Unfortunately, I had to quit my job to do the video because this rock and roll stuff didn't agree with the work schedule my boss had in mind. (2024)

STEVEN TYLER: Aerosmith toured with Run-DMC, so Jay and I got close. Our encore was "Walk This Way"—we'd bring out Run-DMC, and the place would explode! Jay would stand by Joe Perry; I'd sing the first verse, and Jay would be there scratching with his turntables. I'd stick the mic in his face to allow him to sing where he ordinarily wouldn't. The first time I did that, he was so embarrassed. But it became something that we did every night. Jay was the shit, man. He was a beautiful, open guy. Jay was the guy who first grabbed our version of "Walk This Way" and started scratching over it. The sadness of his death pales in comparison to the joy he brought to the world. He was the furthest person from being a gangsta I knew, and I miss him. (2002)

FERNANDO ROSARIO: So, the video happened. The story is that the band planned to hire actors to fill in for the rest of Aerosmith onstage because they didn't know what they were doing. So Sally was like, "We cover a few Aerosmith songs, and we've done 'Same Old Song and Dance,' 'Walk This Way,' and 'Back in The Saddle'"—and that's how we got the video. We each got fifty bucks, and the video shoot lasted 48 hours. We could go home and return, but the crew was there for 48 hours. Anyway, we were never heavily featured in the video. You can barely see me. I'm in the top far right corner. You barely see a giant ball of hair shaking, wearing a red Explorer bass, and that's me. You can barely see the drum set, but Matt's hair is so big and black that you don't see him. His hair obscured him behind the drums. You can see Bart a bit on the left side of the stage. But they didn't feature us at all. Rightfully so, I understand that. (2024)

JOE PERRY: When we filmed the video, we had no idea how important it would be. We didn't know the song would be on the record when we recorded it. It opened the door to a new genre of music, which was important. At the time, MTV mostly played videos of white artists. Michael Jackson, Aretha Franklin, and Prince were the few exceptions. And they weren't playing any rap. (2019)

In retrospect, the "Walk This Way" video plot line came true: kicking off a friendship between two bands with little in common. The video serves as an expression of rock and rap groups collaborating and motivating one another. DMC started wearing cool rock shirts, like those of the Ramones and Motörhead. MTV aired the crossover video twice an hour, which boosted both groups but probably benefited Aerosmith more. Their collaboration on "Walk This Way" ranked higher than the original, hitting #4 on the *Billboard* Hot 100. The *Soul Train Music Awards* named it Rap Single of the Year. The collaboration paved the way for the rap-rock genre for years to come. In 2009, Eminem inducted Aerosmith into the Rock & Roll Hall of Fame.

DMC: Joe Perry was brilliant. He didn't say one word during the session. You would ask, "Joe, are you okay?" He'd nod his head up and down. But when it was time to go in there, he walked in with a cigarette hanging from his mouth and winked his eye. They pushed the record, and we made history. (2016)

WHEN ROCK MET HIP-HOP

CHUCK D: Run-DMC made it possible for all the majors to see that rap music and hip-hop were album-oriented music and rap artists were rock stars. Run-DMC was the complete sacrifice for anything successful after 1986. Run-DMC should be as revered as Aerosmith and have all the spoils. They were the sacrifice for the guys. (2016)

DMC: Some people say it's the most significant rap record ever made and the greatest video. VH-1 did their "Top 50 Videos Of All-Time"—and we were Number One. It was all about bringing generations of music together, which is what music is supposed to do—evolution and unity. (2023)

After their seventh studio album, 2001's *Crown Royal*, Run-DMC was never the same after the tragic murder of Jam Master Jay, shot inside his Jamaica, Queens studio. Run-DMC's career came to a screeching halt, and Simmons and McDaniels were left to pick up the pieces (to McDaniels, Run-DMC ceased to exist that night). The 37-year-old mixmaster Mizell was buried at Ferncliff Cemetery and the Mausoleum in Hartsdale. Simmons and McDaniels tried to recreate the magic as a duo—and often did so successfully—but it was never the same.

JAM MASTER JAY: We'd love to work with Rick Rubin again. He's one of the illest b-boys with the illest brain mentality, making the craziest big rock n' roll records ever. He's sick, he's definitely ill. (1993)

DMC: Seriously, Run-DMC will get back together when the Beatles return. Run-DMC can't do it without Jay as a performing and touring entity. (2023)

DREW STONE: When Run-DMC and Aerosmith collaborated on "Walk This Way," that was a watershed moment where the cat was out of the bag. To me, that's the first rap-metal rock crossover. Sure, there were other instances of rock music rhyming, but "Walk This Way" was when worlds collided. Run-DMC delivered their gritty, urban interpretation of the Aerosmith song without fully understanding the lyrics. But they loved the beat and the groove and rapping to it. I know it's a little later in rap history, but that was the powder keg that exploded. It was like the bomb was set off. And it took a minute for the dust to settle because that was a huge success. Then everybody started running out and trying to do shit like that. (2024)

DEF JAM

> *She studies real hard, all night she'll cram*
> *In school, she majors in Advanced Def Jam*
> —Beastie Boys, "She's On It"

Def Jam was the first record company to successfully blend hip-hop with a rock edge. The label exploded out of the box because it spoke to the need for a fresh new sound reflecting America's browning. The label's founders were Black and white, and as the company grew, it reflected an integrated workplace. Ultimately, Def Jam transformed pop music and established the blueprint for all future sounds.

Beastie Boys, one of Def Jam's first successes, brought together rock and rap, crossing over from the punk side. Over time, they evolved from an ordinary, noisy, hardcore band to a groundbreaking hip-hop group and ultimately to something far beyond. Their iconic sound and style revolutionized music and culture.

Books and films have documented the violent junkie wasteland of early 1980s Downtown Manhattan. Amidst the chaos, the primitive original New York punk and hardcore (NYHC) scenes emerged. The Beastie Boys were part of NYHC's first wave of bratty, misfit teen bands, including Kraut, Reagan Youth, Heart Attack, and the Undead.

WHEN ROCK MET HIP-HOP

Growing up in New York and frequenting the Downtown "rock discos" sparked their interest in club music and early hip-hop. As such, they became the first hardcore band to hit the mainstream—before being embraced by the punk scene.

MIKE D: The only way we could've become the band that we became is because New York had everything going on then. Now, you can get every song that ever influenced us on my phone. But at that time, New York was the only place in the world that had a confluence of all different kinds of music: dub, jazz, and salsa; then new-wave, no-wave, post-punk, and the beginnings of rap. (2018)

Michael "Mike D" Diamond, the original Beastie Boy, grew up in an affluent New York family of art collectors. He fronted a group called the Young Aborigines, which included drummer Kate Schellenbach, guitarist John Berry, and bassist Jeremy Shattuck. Adam "MCA" Yauch, a West Village skateboarder who also attended Brooklyn Friends School, hung out with the Aborigines. On Adam's seventeenth birthday, the Beastie Boys came to form, with Yauch replacing Shattuck on bass.

MIKE D: When I was fourteen years old, we ran around and started playing music. The furthest thing we could see was two weeks ahead, and maybe we could get a gig at CBGB. (1994)

The band became known on the NYHC scene when they started hanging out at 171A, a rehearsal space and recording studio on Avenue A, where the Bad Brains recorded their legendary ROIR cassette with studio owner Jerry "J-Dub" Williams. Jerry imparted wisdom to the young wayward punks about Rastafarianism and Buddhism through the magic of the endless amounts of weed he'd smoke with them.

One of J-Dub's friends was Dave Parsons, who sold indie and imported punk vinyl from his beat-up shopping cart trolling the streets of Alphabet City. Jerry invited Dave's Rat Cage Records to open in his cleared-out cellar. Rat Cage became the epicenter of the nascent New York scene. That's how Dave Parsons saw the Beasties' first gig and loved what he saw, and put out their 1982 debut *Pollywog Stew* 7" EP on his Rat Cage label, recorded upstairs at 171A with Jerry Williams and producer Scott Jarvis. The Beasties also cut two songs for the iconic 1982 *New York Thrash* compilation cassette.

DARRYL JENIFER: We all used to hang out around the Rat Cage Records store on Avenue A. It was like we were in college; Rat Cage was the quad. We were up there eating pistachios, drinking soy milk, selling a little ganja on the strip, and selling our nickel bags to get our music going. And we would yell, "Beast! Beast!" when the cops came. Mike and Adam would be on the stoops, yelling it back to us. That's where I believe "Beastie Boys" came from. (2011)

ADAM YAUCH: I wanted to start a hardcore band, but hardcore hadn't come to New York. We knew there was hardcore in DC, so we said, "Let's start a New York hardcore band!" So we tried to write some faster punk songs. Dave Parsons saw us play and said, "You guys have to make a record for my label." So we went into the studio at 171A with Scott Jarvis, recorded those songs, and then the band broke up. When the record came out, the kids were listening to it. We got offers to do shows, so we got back together and figured out how to play those songs again. After a few gigs, we became a band. We did one show at A7 and one at The Playroom with Even Worse. HR from the Bad Brains was at that show and liked us. He asked us to open for them at Max's Kansas City. It all went from there. (1998)

The Young and the Useless was much like the Beastie Boys in that they were also a comedic NYHC band that hung out at 171A. Adam "Ad-Rock" Horovitz, son of infamous Greenwich Village playwright Israel Horovitz, played guitar in the band fronted by the late Dave Scilken. The band printed 800 copies of a six-song 7" called *Real Men Don't Floss*, recorded by Jerry Williams at 171A. The band, briefly managed by PiL manager Bob Tulipan, played inane thrash covers of "Grease" and "Billy, Don't Be a Hero" at clubs like CBGB, A7, Mudd Club, and Reggae Lounge, opening for the likes of the Bad Brains, Ramones, and Dead Kennedys. The Young and the Useless broke up when Horovitz left to join the Beastie Boys and went on tour with Madonna.

KATE SCHELLENBACH: Sometime in 1982, John Berry left. He wasn't into playing music. He went off on a drug-induced tangent. Horovitz was already hanging around. He already knew all the songs. As he says, Adam came up from the minors. (2011)

> *Pussy crumbs? What are pussy crumbs?*
> *Take me home and eat me, yeah!*
> —Beastie Boys, "Cooky Puss"

Cooky Puss, the Beastie Boys' second record, also released on Parsons' Rat Cage label, delivered a snotty punk attitude with a hip-hop beat. These somewhat Jewish New York punks who became intrigued by rap music's possibilities created an utterly unique 1983 12" record based on a ghetto-style prank phone call to a Carvel Ice Cream shop asking to speak to Cooky Puss, the name of Tom Carvel's iconic ice cream cake.

DOUG POMEROY: The recording was completely spontaneous, with no pre-planning. The studio had a phone line that could be patched directly to any track on the tape recorders. I must have told them this because I don't think they would have known otherwise. What made Horowitz consider calling Carvel to order an ice cream cake? I'll never know! But he did it, and it got recorded without any edits. They also had a Steve Martin comedy LP and did some scratching on it. I thought "Cooky Puss" was a great piece of aggressive comedy, and I loved it. It did not surprise me that it became popular and helped make their reputation. When we mastered the 12" single, I requested the disc-cutting engineer to compress the sound grossly, as a joke, to make fun of over-compressed records. The Beasties didn't ask for that, but they liked it. (2004)

"Beastie Revolution," the B-side, was a cheeky stab at Bad Brains-style dub with primitive beats and scratches. A short while after the release, they saw their song in a British Airways ad, used without their permission. They sued BA and settled out of court for $40,000, which allowed them to move out of their parental homes to share a rat-infested loft in Chinatown. The newly flush copyright plaintiffs could also afford an 808 drum machine, which marked their dive into becoming a rap group. The irony was that the trio admitted years later that "Cooky Puss" was their appropriation of Malcolm McLaren's "Buffalo Gals."

MIKE D: "Cooky Puss" couldn't be replicated live. It was a bunch of segments of stuff that we'd played, chopped up with the phone call. But that started getting played in clubs, and suddenly, we got asked to do shows in places we'd never been. (2011)

KATE SCHELLENBACH: "Cooky Puss" started getting college radio play, and we thought it was time to incorporate some hip-hop experience into the live show. That's when Rick Rubin came aboard. I don't know who found him, but it was like, "This guy goes to NYU and could be our DJ." We called him DJ Double R. (1998)

WHEN ROCK MET HIP-HOP

Like claps of thunder from a cumulus cloud
Double R pump the beat and make it real loud
—Beastie Boys, "Rock Hard"

Rick Rubin (Frederick Rubin) was the most unlikely of hip-hop pioneers. He grew up in upper-middle-class Lido Beach, Long Island, where he learned the basics of music from his music teachers. As a member of the AV Club, he played at birthday parties when he was twelve or thirteeen. Rick became the guitarist of a Long Beach High School punk band called the Pricks, with his first credited production being the band's eight-song single. At a gig at CBGB, they tried to get thrown out. So they had friends heckle them onstage and started a brawl. A "cop" wanted to arrest them, impersonated by Rick's shoe salesman dad, Michael Rubin.

RICK RUBIN: I was the only punk rocker at my high school; at least a handful of Black kids liked hip-hop. Both were the new music of the day. Being the only punk was lonely. Because of where I lived and the lack of a community to be a punk with, I started hanging out with kids who liked hip-hop. And I learned it through them. (2013)

In the fall of 1981, Rick attended New York University (NYU) in Greenwich Village. As a freshman from his Weinstein Hall dorm room #712, Rubin rolled out Hose, a grating PiL/Flipper-style "noise" band that played the Downtown new wave and hardcore clubs. His quartet of classmates made two records: 1982's *Mobo* (a 7" EP sold in a paper bag) with singer Rick Rosen and 1983's *Hose* 12" EP with singer Michael Espindle. The latter presented a Rubin-designed faux-Mondrian front cover and slow, grinding renditions of Rick James' "Super Freak," Black Sabbath's "Sweet Leaf," Hot Chocolate's "You

Sexy Thang," and Ohio Players' "Fire." These were the first releases on Def Jam Recordings.

ERIC HOFFERT: Rick Rubin was in a hardcore band called Hose. They would play in the cafeteria of the Weinstein dorm. It was crazed, almost Charles Manson-like. They were pretty awful. People couldn't understand what he was onto—the fact that he was in this band, and then he'd go out to these hip-hop clubs at night. He was a budding impresario. He was a powerhouse; he worked fourteen, sixteen hours a day. (2011)

Rick spent his nights at trendy clubs like Danceteria and the Peppermint Lounge, where he saw early rap groups like DJ Jazzy Jay and the Treacherous Three. He instantly understood that, like punk, hip-hop is about having something to say, rather than being a virtuoso. He immersed himself in a world of DJs, MCs, and like-minded fans.

AD-ROCK: For one thing, Rick was a little older, so that was kinda cool. He's just one of these people who would let you know, like, "Oh, I'm really cool and really smart, and my opinion is the right opinion." And when you're a kid, you're cool with it. But, in retrospect, he's interesting. You want to believe things when you're a kid, you know? (2020)

At the age of nineteen, Rick Rubin made his first inroads into the music business with his father's financial support. Before connecting with Russell Simmons, he tried to buy into working with Arthur Baker and the Washington, DC, go-go band Trouble Funk.

Russell Simmons was one of the biggest names in the emerging rap industry. Rick's chance meeting with Russell at Danceteria through DJ Jazzy Jay forever changed Rick's career trajectory. [Jay introduced Rick to many early rap legends, taught Rick how to make beats on a drum machine, and built a world-class sound system into Rick's car.] Simmons was five years older than Rubin. But he immediately recognized the young producer's skills. The two showed mutual admiration and formed a partnership.

RUSSELL SIMMONS: The more I got to know Rick, the more I felt that my efforts should go into a partnership. Rick wanted to start a record company as an independent entity, as opposed to a distribution deal, which made sense. I put the money in with him — it was only a few dollars — and the first record, "I Need a Beat," sold so well. And it was not the sales of the records; it was the sound of the records that inspired me to be his partner. He's a great producer, and I thought, "We can do a lot together." (2011)

It's incredible how an aspiring Black hip-hop entrepreneur and a white Jewish punk created the new school of rap, dominating 1980s pop music by working with rising artists like Run-DMC, the Beastie Boys, and Public Enemy.

DREW STONE: You have to connect the dots between Rick Rubin, Russell Simmons, Lyor Cohen, Scott Koenig, Rush Management, Def Jam, Slayer, Danzig, LL Cool J, Run-DMC, and Profile Records. You see that this stuff didn't happen magically. Lyor Cohen tour managed Slayer before he was behind Rush Management. Russell Simmons is Run's brother. So, things fell into each other. It was all very interconnected. (2024)

BILL ADLER: The label was a new opportunity created by people committed to the culture. There was no way to predict that what we did would blow the fuck up. (2024)

*Commentating, illustrating, description giving, adjective
expert, analyzing, surmising
Musical myth-seeking people of the universe, this is yours*
—T La Rock, "It's Yours"

T La Rock (Terry Keaton) was the first rapper signed by Rick Rubin. He dated back to hip-hop's earliest days in the Bronx, attending Kool Herc parties and MCing, scratching, and breakdancing in the parks. That's where he introduced his brother Special K of the Treacherous Three to the scene. By age twenty-one, Terry, who'd been performing with Afrika Bambaataa's Soul Sonic Force, went solo. Through Bambaataa, T knew Jazzy Jay, the top DJ on KISS-FM. The two immediately clicked. The result was one of the most noteworthy early b-boy records.

T LA ROCK: My brother Special K introduced me to Rick Rubin. He was going to make a record with Rick, but he couldn't because Sugarhill Records had already signed The Treacherous Three. So my brother told me that Rick wanted to release a record and start a label. So, I met Rick at NYU. When we did "It's Yours." Def Jam Recordings wasn't a label yet; it was in his dorm room. It was like a production company. (2008)

"It's Yours," the first Rick Rubin rap production, brought Rick and Russell together. The single first came out in 1983 on Arthur Baker Streetwise Records' subsidiary imprint PartyTyme before Rick re-released it in 1984 as the first 12" with a maroon-and-white Def Jam logo. T's fresh, rapid-fire vocals sliced through exploding 808 drum machines. Rubin invited a few NYU friends to the recording session, which involved the punk-era Beastie Boys in the crowd chorus.

WHEN ROCK MET HIP-HOP

RICK RUBIN: Power Play was the studio where we recorded the Hose record, which was really cheap. It was $45 an hour, and we made "It's Yours" in three hours. (2022)

("It's Yours" has been sampled over 300 times, most notably on Public Enemy's "Louder Than a Bomb" and Nas' "The World is Yours." T nearly died in 1994 due to brain trauma in a club fight, in which he suffered loss of memory and motor skills. It took until age sixty to regain his health. Russell began development on a film with 20th Century Fox based on T's story, based on a *GQ* article by Josh Berman entitled: "The Man Who Forgot He Was a Rap Legend.")

RUSSELL SIMMONS: T La Rock has always inspired me and many others in the hip-hop community. This is a man who was beaten to within an inch of his life at the height of his fame. How he regained his memory and recovered from his coma while being cared for and surrounded by the most unlikely group of therapists and friends is a hope-filled and hopeful true story that will appeal to everyone, whether you love rap music or not. (2017)

> *There's no glo-glory for this story-story*
> *It-it rock-rock in any territory-tory*
> —LL Cool J, "I Need A Beat"

LL Cool J came to Def Jam through a teenage Ad-Rock. Adam basically lived at Rubin's dorm, listening to demo tapes and fielding calls for Def Jam. The demo that caught his attention was from a 15-year-old kid from Queens named James Todd Smith, who went by the stage name LL Cool J (Ladies Love Cool J).

In early 1984, LL sent Def Jam his cassette—with cutting and scratching by mixmaster Cut Creator, in which LL gave shout-outs to his friends on Farmers Boulevard in St. Albans—and followed up with a flurry of calls. LL bonded with Adam, who turned on Rick to the recording. Rubin saw he had something special with the young rapper spewing street-tough rhymes with a cocksure attitude. LL's debut 1984 single, "I Need a Beat," made with a young Ad-Rock as drum programmer and engineer Jay "Burzootie" Burnett, became Def Jam's first hit. Between Rick's minimalist production and Russell's industry inroads, the 12" sold over 100,000 copies, instantly establishing Def Jam.

LL COOL J: Ad-Rock of the Beastie Boys was the one who gave my demo to Rick Rubin. That's how I got my break. Ad-Rock used to hang out with Rick in his dorm room every day. Ad-Rock would go through the box when he had nothing to do; he was playing hooky at school. He listened to my tape, liked it, and told Rick. Rick and I went into the studio, and that's when we made "I Need a Beat." At the time, Def Jam Productions had problems collecting their money from PartyTyme/Streetwise, Arthur Baker. That was a tough time for Def Jam. (2023)

> *Got real rock shit, you must admit*
> *Not fake, not false, not counterfeit*
> —Beastie Boys, "Rock Hard"

The ambitious Rubin's next career step came from his connection with the Beastie Boys. Likewise, the Beasties would never have existed as we know them had Rick not stepped in as their DJ and then as their producer and boss at Def Jam.

RUSSELL SIMMONS: I met the Beastie Boys at Danceteria. They were wearing red sweatsuits with stripes, red Pumas, and doo-rags. They were assholes. (1998)

"Rock Hard" was the Beastie Boys' first Def Jam 12". Rick Rubin, credited as "DJ Double R," produced it. They became the first group to create a song that merged raw hip-hop beats with heavy metal riffs—deconstructing AC/DC's "Back In Black." The radically original and childishly simple yet hard-driving jam remains one of the Beastie Boys' essential recordings and a definitive moment when rock and hip-hop met.

RICK RUBIN: Our goal is to combine rap rhythms with the heavy guitar sound of AC/DC. (1985)

Other original Def Jam 12"s to redefine hip-hop included the Beasties' "Jimmy James" with a sample of Jimi Hendrix's "Voodoo Chile (Slight Return)," and Adam Yauch with engineer Jay Burnett, credited as MCA and Burzootie, on "Drum Machine." A comical moment in Def Jam history was on Jazzy Jay's "Def Jam," whose B-side "Cold Chillin' In The Spot" featured a freestyle rap by Russell Simmons (as "Russell Rush.")

BILL ADLER: Def Jam was baptized in hip-hop. Rick was a massive lover of live hip-hop and was dissatisfied with the rap records being made. He thought they were compromised. (2015)

Rubin transformed the Beastie Boys from hardcore punks to sharp-tongued rappers. Gone was drummer Kate Schellenbach, with

Double-R becoming the group's DJ and producer. The Beasties tore it up at the Downtown clubs during this time with mixmaster Rick. That era culminated in their opening slot on Madonna's "Like A Virgin" tour, a hookup with their nightlife friend. It was a pairing comparable to Jimi Hendrix's opening for the Monkees. Madonna asked Russell Simmons about Run-DMC, who were busy, so he convinced her to take out his white rappers. The Material Girl's pubescent fans loathed the vulgar, beer-soaked Beasties so much that it helped her edgy public image.

AD-ROCK: Then the Madonna tour happened. We'd do like three songs, and then I'd do the electric boogaloo for a minute, and then we fucked with the audience. They hated us. Kids were literally in tears; parents wanted to kill us. It was awesome. They wanted to kick us off the tour, but Madonna said, "These guys are staying. These guys are great." We got back to New York, and we were really feeling ourselves. We were crushing our old spots. (2011)

The Beasties exploded under Rubin's direction. The group's first Def Jam/Columbia 12", 1985's "She's on It" b/w "Slow and Low," was their most interesting rock-rap fusion.

ADAM YAUCH: In the future, we'll do anything we want. If you had asked us about our plans after our first hardcore record, we wouldn't have known we'd do "Cooky Puss." When we did "Cooky Puss," we couldn't have told you we'd do "She's On It." (1985)

HIP-HOP AND GRAFFITI: Artist Keith Haring and the Beastie Boys, Madison Square Garden, 1985. MediaPunch Inc / Alamy Stock Photo.

> *I'm schoolin' in the boys' room, coolin' by the locker*
> *All the girls in class know that I'm the cool rocker*
> —Beastie Boys, "She's Crafty"

Licensed To Ill, the Beasties' 1986 debut album, was going to be called *Don't Be a Faggot* until Columbia Records intervened. The record took over a year to complete, with about one song recorded per month. However, that hard work may be what made it such a great album. It reached the Top 10 within two months of its release, becoming the fastest-selling debut in Columbia history. *Licensed to Ill* was the first hip-hop album to go #1 (for seven weeks) and became the first rap record to surpass five million sales. For its time, it was the largest-selling rap album ever made.

CHUCK D: People were so confused about race and hip-hop that they didn't even consider the Beastie Boys one of the greatest rap groups ever because they were white. (2023)

DJ MUGGS: I was the biggest Beastie Boys fan. I bought every Def Jam record; I didn't give a fuck what it was. Anything by Rick Rubin was getting bought. We were trying to tap into that same rock and roll energy that Run-DMC, Public Enemy, and the Beastie Boys had. It was that rock and roll energy that transcended. (2013)

Rooted in window-rattling hard rock tradition, biting humor, bratty prattling, and bawdy party rhymes, rarely had an album been so riddled with references to drugs, alcohol, violence, and objectification of women. Everyone from b-boys to frat boys embraced the deliberately fun and sassy album. *Licensed to Ill* was a riotous exploration of early cut-and-splice sampling techniques and a satirical glimpse of amped-up adolescent sexuality, delivered with an intentionally heavy-handed, trash-talking, irreverent tone.

HANK SHOCKLEE: At that time, hip-hop and rock, especially heavy metal, were so far away from each other. Rick's genius was taking rock and hip-hop and marrying them together. (2008)

MIKE D: We would start with the music, and then Rick would clean it up. Rick had the ability to make things sound legitimate and bigger, to make it sound like a record. (2011)

The *Licensed to Ill* track "She's Crafty" embodied the group's originality, melding punk's jagged edge, rap's staccato prosody, and the drum break from Led Zeppelin's "The Ocean." Their live shows were like

Sodom and Gomorrah, depraved enough to make Caligula smile. For much of 1987, after the album's massive success, their tour opening for Run-DMC became a headlining tour. All this mayhem contributed to an unforeseen resurgence of rock and roll.

DARYL JENIFER: The Beasties, at least Mike D and Adam Yauch, were mainly rock dudes. Ad-Rock was a b-boy the whole time. I used to call him my son when they were young, like 15. He always had that b-boy persona, even back then. Yauch was a total rock dude, and Mike D was like this pimp/rock dude who hung out with a lot of girls; some of them went on to become Luscious Jackson. (2016)

While *Licensed to Ill* made for appalling sociology, as music, it was lovably loud, excellently offensive, and delightfully disgusting. Bad behavior was the lynchpin of the early Beasties. Their audacious behavior led to their banishment from hotels and record label offices. The security team for Tower Records in New York City warned that *Licensed to Ill* was "the most shoplifted item in the stores."

AD-ROCK: What upsets me about that era is that we might have reinforced specific values of some people in our audience when our values differed. At the same time, some of our values were twisted. (1994)

The Beastie Boys' best songs on *Licensed to Ill* were the fourth and fifth singles, featuring raging heavy metal guitar: "(You Gotta) Fight For Your Right (To Party)" and "No Sleep Till Brooklyn." Adam Horovitz and Rick Rubin traded riffs on "Fight For Your Right." Kerry King from Slayer shredded guitar on "No Sleep." Rapping over AC/DC on "Rock Hard" was one thing; King's insane soloing took rap-metal crossover to the next level.

LICENSED TO ILL: Adam Yauch, Mike Diamond, Rick Rubin, Adam Horovitz, 1985. Photofest.

Slayer was one of the heaviest rock bands of all time. They thrashed with such a breakneck tempo and unrelenting attitude that the world has yet to catch up. Slayer's first record with Rick Rubin was their evil opus *Reign in Blood*. The 1986 album first appeared on Def Jam, so the headbangers interacted with unexpected hip-hop peers. Rubin produced Slayer and the Beastie Boys simultaneously—in the same studio but in different rooms—leading to unique interactions. When the Beasties' "No Sleep Till Brooklyn" needed a raging guitar solo, Rubin paid King $250 for the studio session.

KERRY KING: We were in the studio doing *Reign in Blood*. They were doing *Licensed to Ill* right down the hall, and Rick Rubin was doing both. So, he came in and said, "Hey man, we need somebody to do a lead on this track." And that's all it was. (2024)

Kerry was a big-haired Southern California guitar hero but not the brightest bulb on the Christmas tree. Slayer began as an incredible

Judas Priest cover band. Kerry briefly left Slayer to play with Dave Mustaine in the first shows by Megadeth. Rubin hired King because he was a deft Sunset Strip shredder, far beyond his savage Slayer image.

DREW STONE: MTV loved the Beastie Boys, going back to those first *Licensed to Ill* videos. "Fight For Your Right To Party" and "No Sleep Till Brooklyn" were incredible blasts of rap and metal. They were legit because there was the Kerry King of Slayer tie-in. It's hard to explain just how radical it was to have the guitarist of the world's most extreme metal band on a rap track. So, the video drew in people from all sides. (2024)

King's gnarly licks with the Beastie Boys fast-tracked the crossover of the punk, rap, and metal undergrounds. A great byproduct was Public Enemy's 1987 hip-hop track "She Watch Channel Zero?!" slowing down and sampling "Angel of Death," the opening song on *Reign in Blood*. Rubin pushed the envelope, promoting Slayer as a Satanic, possibly Nazi, metal band with the lyrics to "Angel of Death" about Josef Mengele and the horrors of the Holocaust.

KERRY KING: Rick asked me to go in there and make this really obnoxious lead. So that's what I did. I made an obnoxious lead! It sounded terrible—but hey, that's what he wanted! (1986)

> *Your mom busted in and said, "What's that noise?"*
> *Aw, Mom, you're just jealous it's the Beastie Boys*
> —Beastie Boys, "(You Gotta) Fight For Your Right (To Party)"

"(You Gotta) Fight For Your Right (To Party)," the Beastie Boys' raucous anthem of high-energy metallic rap, brought them widespread ("white spread"?) appeal. All of a sudden, rockers rapped, and hip-hop DJs sampled metal. The 1986 song hit instantly; its *Animal House*-style video, directed by Ric Manello and Adam Dubin, showcased the Beasties' irreverent penchant for rhymed vulgarities to MTV's young audience. In the video, Scott Koenig wore an eyepatch and took a pie to the face.

ADAM DUBIN: It was crazy. DJ's were spinning "Fight for Your Right" every hour. On the set of [the Run-DMC movie] *Tougher Than Leather*, MTV executives said, "We're holding a spot in heavy rotation. We need a music video." We shot it in two days. The idea was to present who the Beastie Boys are: They come to your party, they wreck the party, they steal the girl, they drink all the booze, and when all hell breaks loose, they leave. Ric Menello came up with the high-minded idea: It's the party scene from *Breakfast at Tiffany's*. (2011)

JIMMY G: You can find me in the "Fight For Your Right" video. I was in the middle of the room when everybody was dancing and had my Murphy's Law shirt on. My old girlfriend Natalie was in it; she was one of the girls who pulled the nerd into the back room. My guitarist smashed a cake into a guy's face. We shot both days and stayed out all night. The filming occurred at someone's loft. Back then, people made videos that way. (2016)

> *Foot on the pedal, never ever false metal*
> *Engine running hotter than a boiling kettle*
> —Beastie Boys, "No Sleep Till Brooklyn"

"No Sleep Till Brooklyn" became one of the Boys' biggest hits. The metal-rap battle cry featured the Beasties poking fun at heavy metal (the title taken from Motörhead's *No Sleep Till Hammersmith*). Ric Menello directed this video at The World at 254 East 2nd Street. King jammed in a goofy wig as a knock at the era's Hollywood hair metal bands.

WHEN ROCK MET HIP-HOP

KERRY KING: The simplicity of the situation is what's funny about it. We were recording *Reign in Blood*, and the Beastie Boys were working on *Licensed to Ill* down the hall. Rick Rubin was producing both projects. They needed a lead for "No Sleep Till Brooklyn," and I thought, "Why not? I could use a couple hundred bucks." Accepting a one-time payment instead of a percentage of royalties is a common mistake among session musicians, often leading to significant regret years later. But I wasn't well off then, so I did it for the money. In hindsight, I wish I had taken a quarter point or something because now I would be a rich man! (2024)

RICK RUBIN: Kerry King from Slayer did the guitar solo. I don't think he liked the song. I think he just thought it was bizarre. He's a total metalhead. He loves metal, and I don't think he listens to much music outside of metal. At least then, he didn't. I don't think hip-hop spoke to his aesthetic. And honestly, in retrospect, I don't think his metal style spoke to the Beasties' aesthetic. They didn't like him either. It was mutual. (2016)

SCOTT KOENIG: The Slayer guys did not want Kerry in that video. The Beastie Boys wanted him in the monkey suit the whole time, which would not happen. The Beastie Boys looked at "The Slayer Dude" as ridiculous and funny. The Beasties were people who saw themselves as more upscale. (2008)

MIKE SCHNAPP: The "No Sleep" video was shot at The World in the Lower East Side. Scott Koenig invited me, and I showed up properly with 100 White Castle burgers. Scott recommended Rick to sign Slayer. Rick wanted to put things together that most people wouldn't think made sense, so he hired Kerry King to play an insane guitar solo on this Beastie Boys song. Kerry was not at the shoot; his part was done at another time. What we saw was a guy in a gorilla outfit playing guitar, which was Rick's roommate, Adam Dubin. In the final video, Kerry, in his leather and spikes, body-slammed Adam Dubin out of the frame, which was Kerry's way of saying no monkey business with me! (2024)

Chung King House of Metal (later Chung King Studios) was a graffiti-covered, late-night, de facto musical hub for Def Jam in its early days. Located above a Chinese restaurant on Centre Street in Chinatown, Chung King was the sonic cauldron where the collective visions of engineer/owner John King, his beat-making partner Steve Ett, and Rick Rubin cooked up the sounds of Run-DMC, Beastie Boys, LL Cool J, and Public Enemy that took hip-hop to the mainstream and played a significant role in creating the new rap-metal crossover.

JOHN KING: The relationship with Def Jam was actually Russell and me. It wasn't Rick Rubin so much. Russell and I got together early on, and I was working for him for the right price. You know, Russell's a great promoter. He knew when somebody knew what they were doing for the right price. Price was important; we didn't have much money back then. I don't know if you remember the business back then, but all our clients were $400 cash clients—some shady dudes on the corner. Then Sony came along, and everything just blew up. (2017)

Def Jam had become the pinnacle of cool in 1980s rock and rap history. But Simmons and Rubin began to drift apart. Russell started looking backward, signing retro R&B flops like Alyson Williams and The Black Flames. While still associated with Russell and Rush, Rubin spent time between New York and LA, working with Slayer, Danzig, and Masters of Reality, as well as on a failed attempt with an outerborough metal band, Nevermore. Rick also produced the Cult's rock classic *Electric* for Sire Records.

WHEN ROCK MET HIP-HOP

IAN ASTBURY: The Beastie Boys used to come into the studio when Rick Rubin was making *Electric*. They'd be jamming on our fucking gear, and we'd throw them out. They would incorporate drum breaks from Led Zeppelin into their tracks. It was interesting how stripped-down it was. Hip-hop was very stripped-down, and I thought that would be a great way of producing the Cult because, at that time, records were very layered. (2013)

The significance of the culture around Def Jam and Rush Management can't be overstated. Scott Koenig was Rick's friend from NYU, a Staten Island metal fan who became a mainstay at Rush Management, where his desk became the hub of the rock department. Scott helped connect Rick with Aerosmith. He turned Rick on to Slayer and Trouble, a great Black Sabbath-style band from Chicago, with whom Rubin would produce and release albums. Rubin and Koenig's Def Jam Black metal cabal included Georges Sulmers, a half-Black, half-Jewish metalhead whom Rubin saw wearing a Plasmatics shirt at a concert.

PETE NICE: The Rush office was such an important place. We spent a lot of time there. "Rock N' Roll Scott" Koenig, working with Law And Order, Biohazard, and Slayer, was always there. A Black man, Georges Sulmers, was the other rock guy. Me and Serch had the job of going through and answering Slayer's fan mail. You can imagine the crazy shit we pulled with those people! We'd go to Chung King Studio with the crazy Danzig goat-character shit on the wall. The whole rock thing was always going on, which had to do with Rick. Russell had no ties to rock; he was uptown disco R&B before hip-hop. So, every rap group came to Rush. I remember Eric B and Rakim, and Stetsasonic coming in for meetings. We were there when De La Soul signed with Rush. They were responsible for long-running lists of artists and promoters. It was all going on in this one office—along with all the crackheads and crazy shit going on in the neighborhood. Looking back on Rush, it was the

Motown of hip-hop, with all the music created by that label and management office. (2025)

Danzig deeply disturbed the Black rappers recording at Chung King. The band scrawled on the walls the Satanic graffiti of a pentagram declaring "Satan Rules" after a studio session described more like a devilish seance than a studio jam.

GLENN DANZIG: In the beginning, I enjoyed working with Rick. But then things started getting weird. I remember we had lunch, and he was telling me that he enjoyed the business end of it more than the musical end, and I said, "That's not good." It was right when he started getting less involved in the records than he used to be. So we fired him as producer on *Danzig III: How the Gods Kill* and I took over. He was the executive producer. Then he got the picture and got more hands-on. For the next two records, we shared producer credit. (2019)

> *Hip-hoppin' and body rockin', doin' the do*
> *Beer drinking, breath stinking, sniffing glue*
> —Beastie Boys, "Hold It Now, Hit It"

The 1987 arena dates with Run-DMC and the Beastie Boys, at the height of their careers—billed as the "Together Forever Tour"—integrated audiences and created a cultural shift. Each group represented different sides of the rap-rock crossover. The Beasties' strip-club-like shows perfectly fit their X-rated rhymes; their obscene gesticulations were both gross and engrossing. Girls threw their bras, and everyone shouted back the lyrics.

Jon Pareles of the *New York Times* (12/29/86) described the Beasties live: "On stage Friday at The Ritz, the Beastie Boys did their best to live up to *Licensed to Ill*. As they shouted rhymes, they palsy danced

The Jerry Lewis. The Boys, wearing red, white, and blue T-shirts, poured beer on one another's heads and spewed it into the crowd. Meanwhile, two disc jockeys, Hurricane and Mr. Bill, played backup tracks (including a bit of the 'Mister Ed' theme), and a woman wild danced in a cage, while bouncers repulsed the audience members who repeatedly climbed onstage."

The Beasties took out their NYHC friends Murphy's Law and Fishbone for their first headlining tour. Black ska punks Fishbone was the hippest band in LA. There were also theater and arena dates with the Beasties, Murphy's Law, Public Enemy, and Run-DMC.

Murphy's Law became the second NYHC scene band to play arena stages, and America would never be the same again, with frontman Jimmy G (James Drescher) and crew bringing wild stage-diving and slam dancing to people for the first time. They were like what the Beasties may have been like had they never discovered a beatbox. Murphy's Law lacked the Beastie Boys' sense of rhythm and wordplay but made up for it in terms of speed and energy, introducing wild stage-diving and slam dancing to mainstream America.

JIMMY G: Going on the road with the Beasties and Run-DMC was crazy; it was insane. And you could watch how the music scene was changing overnight, or show by show, as we traveled the heartland of America. It was New York on the road, Black and white, punk rock and hip-hop. We blew people's minds diving off the stage and doing "The Creepy Crawl" in front of a crowd of 20,000 in Dubuque, Iowa, or wherever. (1988)

The Beasties came to detest *Licensed to Ill* and their dumb displays of chauvinism—be it the 21-foot-tall onstage phallus or the bare buttocks that adorned their stage set, or the scantily clad strippers in go-go cages, or speaking to their female fans not in the most complimentary tones, imploring them to take off their shirts, or dousing crowds with geyser shots of shaken beer cans, or the explicit profanity, or their puerile days destroying hotel rooms, or riding their drug-and-alcohol frat-boy carnage to fame and fortune. Their sheer nerve gave way to a modicum of maturity, seeking to move on from the socially irresponsible vulgarity and exhilarating rap-metal melding of *Licensed to Ill*.

RICK RUBIN: *Licensed to Ill* was a funny album. But it ended up being a bone of contention for the band. They were disappointed that not everyone got the joke. (2014)

MCA: In many ways, our early period—overblown in the media—was us goofing around, almost mimicking a lifestyle. Maybe it went too far. Perhaps we became what we were mimicking. Like to write something as stupid as "(You Gotta) Fight For Your Right (To Party)," and seeing it get as big as it did could change anybody. But it's an exciting experience to see something you made as a goof become so successful. (1992)

SCOTT IAN: I know the guys grew to hate everything about that first record and who they were back then, and I get it. The drinking and partying, that shit gets old after a while. It's easy to look at yourself and go, "Who the fuck is that guy?" But sometimes, you have to ride the wave. They were different from all other hip-hop. They could rap, they had the songs, and they offered something different than Run-DMC, Public Enemy, or LL Cool J. (2021)

This explosive era led to the Beasties' bitter departure from Rick Rubin, Rush Management, and their Def Jam deal through Columbia. Despite selling millions of albums, the Boys were on the verge of bankruptcy and internal collapse. At that point, they'd become like the Sex Pistols, who'd taken their brand of madness as far as it could go. The trio rightfully felt taken advantage of by Rick, to which Rubin replied that they could have negotiated a better deal. Plus, the innocent good vibes of early Def Jam had devolved into Russell Simmons' bloodthirsty hip-hop enterprise.

RICK RUBIN: The Beastie Boys said they were leaving Def Jam. When they said they were leaving, Def Jam had an exclusive relationship with Columbia Records, which is part of CBS. So we and the artists were signed to CBS. Being signed to CBS, we were guaranteed to deliver whatever act we signed. That was our obligation to them. So when the Beastie Boys announced that they were leaving Def Jam and started shopping a deal, CBS cut off all royalties, not only going to the Beastie Boys. They cut off all royalties going to Def Jam and all our artists. (2020)

Back in the day, it was war. But now that both Rick Rubin and the Beastie Boys have become wildly wealthy cultural figures and industry insiders, it's all water under the bridge. At press time, Rubin, the philosopher of creativity, has been involved in over 150 million albums sold and has worked with ten percent of all Rock and Roll Hall of Fame inductees.

BILL STEPHNEY: There was a time around 1988 when the Beastie Boys were persona non grata by the hardcore rappers and cognoscenti. They got dismissed as "just white rappers." As more attempts by other white rappers followed, people began reappraising the Beastie Boys. While most hardcore rap radio doesn't play them, nobody's mad at them either. They earned respect. (1994)

Rick and Russell locked into a long, bitter dispute between financial differences and legal delays. Some have suggested that Rick's nemesis, Lyor Cohen, was responsible for pushing Rubin out. But when Rick departed Def Jam, he symbolically buried his old label with a footstone at the Hollywood Forever Cemetery that read: "DEF: Laid To Rest

August 27, 1993," as he launched his next label venture, American Recordings. Bomb Squad producer Bill Stephney, previously recruited by Rubin to run radio promotions, became the first president of the first legendary hip-hop label, Def Jam Records.

BILL STEPHNEY: I've always said that we essentially had two labels: Def Records and Jam Records. Def Records was Rick, with the rap and the rock, and Jam Records was the R&B stuff Russell liked because that was his music from day one. What they had in common was a desire to be at the cutting edge. (2023)

By 1987, Adam Yauch spent much of his time with his hero, Bad Brains bassist Darryl Jenifer. Both bands came off iconic 1986 albums, *Licensed to Ill* and *I Against I*. So when Adam and Darryl began a band called Brooklyn with Murphy's Law drummer Doug E. Beans and guitarist Tom Cushman, there was instant interest from those in the know. Brooklyn's music was unlike their collective punk, rap, and reggae past, with Yauch on guitar and vocals crooning an angst-ridden Americana rock sound. Adam funded their demo dubbed on twenty-five Maxell XL tapes. Once the BBs developed their post-Def Jam game plan, Yauch never pursued Brooklyn again.

ADAM YAUCH: In 1987, after finishing the *Licensed to Ill* tour, we were fed up with everything, with each other, with Def Jam. I always looked up to Darryl as my idol, the greatest bass player in the world. It seemed like a great idea to form a band. Darryl felt strongly that the music should be recorded in a good studio. We spent the little money I had from touring, around twenty grand, thinking that I'd get paid by Def Jam shortly. The tape was recorded tightly and cleanly, but it sounded stupid because I couldn't sing. I sent it to a few labels, but I'm glad it never came out. Then, Def Jam didn't pay us. Russell Simmons pressured us to go back to the studio with Rick. I didn't want to go in the fucking studio with Rick. I thought he ripped us off, and I didn't get along with him that well. (2001)

The trio knew they needed a change of atmosphere, away from Rubin, Rush, and Def Jam. So they relocated to Los Angeles, a city just coming into its own, with a new energy of nightclubs and restaurants and an evolving West Coast hip-hop culture.

DMC: I commend the Beastie Boys for leaving Def Jam. They were able to go away and maintain their identity. It wasn't defined by, "Oh, the label wants this song." That's why they still have their following. I'm jealous. (2011)

RUSSELL SIMMONS: Rick wanted to make Slayer and his loud rock records. Meanwhile, he lost the Beasties, and here's his hardcore rapper, LL Cool J, who is making "I Need Love." It was a fucking mess. (2011)

BILL STEPHNEY: It was Rick who built Def Jam, without question. In terms of its musical vision, attitude, and logo, it all came from Rick. But if Rick built Def Jam, it's still subordinate to Russell's building hip-hop. Russell built the hip-hop culture. (2011)

PAUL'S BOUTIQUE AND BEYOND

> *I'm mad at my desk, and I'll be writing all curse words*
> *Expressing my aggressions through my schizophrenic verse words*
> —Beastie Boys, "Looking Down The Barrel Of A Gun"

Paul's Boutique, the Beasties' second album, would become their most significant recording. Unlike their debut record's cock-rock stylings, *Paul's Boutique* was a sampling orgy reflective of their musical and personal growth. While *Licensed to Ill* put the Beasties on the map and brought them fame and fortune, *Paul's Boutique* saved them from one-hit wonder status and elevated them to rock star status. After spending 1987 touring the world, the burned-out Boys left New York to escape Def Jam. They made a definitive Los Angeles record during the earliest days of LA's rap ascendancy.

Dust Brothers were the top producers at Matt Dike's LA-based Delicious Vinyl Records, at the time considered "the Def Jam of LA," with Dike being their "Rick Rubin." Mike Simpson and John King started playing rap on California's first weekly rap show at KSPC at

Pomona College. A listener named Tone Loc sent his demo, "Cheeba Cheeba" (based on the George Benson song), so they had him on their show and produced him to fame and fortune. The Dust Brothers were behind Delicious Vinyl's biggest crossover dance hits: Tone Loc's "Wild Thing" (based on a heavy metal sample of Van Halen's "Jamie's Cryin'") and Young MC's "Bust A Move." Dike's adept ear, massive record collection, and memory of all things rock, funk, and soul were short-lived as his career devolved into drugs and an early demise.

MIKE SIMPSON: I'm sure people thought the Beasties were a one-hit wonder, but I knew better. "Fight For Your Right (To Party)," was one of their worst songs. (2016)

Upon moving to LA in the summer of 1988, the Beasties happened to walk into the Delicious Vinyl studio. They heard the songs that the Dust Brothers were planning to release as their album—a low-tech amalgam of sly 1970s soul for Matt Dike and Delicious Vinyl. The Beasties asked if they could rhyme over a few of these songs. The rest was history.

MARIO CALDATO, JR.: Recording *Paul's Boutique* was a fantastic ride because we were still getting over the Tone Loc and Young MC high and getting all this attention. Then, the Beastie Boys came into town excited about the songs. They did the two songs first and said, "We have to make a record immediately. We're going to New York and will be back in a month. Get the very best studio; get everything you need." They spared no expense. So we went to the Record Plant and spent three thousand dollars daily. Since there were no instruments, we had a huge room where they recorded drums. We also rented a ping-pong table, a pool table, air hockey, and a pinball machine and filled it up with junk that wasn't music-related. That was the environment; we could hang out and have fun. All they had to do was the vocals, and the Dust Brothers provided all the music. (2023)

Most of those Dust Brothers tracks ended up on 1989's ambitious Capitol Records comeback *Paul's Boutique*, with a deft, dense, funky new sound never heard before. The LA producers created a captivating pastiche that surpasses the swiped sounds achieved by Rick Rubin on *Licensed to Ill*.

JOHN KING: We were excited to work with them. We had been fans for a while. We were blending shit like Black Oak Arkansas with Sly & The Family Stone or Alice Cooper with the Crash Crew. At that time, the production of hip-hop records was quite minimal. We aimed to create edgier, more emotional records that would sound slightly different each time you listened to them. (2016)

Paul's Boutique was the Beasties' masterwork, an ambitious sleeper above most people's heads at the time. The Three Stooges of hip-hop—whose smash debut album was a bad boy shout-out to Party Hearty—made a significant shift the second time. They abandoned their metal-rap meltdown for a latticework of *Shaft/Superfly* rhythms, intricate melodies, and a flood of pop-cultural wordplay to create one of the most exciting hip-hop records ever. The clever verbiage and pointed observations proved that the drunken teens had evolved into rap visionaries. The about-face was so ahead of the curve that most legacy media of the day savaged or outright dismissed the release.

MIKE SIMPSON: We would find a groove, loop it, and then print that to tape. We'd go for five minutes on one track of the tape. Then, we'd find another loop and spend hours getting that second loop to sync up with the first loop. Once we had it in sync, we'd print it for five minutes on another track. And we'd load up the tape like that. (2006)

WHEN ROCK MET HIP-HOP

Paul's Boutique was a literal variety store of street surrealism; dirge-like art-pop churned out of phat grooves. The unprecedented quadruple-fold color album jacket depicted the New York neighborhood around a shop called Paul's Boutique, a spoof on the name of Paul McCartney's boutique he owned at the time of *Abbey Road*. *Rolling Stone* called *Paul's Boutique:* "The *Sgt. Pepper's* of rap." *Q Magazine* quipped: "*Paul's Boutique* is one of the top 10 most influential records ever made." Before his passing, Miles Davis said that he never got tired of listening to it.

EAZY-E: Beastie Boys are pretty cool. But I'm not so into that second record. They needed to come back out with that shit they had when they started. They should always be bringing that "I don't give a fuck" attitude. (1994)

The album created an aural landscape that celebrated both good times and bad, merging the sampling sophistication of Public Enemy's pop reference library (the Beatles, the Wailers, Jimi, etc.), Dr. Seuss's poetry, and their mildly mature sense of fool's cool, verbally motoring down the rap and roll highway. This mighty mix of lyrical and musical innovation squeezed through the eye of a turntable needle, ambitiously stitched together song fragments in a way unheard before or since. They traded their fraternity humor for dense samples, oblique sound collages, and abstract lyrical themes.

The record's genius was in raising sampling to an art form, with its mosaic of disparate sound sources; the sample-delic odyssey of rhymes, skits, and beats remains unrivaled. The rhymes were robust, clean, and comical. A dollop of punkish free-form poetry swerved from raucous chaos to strange head-pounding delirium. The Boys re-seized their rap cred because there could be no doubt that hip-hop was in their hearts.

MIKE D: We were excited about this record. So we thought, "Of course, it's going to connect with people because that's what happened with our last one." But then it came out and absolutely did not. Looking back on it now, it makes a lot of sense to us why it didn't, because even though we were super into it, and eventually other people were too, it's nothing like Licensed to Ill. In hindsight, it worked in our favor. (2019)

The album failed to resonate, as most people were unsure of how to interpret it. Due to poor promotion—Capitol was more into a new Donny Osmond album—and the group's deviation from their signature sound, *Paul's Boutique* flopped out of the box. The industry dismissed the album because it only sold a million copies in its first year, compared to *Licensed to Ill*, which had sold over five million copies by then. A decade later, *Paul's Boutique* was considered a classic and sold over five million units. In their conscious move away from the crass irresponsibility of their earlier dust-smoking daze, the Beasties' new-found deep-thinking blew minds and tore down all previous limitations on rock and hip-hop.

ADAM YAUCH: When we were working on *Paul's Boutique*, we started listening to a lot of funk and jazz and looking for samples. We were trying to find records to sample, and just listening to that kind of playing gets you back into the frame of mind to play music. So, when we finished *Paul's Boutique*, we started jamming and playing again. That was around 1989. We started trying to play funk and wound up with something else. But that's what we were trying to do. (1995)

> *What's running through my mind comes through in my walk*
> *True feelings are shown from the way that I talk*
> —Beastie Boys, "Pass The Mic"

Check Your Head, released in 1992, marked a turning point for the Beastie Boys, who began to trust their instincts, resulting in their most compelling work to date. The album's grooves landed in cosmic alignment with the exploding grunge and hip-hop movements. The era saw the band picking up instruments again and reintroducing elements of their NYHC past to their sonic clash of rap, punk, jazz, soul, and futuristic turntablism. The free-for-all incorporated the Beasties' hip-hop braggadocio with a more sophisticated attitude. In many ways, they quit being a hip-hop crew. They created a unique rock crossover, with an intense edge of sonic anarchy redefining musical boundaries and an uneasy calm on the verge of explosion.

MARIO CALDATO, JR.: It was two and a half years of jamming and horsing around to come up with *Check Your Head*. It was a lot of work, reworking, and arranging. But there was no pressure. Nobody came in and said, "Hey, turn in the record next week." There was none of that, and it was great. It came out exactly how we wanted it when we had it done. And from that point on, we were always in control. (2017)

The album was a thick gumbo of 1970s funk and blues grooves, hard rock bombast, and b-boy beats, all in cosmic alignment with the 1990s alternative culture. A pivotal part of the Beastie Boys' sound was keyboardist "Money Mark" Nishita, who was primarily responsible for recording and producing *Check Your Head*. This labor resulted in a diverse and audacious record—and an unsuspected commercial success that allowed them to spread their wings.

Check Your Head's twenty deeply layered tracks were defined by crunchy guitar distortion, crackling Afro-Cuban percussion, rare-groove keyboards, punky three-chord bash, psychedelic freakout, and discordant funk jams. The music was deliberately wayward and askew, yet prodigally pushing big ideas. They exploited all the possible opportunities for idiosyncratic self-expression that hip-hop's unique merging of bluster and etiquette could supply.

MONEY MARK: On *Check Your Head*, we sampled ourselves, and that's how I sampled then. When sampling other people's music, I consider those "found sounds." If I found it on a record, I would see it like this: I found this seashell on the beach, and now I'm going to bring it home, polish it, and create something from it. (2015)

The album's significant Rock-met-rap moments were "Time For Livin'," an amalgam of Sly Stone and the NYHC band Frontline, and "The Biz vs. The Nuge," Biz Markie's reworking of Ted Nugent's "Home Bound" instrumental off *Cat Scratch Fever*. The third album in the original Beasties' "trilogy," *Check Your Head*, became a musical roadmap through the end of their career—debuting in the Top 10 and selling out every concert from that point forward.

> *Strictly handheld is the style I go*
> *Never rock the mic with the pantyhose*
> —Beastie Boys, "Sure Shot"

Ill Communication, from 1994, was the first Beastie Boys release not to represent a radical break from their past. It was a similarly dazzling sound collage of tape loops and live instruments, like a more eclectic *Check Your Head*. The jumble of disparate ideas seemed expertly juxtaposed with a wired minefield of hard beats, jazz-funk interludes, and a healthy dose of bad-boy posturing that kept listeners locked. It was not a new sound, but a good one. The record debuted at #1 and spawned "Sabotage," a vitriolic rap and punk/rock hybrid that became a hit video directed by Spike Jonze. The "Sabotage" video featured guest appearances by their friends Q-Tip and Biz Markie.

WHEN ROCK MET HIP-HOP

Q-TIP: The album title comes from my rap on "Get It Together," where I go, "Like Ma Bell, I got ill communication." They gave me a mic, and I freestyled for five or six minutes. Did I mention how high I was? I was dumb high. (2021)

The Mario Caldato, Jr. co-production was another party rocker. Their most subtle shift was cannonballing into new realms of ambient jams, hyperbolic raps, and alt-rock hooks; ready to rock, full of funk, and anxious to move the crowd.

MARIO CALDATO, JR.: Sometimes we wouldn't tell each other where we were going. You'd show up at a record shop, see one of the guys, and be like, "What are you doing here?" Sometimes, you knew someone was looking for a particular record. You'd find it and say, "Hey, weren't you looking for this Meters record? Found it for you." (2021)

In between recordings, the Beasties were dynamic. Mike D was the force behind X-Large, the band's successful clothing line, and *Grand Royal* Magazine, which was founded with the late great editor Bob Mack. The magazine merged rap, rock, metal, and hip-hop cultures. Issue #1 featured a Bruce Lee cover and included interviews with Q-Tip, Coxsone Dodd, George Clinton, and Kareem Abdul-Jabbar. Grand Royal Records, their Capitol-distributed alt-rock label, released cool genre-less scree like Luscious Jackson, Cibo Matto, and Atari Teenage Riot. On Grand Royal, Beastie Boys released the *Some Old Bullshit* CD of their early NYHC roots.

ADAM YAUCH: I don't know if we're moving away from hip-hop more than ever. It's more like all these other influences have come back to us. We still love and respect hip-hop as much as ever. We're just expanding. (1997)

> *Most illingest b-boy, well, I got that feeling*
> *I am most ill, and I'm rhymin' and stealin'*
> —Beastie Boys, "Rhymin' and Stealin'"

Yauch remained the band's artistic heart and soul, creating videos and films under the pseudonym Nathaniel Hornblower. After a trip to Nepal, he devoted his life to the Milarepa Foundation, the Tibet Freedom Concert series, and raising a Buddhist family. Mike D ran the operation in that vacuum without the same spiritualism. Mike D was a witty rapper and a stylish culture vulture, sporting a silver-chained VW medallion. But there were unfortunate stories: viciously battling the sampling lawsuits by older artists, funk star Jimmy Castor, and jazz flutist James Newton; the odd, epic fail of the Grand Royal empire, reportedly firing its label employees on a few days' notice, and then listing the label for sale on an online auction; and the bitter expulsion of devastated insiders like editor Bob Mack, producer Jerry Williams, and photographer Ricky Powell.

Ultimately, the Beasties' strength lay in their postmodern ability to distill pop culture and to connect cultural reference points, finding humor in the overload of names and images from the worlds of music, sports, film, fashion, and TV. The threesome, with an image that was part slacker, part nerd, and part b-boy, incorporated such pop aspects. They diced the music they loved without regard to demographics, categories, or boundaries. But rather than making sense of the confusion, they made fun of it. There may never have been another group to pack so many snippets of ideas and information into a single song.

SCOTT IAN: The best thing you could say about any band is that they did something new and original. The Beastie Boys took all their influences: punk rock, hardcore, rock, and rap, threw it all in a pot, and look what came out! They put their branch on the tree of hip-hop. They were the authentic originals. (2021)

Like most rock and roll greats, the Beastie Boys transformed their love of Black music into a sound distinct from the one they initially mimicked. In doing so, they became ambassadors of Black music to white audiences. Their music did more than anyone to provide a safe harbor for the cross-collision of rock and hip-hop. The moral of the Beasties' story is that culture and commerce, if properly handled, do not have to be mutually antagonistic. The death of #1 soul brother Adam Yauch on May 4, 2012, at age forty-seven, after a three-year battle with salivary gland cancer, etched their legacy in history.

DANTE ROSS: Beastie Boys made millions and millions of dollars but lived humble lives. They never bought fancy sports cars; it was never a rock and roll fantasy for those guys. They were grounded people. It comes from their aesthetics and their mutual respect. It reflects their values. (2023)

PUBLIC ENEMY

A cell is hell—I'm a rebel, so I rebel
Between bars, got me thinkin' like an animal
—Public Enemy, "Black Steel In The Hour Of Chaos"

Public Enemy was a group that transcended the limitations of its genre. They were the world's most militant rap group of their time. At their best, they spewed seething venom. When they offended, they did so with purpose. Respected for their innovation and integrity, PE delivered brutal beats louder than any other rap act—partly explaining their appeal to the rock scene.

CHUCK D: When I started this project, I said each album would be more profound until it raises hell. I'm naming names. When you say that the CIA and the FBI were responsible for the murders of Martin Luther King and Malcolm X, you're treading into some deep shit. (1988)

PE began at Adelphi University in Long Island, where art students Chuck D and Hank Shocklee cohosted a college radio show. Shocklee, a fan of progressive rock stars like Yes and Pink Floyd, managed the local vinyl shop Record World, where he was the only Black employee. In 1982, Chuck D (Carlton Ridenhour), Bill Stephney, and Harry

Rock The Bells, Public Enemy live, Author's collection.

Allen were all excited by an Adelphi class called "Black Music and Musicians." Shocklee urged Chuck to become a rapper, and they cut the first PE song, "Public Enemy No. 1."

RICK RUBIN: DMC from Run-DMC played me a tape of Chuck D hosting a radio show. The show was titled "Public Enemy Number One." The show's first minute was "Public Enemy No. 1," his theme song. We listened to it over and over again. He sounded different. He had a deep voice and an intellectual side. He didn't sound like a kid. He sounded more mature. And angry. So I called him every day for six months. He worked at a record store and would tell whoever was there, "Tell Rick I'm not here." Eventually, I got a message: Chuck wanted to meet. He came in, and he's like, "I'm willing to do it under these terms: It's called Public Enemy. It's a group. It's more like The Clash than a rap group. It's me, Flavor Flav, Griff and Hank." That's how it started. (2013)

The magic of Public Enemy was in its assemblage: Their "schizo style" reflected the random, dangerous energy of the streets, while Chuck, the group's focal point and image creator, ably handled his role as a passionate, agitated social commentator. Chuck's lyrical attack pulled no punches. His deep, heavy voice was rich in inflection and intent. His mouth was his gun; his words were his bullets, with lyrics that elevated rap artistry and hip-hop legitimacy beyond its core following. Flavor Flavor (William Drayton) delivered enthusiastic cheerleading and comic relief. The physicality of scratch master DJ Terminator X (Norman Rogers) mixed fierce samples that defied the crowd to dance while hammering home sociopolitical slogans. Professor Griff (Richard Griffin) and his S1W ("Security of the First World") dancers, dressed in Che Guevara-style attire of jackboots and fatigues, ratcheted up the urgency with an amalgam of karate "vogue" poses and synchronized military marches, accompanied by plastic Uzis.

RUSSELL SIMMONS: Being rebellious just to be rebellious isn't that interesting. Public Enemy had things to say. They influenced a whole generation of Black Americans to be more conscious. (2014)

PE wasn't what most people would call rock and roll because it was more of a studio creation than a band. Their visionary Bomb Squad production team—Hank Shocklee, Keith Shocklee, Eric "Vietnam" Sadler, Bill Stephney, Gary G-Wiz, and Chuck D—created a "wall of sound." Hank Shocklee dubbed Chuck "The Phil Spector of Noize."

It was a landscape of turmoil: a creative, complex, timely, funky, and intoxicating aural collage of sirens, beats, buzzes, scratches, knife-edged guitar licks, and brutal rhythms. Bomb Squad recordings were sometimes dismissed as random noise collages, but nothing about them was random. The interaction of music and vocals was deftly composed, with the music responding phrase by phrase to the raps, as the sonic assault reacted to the lyrical flow.

CHUCK D: Everything is rock, and rap is more rock and roll than a lot of music that considers itself rock and roll. We are a group that dared to bring something that was looked down upon as being unimportant music. We're just saying, "Yo, I'm taking it to our audience, whether or not they like it." (2002)

There had never been a Black group that fit their profile, and their motivations changed the direction of rap music. Fueled by their righteous anger at the state of Black America, PE created a controversial sound that articulated rage and aggression like never before. In doing so, music's most feared and misunderstood group came to represent something far more threatening than Black empowerment. They based their image on the Black Panthers, delivering a funky street beat full of Black pride. The rap firebrands spewed intensity and energy, but the music was danceable. Most importantly, just as many whites were interested in such ideas and messages—some ideas as old as rock and roll's anti-establishment themes like "Fight The Power."

RICK RUBIN: I played an advisory role with Public Enemy. I trusted them to make the music they wanted to make. The way The Bomb Squad worked with them, they created their world of music. They'd ask me to come to the studio, and I'd check in and make suggestions. But for the most part, the closer it was to Chuck's vision, the better. Chuck didn't sound like anyone else. He had authority in his voice and an anger not many MCs had at that time. He seemed more literate when there were not many great hip-hop artists. I could tell he was special and needed to be heard. I think Chuck's always had a great viewpoint and interesting things to say, which separated him from all other MCs. (2013)

From the outset, Public Enemy wanted to be a pro-Black group, with plans to evolve into a quasi-rainbow coalition. 1987's *Yo! Bum Rush the Show* was full of menace and violence, propelled by pounding beats, crazed samples, and a pre-Living Colour guitarist Vernon Reid on the PE anthem "Sophisticated Bitch." On the pulverizing riff on 1987's "She Watch Channel Zero?!" PE sampled and slowed Slayer's "Angel of Death." Shocklee, needing a rock track, first tried Bad Brains' "Re-ignition," but it didn't work. They required a darker guitar break—something louder than a bomb—and looped Slayer. Their rap-metal crossover was ahead of its time, making Slayer one of the godfathers of hip-hop.

HANK SHOCKLEE: I learned a lot from managing a heavy metal record store. I was interested in Iron Maiden, Megadeth, Dead Kennedys, and Black Flag. Bands like that, everything they did was conceptual. Public Enemy followed in those footsteps. PE was never a hip-hop group. To accomplish that, everything had to be tactical. We thought of it as a rock band that lived in the hip-hop world. Everything PE did was conceptual. (2015)

In 1988, *It Takes a Nation of Millions to Hold Us Back*—one of the best and best-recorded albums of the decade—featured a thick maze of programmed beats, sold over two million copies, and led to their music propelling Spike Lee's *Do the Right Thing* ("Fight the Power" became the biggest-selling 12" in Motown Records history). In 1990,

IT TAKES A NATION: Public Enemy blended hip-hop beats and thrash metal, 1985. Photofest

Fear of a Black Planet, focused on white racism, gave rappers a new sense of self-confidence and African American ambition. By 1991, *Apocalypse '91 . . . The Enemy Strikes Black* with "By The Time I Get to Arizona"—about that state's initial denial of MLK Day—looked at failures in the Black community, from dope dealers to deadbeat dads. "Shut Em Down" became the ultimate rap-rock fusion, characterized by the sound of scraping metal rhythms and percussion. PE was one of the first rap acts to maintain mainstream and inner-city credibility because they practiced what they preached.

SCOTT IAN: Every generation needs its music, and nothing comes close to moving me as much as Public Enemy did. They created something new. We added a new branch to the heavy metal tree, but they grew a whole tree! (2016)

PUBLIC ENEMY

Solid like rock, above your level
Lethal like a bomb, heavy like metal
—UTFO featuring ANTHRAX, "Lethal"

Anthrax—frontman Joey Belladonna, guitarists Scott Ian and Danny Spitz, bassist Frank Bello, and drummer Charlie Benante—came from Bayside, Queens, so as New Yorkers, they were exposed to hip-hop early on. The band recorded for Megaforce, the label of Jonny Z, who rapped on the first metal-rap vinyl as the Lone Rager. For the B-side of their 1987 "I am the Law" single, Anthrax created their metal-rap track called "I am the Man." The Bronx-bred Bello wrote the song, which never came out on an album, and he rapped over it in a manic, tongue-in-cheek style. The single's cover shot was the band posing metal-tough with a homeboy-style in backward baseball hats, et al.

UTFO was famous for one of the all-time rap hits, "Roxanne, Roxanne," a song based on a sample by Billy Squier. Their next step was to record with a rock band, culminating in the 1987 "Lethal" single with Anthrax. The UTFO-Anthrax "Lethal" 12"—also the opening track on UTFO's *Lethal* album—was recorded in Bayside at David Eng's Bayside Sound and produced by the late great Full Force. UTFO members Mix Master Ice, Doctor Ice, Kangol Kid, and EMD (The Educated Rapper)—with roots as backup dancers for Whodini—came out strong with primitive beatbox rhythms and a dated rap style, joined by Anthrax on background vocals and crunchy metal riffs that enhanced the sheer dopeness. *Ego Trip's Book of Rap Lists* rated it "one of the worst rap-rock collaborations of all time." Today, the band laughs off the collaboration, saying it is not their shining moment. Four years later came "Bring the Noise."

KANGOL KID: We didn't know Anthrax. We just knew we wanted some crazy rock and roll sound on "Lethal." I thought they were gonna be some crazy devil shit people, but they were very cool. I could tell they had no idea what they were getting into. But then again, neither did we. (1989)

BRING THE NOISE

BRING THE NOISE: Chuck D and Flavor Flav of Public Enemy, rock n' rap with Anthrax guitarist Scott Ian, 1997. *WENN Rights Ltd / Alamy Stock Photo.*

> *Never badder than bad*
> *'Cause the brother is madder than mad*
> —ANTHRAX & PUBLIC ENEMY, "Bring the Noise"

Anthrax, while recording their fifth album, 1990's *Persistence of Time*, guitarist Scott Ian convinced his band—one of the gnarliest, hardcore metal groups ever to blow an eardrum—to deliver their assault on ears and minds with a punk/grind cover version of Public Enemy's "Bring the Noise," a song that originally appeared on the soundtrack for the 1987 movie *Less Than Zero* and on Public Enemy's second album *It Takes a Nation of Millions to Hold Us Back*. Unlike Run-DMC-Aerosmith's "Walk This Way," the twist here was headbangers covering a hip-hop track, merging extreme rock and rap like never before. Scott loved the idea of a speed-metal version of the rap song, coalescing the band's brutal riffage with Chuck D's hardcore hip-hop vocal flow.

SCOTT IAN: Some people said it would alienate our audience if we had Chuck D on our record. Alienate who? This is the heaviest song we've ever played! (1991)

MARIA FERRERO: Anthrax were, and are, bold, ballsy, brave, fearless New Yorkers. Their music was pumpin', and they took no shit from anyone. They reinvigorated Public Enemy's "Bring the Noise" because it was music they loved. The collaboration was legendary; "Bring the Noise," and Run-DMC with Aerosmith updating "Walk This Way," changed the face of rock and rap. (2024)

Public Enemy name-checked Anthrax in their lyrics ["Wax is for Anthrax, still it can rock bells"] after Chuck saw a 1987 *Melody Maker* cover photo of Scott onstage at the Monsters of Rock festival wearing a PE shirt. Therefore, the collaboration made sense on several levels. As it was born of a love for PE music, it was not an artificial construct built on marketing or gimmickry; "Bring the Noise" was a great song worthy of transformative performance. Additionally, the PE original had an infectious groove that Scott Ian and Anthrax pulverized, upping the tension until it exploded in palpable white noise. The collaboration delivered a hit single, a noisy national tour, and a sound that would forever transform heavy music.

SCOTT IAN: We all were into hip-hop and listened to that. Public Enemy was our favorite band at that time. We couldn't believe our favorite rap band was name-checking us in a song. That was such a giant kick in the ass! But all we did—or Run-DMC and Aerosmith did—was dabbling and treading lightly in it. We weren't a crossover group. (2020)

CHUCK D: I checked out my first heavy metal show in 1987, and Anthrax was on it. We got to know each other, and I name-checked them in the original 1987 single "Bring the Noise" because I thought they were cool. They had that hip-hop tip, that hip-hop feel. When they wanted to make a heavy metal-type version, at first, I was like, "Damn, I don't know." But as time went on, we said we were with it. We said, "Why not do something that will show both audiences that it's the same thing?" It's attitude, speed, and still being hard without being soft. (2020)

HANK SHOCKLEE: Public Enemy's whole concept, to me, came from Megadeth. Megadeth made one record that fucked my entire head up: *Peace Sells ... But Who's Buying?* That shit is crazy! (2008)

Once Anthrax cut the demo, Scott sent a tape to Chuck and Flav and pitched the rap firebrands on re-recording "Bring the Noise" with his band of comic-book-obsessed Queens headbangers delivering intense volume and breakneck speed. Both groups had built sizable cult followings for their unrelenting sound and attitude. When Chuck D heard the demo, he loved the raw noise and recognized the political impact of both crowds coming together. Scott Ian never considered the social impact or the unified racial front. However, the video became the first to have a world premiere twice on MTV: first on "Yo! MTV Raps" and then on their hard rock show, "Headbanger's Ball."

CHUCK D: I was approached by the guys about me rapping over a version of "Bring the Noise" that Anthrax had decided to "metallize." I said, "Why don't you guys just record it? Because I already did it." I didn't understand why I had to get down and do it again because the original "Bring the Noise" was not too long before that. (2016)

SCOTT IAN: We recorded my riff and the drums and made a fucking crushing track. We thought we'd use it for Anthrax if it didn't work out with Public Enemy. We sent over a cassette, and Chuck called us and said, "We love it. How do we do it?" We spent months trying and failing to get into the studio. So they sent us the vocals, and Charlie [Benante] and I spent a week cutting and pasting them on the instrumental tracks. A whole week! That'd take five minutes now, but it took hours and hours a day. Everybody thought we were crazy, but we kept going until it was perfect. For years, we never told anybody how it was done. Everybody assumed that the bands were in a room together. (2016)

CHARLIE BENANTE: Public Enemy had this incredible musical vocabulary. For example, Flavor Flav is excellent on drums. Every day on the Anthrax-Public Enemy tour of 1991, and when we appeared together in that video for "Bring the Noise," I had a drum kit set up in the dressing room, a warm-up kit, and he would come in every day, and bang the hell out of those drums. He was really good. (2017)

Chuck and Flav joined Anthrax onstage at Madison Square Garden. Then PE took the Anthrax guys to a playground in the Southside of Chicago to film a video. By the end of 1991, the scorching new "Bring the Noise" with Chuck, Flav, and Anthrax came out on both

Anthrax's *Attack of the Killer B's* and PE's *Apocalypse 91 . . . The Enemy Strikes Black*. The video featuring both bands onstage in front of a mixed crowd was not contrived. The song blew up, three minutes of unadulterated rap and roll, breaking down barriers and inflicting tinnitus, nominated for a Grammy for "Best Metal Performance." Later that year, the bands toured together, as Anthrax matched PE cuss for cuss. The "Bring the Noise Tour" (Anthrax, Public Enemy, Primus, and Young Black Teenagers) closed every show, with Anthrax and PE doing their new rap-metal anthem, "Bring the Noise."

HANK SHOCKLEE: Black R&B radio was not educating, and they were not stimulating. They were soothing with the typical "smooth" bullshit. That's what "Bring the Noise" was about. If they're callin' our music "noise." If they're saying we're getting out of character being a Black person in America, then we're bringin' more noise. The message was aimed at Black youth and, at the same time, at the Black bourgeoisie because they didn't give a damn about the Black youth—whether they said so or not. Public Enemy was the new rock and roll. (1988)

CHARLIE BENANTE: Scott and I loved Public Enemy. We were fond of hip-hop in general, and Public Enemy was the epitome of rap music. It was talking about important issues. Some people deemed Public Enemy as a racist group. I never took what Chuck D was saying as being racist. I saw it as Chuck D talking about what he knew, felt, and saw. To me, Public Enemy hit the nail on the head. The Anthrax name-check in the original "Bring the Noise" was one of the reasons we wanted to do that cover. We wanted to pay it back to them. I remember sending the track to Chuck, and he called to say how much he loved it. In his exact words, "This track is slammin'!" Then the ball just rolled from there. I remember talking to Chuck, and we agreed to go out and do some shows together. It was one of those great things that came together in an organic way. No, "I can't do it unless I get paid this." It was how it should be. (2008)

CHUCK D: The key to the new version was that Flavor Flav had vocals that cut through the guitars. In hip-hop, it's about the voice on top of the music, and we could take more "noise"—as we called it—because we felt that our voices could cut through anything . . . Then we said, "We have this song, why not do a tour?" We made up our minds in less than five minutes. We said, "What can stop us? Let's do it!" And the tour was magic. (2016)

Live on tour, both groups and their entourages stomped wildly around the stage, ending the night on a fever pitch. The heaviest groups in thrash metal and urban hip-hop delivered an adrenaline rush of epic proportions, and their touring package benefited from a sizable audience. The sight of rap and metal fans going berserk together proudly (and profanely) proclaimed the tour a complete success. The groups loved working together, from both musical and social points of view—kickstarting a new generation of in-your-face metal with relentless rap swagger. Interestingly, the Anthrax/PE bill only drew undersold crowds when they added Goth icons Sisters Of Mercy to the bill. The irony of these concerts was the political incorrectness of headliners Anthrax performing their song "Indians," with singer Joey Belladonna running around the stage in a Native American headdress. It wasn't long until bands like Limp Bizkit took Anthrax's metal guitars and Public Enemy's rhymes to create the definitive new rap-metal mashup: "Nu-Metal," the sound that dominated the late 1990s and through the early twenty-first century.

SCOTT IAN: A lightbulb went on over many people's heads at the end of the night of each show when we played "Bring the Noise" together.

The rap fans were polite to us, and the rock fans were respectful to Public Enemy. A lot of mutual respect was shown. (2020)

JOEY BELLADONNA: Scott Ian never even told me. I remember we were rehearsing for *Persistence of Time* when he played this riff, and I was like: "Wow. What's that? That's pretty cool." Scott said, "Uh, that's just something we're working on." Okay, no problem. The next thing you know, Chuck D and Flav are in the studio. I was kind of in the dark with it all. That part of it did suck. But the outcome was great. (2020)

SCOTT IAN: People ask us if we think we created a particular genre of music that the press named after we did what we did with Public Enemy. I never thought we invented it. It opened a door, even just a window for people to jump out of. I truly believe that Rage Against the Machine was the band that drove a train through that door—they took the influences in their individuals and came together to make a band out of it. Meanwhile, with us and Public Enemy, it's not like Anthrax became a rap group, and it's not like Public Enemy became a metal group. We just collaborated and did something incredible. We didn't then become one unit and continue to make music like that. Rage was that band, and this is the music they created from their souls, which blew up worldwide. (2013)

NEW YORK

New York City, shifty low-down gritty
You punk niggas yell pity and smell shitty
—Onyx, "Walk In New York"

In New York, a generation or two of rap supremacy permeated the city's musical landscape. Homeboys of all persuasions loved and embraced hip-hop culture to its fullest. New York crews, such as Run-DMC, the Beastie Boys, and Public Enemy, infused their hip-hop with shades of rock, punk, and metal from their earliest days of MTV airplay. That melting pot crossover spanned from the Black Rock Coalition, a collective founded in late 1985 by Living Colour guitarist Vernon Reid, to the multicultural b-boys who simplified the English language to convey a city street-tough image.

DMC: We never lost that desire for rap when we started making money with this thing. We love doing it. We love doing live shows. We never let the fortune take away from the art form, you know, the culture of hip-hop. What hip-hop really stands for. (2023)

WHEN ROCK MET HIP-HOP

URBAN DISCIPLINE: Biohazard fused punk-metal with hardcore rap, on Onyx's "Slam," Evan Seinfeld (center), 1989. Mercury/Photofest ¾Mercury.

> *Coming through with a scam, fool-proof plan*
> *B-boys make some noise and just SLAM*
> —Onyx & Biohazard, "Slam" (Bionyx Remix)

Biohazard unleashed an intense amalgam of brutal punk, urban metal, and hardcore hip-hop. The mixture of tattoos, piercings, attitude, lyrics, and hooks were ahead of their time. The Canarsie, Brooklyn quartet begun by bassist/vocalist Evan Seinfeld (related to Jerry Seinfeld), who idolized Geezer Butler, Steve Harris, and Cliff Burton, learned the game as a roadie for the late great Pete Steele of Carnivore and Type

O Negative; Steele named Evan's band for the "biohazard" symbol. Seinfeld teamed with Scott Koenig at Rush, who made them the rap management stable's top rock band (Law & Order, a local hair band that hit with 1989's *Guilty of Innocence* for MCA, was the other).

EVAN SEINFELD: People used to call us rap-metal, but we never called ourselves that. Our music organically has hip-hop in it. We made music from scratch when we did "Slam" and *Judgment Night* with Onyx. We went in the studio with Jam Master Jay in Hollis, Queens, with motherfuckers wearing rope chains and bulletproof vests with their guns out. And none of us were strangers to guns, but we weren't known for coming to the studio with fucking Uzis. You know what I mean? But that was the vibe, man. Onyx rolled in with a posse, so we had all these motherfuckers in the studio. And they were intent on showing up totally hardcore to match our fucking energy. (2024)

Onyx was a Queens crew of gangster rappers friends with Jam Master Jay, who brought them into the Def Jam world and put them on his JMJ imprint. Onyx, led by Fredro Starr (Fred Scruggs, Jr.) and his younger cousin Sticky Fingaz (Kirk Jones), pushed the genre to the level of a cartoon. The group realized the hit potential of "Slam," which was probably the reason it was the only tune on 1992's *Bacdafucup* that was not full of profanity, keeping it off the radio. Lyor Cohen of Rush Management proposed a rap-rock metal remix with Biohazard of Onyx's "Slam," which became the summer's urban catchphrase. The four madfaced baldies' rapping style drew from chaotic reggae dancehall madness but took it to further extremes. Onyx did not sound pretty or ugly, but they did sound urgent. Biohazard delivered with their heaviest rhythms. There were only a handful of seminal records that merged rock and hip-hop, and these groups made two: "Slam" (remixed by Billy "Bio" Graziadei) and the title track to the *Judgment Night* soundtrack.

WHEN ROCK MET HIP-HOP

STICKY FINGAZ: The president of Def Jam at the time was Lyor Cohen. He said, "'Slam' is getting big, but I think you guys can do it even bigger than what Run-DMC did if you hook up with these guys Biohazard and do a rock and roll version." We were anti at first, "Nah, we're on that hood shit homie. We don't want to do no rock and roll." But we listened to him, and it worked. It was a great idea. Biohazard is not your regular rock group. They're hard. They're like the white Onyx. (2002)

The shooting of the "Slam (Bionyx Remix)" video took place at The Academy in NYC on May 24, 1993. It starred the gangsta groups and their crews in a mosh pit, with everyone from Redman to other Rush artists to NYHC insiders like Danny Diablo, Madball, and 25 Ta Life. Original Cro-Mags guitarist Parris Mayhew shot and directed the video, with the Stone Brothers producing it. The tribute to male bonding through slam dancing contained one of the most incredible raps ever at the end of the song by Sticky Fingaz. When their worlds collided, both Onyx and Biohazard rose to fame.

EVAN SEINFELD: There was no foreshadowing of how Biohazard came to be because it's really ironic. How did we get credited for rap-style vocals in metal, hardcore music, and accidental, incidental—call it what you like? I mean, I'm just a bass player. (2024)

DREW STONE: Biohazard from Brooklyn, New York, had a lot of elements, including hip-hop. That's what made them incredibly unique at the time. They happened organically for a band like that, coming from the Canarsie neighborhood and the heavy metal club L'Amour. It just goes to show that white street kids were influenced by the early hip-hop that was around them. (2024)

BILLY GRAZIADEI: I got asked to do a remix of "Slam," so I did that. Then they asked us to perform a live version of the song, so we recorded a video and became good friends with them. Then we did the title track to *Judgment Night*, the film. In management, we were helped by similar people, so there were connections to the New York hip-hop scene. (1994)

DANNY SCHULER: It was a natural thing. Def Jam managed us; we were their company's only heavy white band. Those people didn't like us too much because we were a real street band. We weren't silly. Billy was approached about doing the remix, and I played drums on the track; we also appeared in the video. That led to some great shows with Onyx and working together on the *Judgment Night* soundtrack. We got along well with those guys because we were all from New York. There were many parallels between what we were saying and what hip-hop was saying through music. (2011)

BOBBY HAMBEL: That was a great time, and those guys were cool. We were both underground bands—a mix of what came from the New York streets—and they were very hardcore in their way. (2013)

FREDRO STARR: Onyx brought "Slam" to hip-hop. "Slam" was one of the most successful records and still is. When we first did "Slam," it was to get people to release their energy and have a good time on the dance floor. We brought that to the game. Of course, there were the Beastie Boys, Public Enemy, and Run-DMC—they integrated rock music and hip-hop culture. But as far as "Slam" the record and slam dancing, we brought that to the game. (2023)

BILLY GRAZIADEI: We and Onyx did a few shows together. I remember one show where they showed up with fuckin' vests on. And we're like,

"What you got vests on?" They're like, "Yo, your fuckin' crowd's crazy. We don't wanna get fuckin' stabbed or shot." Like, no, it's all family here. We're like, "Take that shit off, man, you guys are sweating like pigs, you don't need it." Our crowd accepted them as hip-hop fans. (2018)

EVAN SEINFELD: The guys from Onyx got in the pit, and then Sticky Fingaz did a crazy flip off the monitor into the crowd. At that point, the crushing riff and the people jumping in unison were one. It was awesome to watch Onyx thrashing around, smacking each other, and loving each other. It was Black people fucking with rock and metal in all the right ways. (2024)

> *What we gotta say*
> *We could hit this jam in the old-school way*
> —Dog Eat Dog, "No Fronts"

Dog Eat Dog emerged from Mucky Pup, a late 1980s punk/metal band with a comedic edge from Bergenfield, NJ, that played a few times at CBGB. Dog Eat Dog came together in 1991 in Mucky bassist Dave Neabore's mother's cellar in nearby Hillsdale with drummer David Maltby and guitarist Sean Kilkenny (RIP) with hip-hop-style singer John Connor. They became known as an exciting and original band mixing NYHC riffs and rock rhymes, equal parts Beastie Boys and Bad Brains. The six-piece band smacked crowds over the head with an authentically brutal, urban sound, having graduated from the same New York City metal school of hard knocks as Biohazard and Type O Negative.

In 1992, Biohazard's Billy "Bio" Graziadei gave Roadrunner Records the band's four-song demo. Dog Eat Dog called their 1993 debut EP *Warrant* because the hair metal band Warrant had just released a record called *Dog Eat Dog*. Around that time, former Cro-Mags guitarist Parris Mayhew joined the band. In 1994, *All Boro Kings*, produced by late NJ legend Jason Corsaro, contained their 1995 MTV hit "No Fronts," released on *No Fronts: The Remixes*, with two remixes by Jam Master Jay of Run-DMC, one by The Beatnuts, and the B-side "Who's the King?" with vocals by Bad Brains' Daryl Jenifer. Wu-Tang Clan and Ronnie James Dio sang on 1996's follow-up *Play Games*. The band was shocked to be the 1995 winner of MTV Europe's Best Breakthrough Artist award, defeating Weezer, Portishead, and Alanis Morissette. Their inroads across the Atlantic enabled relentless European touring and tapping into the exploding European skate-snowboarding crossover. Unlike metal bands that rapped, Dog Eat Dog brought a rap flow to every metal cut.

JOHN CONNOR: We're a crossover band. We're a cross-hybrid of styles and influences: rock, rapid hardcore. So much of it is kicking now. (1995)

> *You must understand that I'm made this way*
> *Don't give a damn if you can't change your*
> *little narrow mind today*
> —24-7 Spyz, "Social Plague"

24-7 Spyz, a ferocious South Bronx African American foursome with unrelenting power and cathartic energy, won a devout crowd with its distinctive brand of "heavy metal soul." Guitarist Jimi Hazel (Wayne Richardson) saw Jimi Hendrix play at the New York Pop Festival in 1970 when he was six and his brother was fourteen. That was a significant reason they were, first and foremost, a guitar band, like a punk P-Funk, melding rock and hip-hop.

PETER FLUID: The band's musical diversity came naturally. We all had older brothers and sisters who shared their musical knowledge with us, so we listened to everything from soul music to Led Zeppelin. Then, when we got older, we'd ride down to Greenwich Village and go to CBGB. We were always into rap; the music was old music to us because rap has been around since the early 1970s in the Bronx. (1989)

The core four (Peter Fluid, Jimi Hazel, Rick Skatore, Anthony Johnson) began in 1986, melding hardcore stomp, jazz fusion, dub reggae, and thrash metal. Their 1989 debut, *Harder Than You*, came out at a time when, as the *LA Times* put it, "black groups are expected to play rap or R&B." The band that never pigeonhole themselves by racial tradition never fully recovered from firing poetic frontman Peter Fluid and ex-drummer Anthony Johnson after 1990's *Gumbo Millennium* (with "John Connelly's Theory," an ode to the Nuclear Assault singer)—with righteous but never indulgent rapping and lyrics that explored the motivations of society's debris. They closed shows with their cover of Kool & The Gang's "Jungle Boogie," put out as a 1989 single that hit big on MTV, with a chorus shouted in punk-chant style.

To introduce the second lineup for the Atlantic Records-related EastWest imprint, with singer Jeff Brodnax, drummer Joel Maitoza, and returning bassist Rick Skatore, the band released 1991's high-powered *This Is . . . 24/7 Spyz!* five-song EP, and 1992's *Strength In Numbers*—lean, flexible alloys of speed-metal guitar, NYHC vitriol, and melodic pop undertow, integrating a brutal Bad Brains rasta stomp with roaring curiosity and exploration. Spyz and all their fellow "Black Rock Coalition" bands suffered from getting racially stratified radio and video airplay. They endured not-always-friendly battles over constant comparisons to New York City rivals Living Colour, the other significant hard-edged Black rock band of the era, like when *Spin* (12/90) wrote: "If Living Colour make Black metal possible, 24-7 Spyz make it powerful."

JIMI HAZEL: The first year on tour was the most mind-blowing tour of our lives because we'd never been outside New York. Our booking agent decided to build our reputation the old-fashioned way: through grassroots efforts, a headlining tour. So, we went to places where there were 20 people one night, 250 people on another night, and 500 people on yet another night. Our audiences at that point were 90 percent white. Our road crew was white, so in the South, we dubbed them the "cracker crew." What was deep was that we all understood who we were and that we were all good people. There was no racism on our bus, at our camp, or among our crew. So, we would do things that would freak other people out because they weren't ready for how free we were. (2022)

> *Black cat is bad luck, bad guys wear black*
> *Musta been a white guy who started all that*
> —3rd Bass, "The Gas Face"

3rd Bass—MC Serch (Michael Berrin) and Prime Minister Pete Nice (Peter Nash)—was a white rap crew focused on the b-boy scene. Rush Management marketed them as their next Beastie Boys, which caused bad blood with the Beasties. Their 1989 debut record, *The Cactus Album*, crossed over to punk and alt-rock with Henry Rollins in their MTV hit video "The Gas Face." The credits read: "The cactus stands firm on the desert plain, juicing fluids from its desolate environment. Two solo MCs absorbed and deciphered culture from Far Rockaway to Bedford-Stuyvesant, like the desert plant, stood alone." Famed rapper Nas started with 3rd Bass as "Nasty Nas." Serch "discovered" Nas and retained a 2 percent ownership stake in the first two hit Nas albums.

MC SERCH: I am not what you'd call a metalhead, but I have an acute connection to Slayer. We were all connected through Rush Management and Def Jam Records in the 1980s. I would open Slayer's fan mail and respond to their fans to kill time. I learned valuable lessons from those letters that I still hold dear. The biggest lesson I learned was that Slayer fans are out of their fucking minds! (2013)

The Cactus Album producer, Sam Sever (Citrin), started working with Curtis Mantronik behind the 1985 club hit "Fresh is the Word" by Mantronix. Russell Simmons hired Sever to work on Run-DMC's classic *Raising Hell*. Sam then joined a hip-hop duo with Bosco Money (Ken Carabello) managed by Rush called Downtown Science that fell apart after an incredible 12" called "Radioactive" and an eponymous album for Columbia. In 1996, Sam Sever And The Raiders Of The Lost Art reappeared with the opening track on the seminal 1996 techno comp *Brit Hop and Amyl House* called "What's That Sound? (Fucked Up Sound)." That b-boy cred resulted in Sever and original Downtown Science rapper Jonathan Hoffman reworking the Beasties' "Intergalactic" (Fuzzy Logic Remix) 12" released by Grand Royal in 1998.

DANTE ROSS: Although I'm not credited, and unbeknownst to me, I helped A&R 3rd Bass. It was by accident. They were my friends. Sam Sever was my friend. I put them together. (2023)

Their overriding issue was that as white kids, people misunderstood their purist hardcore hip-hop attitude—derided by scene insiders, Black and white, and not afforded the niceties the Beasties enjoyed. Ultimately, 3rd Bass was one of the most influential hip-hop acts of all time.

PETE NICE: Me and Serch were signed to Rush as soloists before 3rd Bass. Being signed to Rush was a big deal, and my claim to fame was that I had a popular radio show at Columbia. We met at the Latin Quarter before we had any prior relationship. He had a record before that, and I knew he had a checkered history. We started hanging out with Dante Ross and Sam Sever, who were behind bringing us together. I knew Red Alert and us being on Red's radio show was the epitome. We could have died and gone to heaven. The next thing I remember is that we played football in the streets with Run-DMC across from Rush to celebrate a tour that never happened. We spent a long time in the studio on our first album, which came out in May 1989, and the fallback plan was to release it on Def Jam. Most labels wanted to hear this rock-rap fusion, which we didn't have. The Beasties were about to leave Russell and Rick and Def Jam, and we just happened to be these white MCs doing our thing at Rush. The narrative that Russell had of us replacing the Beastie Boys was a fantasy. The first album went Gold, and we were satisfied to stay on that true b-boy path. We broke up while making the second album; we tried to sabotage our art. In "Pop Goes The Weasel," we were mocking pop-rap. Suddenly, everyone wanted us to be a pop-rap group. We were offered all these big gigs like we were about to be on *Beverly Hills 90210*, but we turned it down. We were fighting it all. (2024)

Born of the caucasian persuasion
To some, I'm a threat, to others, it's amazin'
—Young Black Teenagers, "Proud To Be Black"

Young Black Teenagers was the brainchild of The Bomb Squad (Hank and Keith Shocklee, Eric Sadler, and Bill Stephney), who'd become the biggest name in hip-hop production. In an almost cruel move, they bestowed the black-ish moniker on the all-white hip-hop group from ethnically diverse Freeport, Long Island. Young Black Teenagers was so ill-conceived that it overshadowed their solid 1991 self-titled debut, which featured Beatlesque cover art. The group featured Kamron (Ron Winge), Tommy Never (Thomas Barbaccia), and Firstborn (Adam Wiener) on the mics, with DJ Skribble (Scott Ialacci) on the turntables, accompanied by ATA. Their record was released through MCA on the producers' imprint, SOUL (Sound Of Urban Listeners). It became a big deal around New York for a New York minute. Beyond the confusing name and lack of MTV play, YBT came out at the wrong time in rap history amid Vanilla Ice's symbolic whitewashing of hip-hop.

FIRSTBORN: We get sick of people asking if Caucasians can rap. We were down with hip-hop from the very beginning. It's not just African Americans. (1990)

Do you think modern cancel culture would've let Chuck D and The Bomb Squad get away with calling a white rap crew Young Black Teenagers that made liberal use of the N-word? However, YBT never caused controversy because they never had a pop hit, so no backlash would have likely occurred if they'd been successful. Few people knew who they were, and African American artists did not speak out about their names. The group's second and final album, 1993's *Dead End Kids Doin' Lifetime Bidz*, with songs produced by Grandmaster Flash and Terminator X and samples of "Tom Sawyer" by Rush and "Monkey Man" by the Rolling Stones, contained their only minor hit, "Tap The Bottle."

KAMRON: Hip-hop culture came from African Americans. It's a Black culture, per se. Where everything is now, compared to then, I think the transracial issue is deep. The whole race thing, to me, is blurred lines. Separating people by race at this point can only breed a lot of hate and bullshit. (2015)

NEW YORK

Check out my rhyme, fuckin' up your mind
Diggin' in your soul with the rock and roll
—Shootyz Groove, "The Craze"

Shootyz Groove was a multi-racial musical beast from the mean New York streets of the Bronx and Washington Heights, fueled by two Puerto Rican MCs and three funky punk-metal players of Dominican, Italian, and Croatian descent. The musicians offered a distinctive style that seamlessly blended rap-rock with a potent combination of funk-metal grooves, hip-hop mixology, socially conscious lyrics, rare samples, and alt-rock melody. They exuded a kinetic flow of intense energy, fueling an exuberant mosh pit with a streak of good-time madness that made you party like it was 1999. The magic was its merger of intricate flourishes from Coltrane jazz, Hendrix rock, and Cro-Mags punk-metal, all while putting a positive spin on everyday urban struggles, such as racism and oppression. The raw immediacy of their funky soul made them hard to ignore, and they never lacked a slammin' groove or bracing wash of savage metal guitar. 1993's *Respect* live EP, mixed by Phil Greene, spun off their breakout 12", "Buddhaful Day."

The buzz led to a deal with Mercury Records with 1994's first full-length *Jammin' In Vicious Environments (J.I.V.E.)*, produced by metalhead Mark Dodson (Judas Priest, Anthrax), delivered with metal-edged rock, no-frills rap, rapid-fire rhymes, and reggae riddims, and 1995's Roy Z-produced *Generation of Hope* split EP with Downset. Then came 1997's Daniel Wise-produced *Hipnosis* for Roadrunner and 1999's *High Definition* full-length for Kinetic/Reprise that contained an MTV hit video with "L Train" and an out-of-left-field freestyle rendition of XTC's "Dear God." The following year, they teamed up with Big Pun on a rendition of his drug anthem "Caribbean Connection" and appeared in a well-received HBO special, performing alongside Kid Rock and Disturbed. In their heyday, Shootyz shared stages with groups ranging from De La Soul and The Mighty Mighty Bosstones to Slayer and 311. Whether one was looking for an alternative to rap or enjoyed alternative rap, Shootyz Groove was so tight that they seamlessly weaved everything into their mix.

DONNY RADELJIC: This is a war; the stage is our battlefield. As artful as the music is, we're here to maraud. (1998)

> *I'm not a man with a grasp on reality*
> *Kerouac is wack, and I'm down with Dostoevsky*
> —Fun Lovin' Criminals, "Come Find Yourself"

Fun Lovin' Criminals centered around Huey (Hugh Morgan), an Irish/Puerto Rican sweet tough from New York's dangerous Lower East Side. Huey got busted for dealing heroin in the LES but lucked out when his FBI agent stepfather intervened to speak with the judge. So, instead of prison time, Huey enlisted in the Marines during Operation Desert Storm. He served in Kuwait until a parachuting accident in which he broke both of his legs and got discharged.

HUEY MORGAN: I've got three Marshall stacks on stage; I don't think there's anything not rock about that. We're a rock band in our minds. You can't have just one stack, and you can't have two. Three is the number you need. When we saw ZZ Top, Billy Gibbons was my favorite guitarist. In Japan, there were three Marshall stacks on one side, a drum kit, and three stacks on the other side. They came out and destroyed. That's my goal with Fun Lovin' Criminals. (2001)

The original trio came together in 1993 with guitarist Huey, multi-instrumentalist Fast (Brian Leiser), and drummer Steve Borgovini working or hanging out at The Limelight, the *Caligula* of indulgent late-night dance clubs. They pestered owner Peter Gatien and booker Neville Wells into filling in for any cancelations, and at one point, they were playing weekly at 1:00 a.m. on Wednesdays. After their sixth show, EMI A&R man Mike Schnapp signed them to the label.

MIKE SCHNAPP: Fun Lovin' Criminals were a quintessential New York music ensemble. A melting pot of styles and cultures came out of this mix—rap, rock, funk, R&B, and film noir. As something very New York, they represented that mix. Their diversity was amazing, but their biggest handicap was that they were difficult to categorize and market. People thought Huey was Black with his deep vocal delivery, whereas the Beasties were obviously white kids. (2024)

At the height of the indie-rock craze, for the 1996 release of *Come Find Yourself*, EMI created a fake indie label front called DiFontaine Carting & Asbestos Removal Co. to convince people they were buying a legit indie band. 1996's *Fun Lovin' Criminals*, with their rock-rap weed homage "Smoke Em (If You Got Em)," "Bombin' The L" (about graffitiing the elevated subway trains) with Lynyrd Skynyrd and Deep Purple samples, and "Scooby Snacks," their biggest selling single—somewhere between a novelty song and a sleek danceable hip-hop jam with samples from *Reservoir Dogs* and *Pulp Fiction* that broke them in the United Kingdom. They developed a potent formula: Huey wrote the lyrics, and Fast wrote the music. 1998's *100% Columbian* with "Love Unlimited" and "Korean Bodega" was written, arranged, and produced by the band. A career highlight came on the 2000 compilation *Take a Bite Out of Rhyme: A Rock Tribute to Rap* with FLC's breakdown of Eric B and Rakim's "Microphone Fiend," with funky rap beats combined into rock culture. 1999's *Mimosa* brought their rap-rock formula full circle with Huey's slow, funky groove on Ozzy Osbourne's "Crazy Train."

FAST: We would take a Deep Purple sample, speed it up three keys, play another sample straight, like by Steve Miller, put the beat behind it, and it was done. (1997)

FLC never gained significant popularity in America but found huge fame in Europe, particularly in England and Ireland. FLC toured often with and befriended U2. Huey got involved in ventures beyond music, took time off from the band, married their manager, and became an on-air personality at BBC Radio. Fast, tired of waiting, tours with a new vocalist/guitarist, Naim Cortazzi—their drummer since 2003 Frank Benbini's cousin, who looks and sounds like Morgan. Huey was the band's main attraction, but he got jammed out of his own group. So he now cynically bills his occasional solo concerts as "Huey Morgan The Fun Lovin' Criminal and His Newest Band" with a crew of London and New York friends. FLC represented New Yorkers to European people—and charming New York bands are charming to everyone except New Yorkers.

D.X. FERRIS: Fun Lovin' Criminals were like the New York answer to Sublime, an ultra-cool distillation of multicultural shards of culture, music, and everyday life. Their chill grooves and hooks tapped into rap, jazz, blues, club music, and big hip-hop beats. They covered Louis Armstrong, Tom Petty, Jimmy Durante, and the Notorious B.I.G. They've got a schmoozy soulful groove, sophisticated and lush as hell, with cool sample action and loops and tight live music. When discussing their gangster style, we discuss Frank Sinatra or John Gotti. They were iconic, one of the best bands of the 1990s. Huey also wrote insightful, sophisticated lyrics, so their records only get better with time. (2024)

WEST COAST

With this mic device, I spit nonfiction
Who got the power? This be my question
—Rage Against the Machine, "Mic Check"

West Coast hip-hop was late to the rap game, which likely had much to do with the slow browning of white California. The early 1980s LA scene was cheesy by modern standards, with groups like World Class Wreckin' Cru, starring a young Dr. Dre first on turntables, or records like "The Gigolo Rapp" by Disco Daddy and Captain Rapp. That all changed in 1988 with N.W.A's *Straight Outta Compton*.

The iconography of the California rock band dates back to the early 1960s surf rock scene. In the 1970s and 1980s, California became synonymous with rock and roll and heavy metal culture. The West Coast rock-rap crossover first manifested in punk bands, who pioneered the first funk metal, characterized by crashing guitars and tribal rhythms delivered with a rapid-fire rap cadence inspired by jagged post-punk and "rock disco" dance floors. The Red Hot Chili Peppers and Faith No More emerged in the mid-1980s from Los Angeles and San Francisco, not closely tied to DJ culture. The rock-driven rap of Cypress

Hill and House of Pain, featuring legendary mixmasters DJ Muggs and DJ Lethal, and Rage Against the Machine, with scratching guitarist Tom Morello, upped the ante forever.

MICHAEL FRANTI: The Bay Area and San Francisco—and California as a whole—is my home. There's still a sense of frontierism here, along with an optimism that doesn't exist in other parts of the country or world. It comes through in the music, especially hip-hop, which has a rock feel. (2014)

HOLLYWOOD SWINGIN': The original Red Hot Chili Peppers, over forty years ago, 1985. MiRafoto.com / Alamy Stock Photo.

> *Not to your death and not to your grave,*
> *I'm talkin' 'bout that freedom, fight like a brave*
> —Red Hot Chili Peppers, "Fight Like a Brave"

Red Hot Chili Peppers was the original rap-rock band. Their "Rock Out with Your Cock Out" style incorporates funk, punk, post-punk, psychedelia, hard rock, and new wave. They inspired future genres like funk metal, rap metal, and nu-metal. The Hollywood band's core sound was a rhythmic punk/metal band centered on bassist Flea, one of the greatest musicians of our time, driving rap vocalist Anthony Kiedis—often regarded as the most underrated rapper ever. They played live breakbeats that did not require a DJ.

ANTHONY KIEDIS: We never get hassles from Black people. But there's a minority of small-minded white people who think we should play rock and roll because we're white. (1986)

One could hear tinges of their future rock-rap style on 1984's *Red Hot Chili Peppers*, produced by Andy Gill of Gang of Four. But on 1985's follow-up, *Freaky Styley*, produced by P-Funk icon George Clinton, the quartet first shone with dexterous punk-funk-metal with hip-hop delivery. That had most to do with the return of original guitarist Hillel Slovak, who brought to the band its brotherly bond and furious riffs. The album consisted of a killer cover of Sly and the Family Stone's "If You Want Me to Stay" and their epic "Yertle the Turtle," based on a Dr. Seuss book. 1987's *The Uplift Mojo Party Plan* represented the Chili Peppers at their artistic apex and their height of decadence, with Kiedis and Slovak on drug trips that took the 26-year-old Hillel's life on June 25, 1988.

The Uplift Mojo Party Plan producer Michael Beinhorn also worked on 1989's *Mother's Milk* with new guitarist John Frusciante, which contained their first hits, a rockin' rendition of Stevie Wonder's "Higher Ground" and their alt-rock anthem "Knock Me Down." After a fallout with Beinhorn, the Chili Peppers balanced their sound with Rick Rubin on 1991's breakout *Blood Sugar Sex Magik*.

Blood Sugar Sex Magik transformed the band from struggling artists to global success. The recording was more like a group art therapy session than a studio one. Rick took the band away from typical studio environs to record in his palatial estate in Laurel Canyon, a haunted mansion brimming with infamy. (The album's hit ballad "Under the Bridge" was about Anthony's remorse over Hillel's death, still using heroin, and missing the funeral.)

FLEA: I knew the music on *Freaky Styley* was way too obscure to ever be popular in a mainstream kind of way. But to me, it is a definitive and substantial musical statement. More than any other record we made, it falls into the category of "too funky for white radio, too punk rockin' for black." (2003)

The band always caught a beat with a run of great guitarists, be it Jack Sherman, Hillel Slovak, John Frusciante, Dave Navarro, or Josh Klinghoffer. The Navarro-era Peppers recorded "Uncle L" for the Howard Stern film soundtrack. Anthony Kiedis hated Faith No More's Mike Patton for "copping his style," so he eventually didn't allow Patton to tour with them.

ANTHONY KIEDIS: My drummer says he's gonna kidnap Patton, shave his hair off, and cut off one of his feet, so he'll be forced to find a style of his own. (1990)

> *We care a lot about you people, about your guns*
> *About the wars you're fighting, gee that looks like fun*
> —Faith No More, "We Care a Lot"

HATE ASHBURY: Faith No More's eclectic metal-rap of "Epic" proportions continues to influence modern rock music, 1988. Pictorial Press Ltd / Alamy Stock Photo.

Faith No More was one of the most significant influences on modern musicians, with a sound that incorporated elements of rock, rap, metal, and alternative rock. Their crossover material was a blend of melodic dance rock, brutal thrash metal, hip-hop drive, and punk attitude. FNM was like the Mothers of Invention of the 1990s, with a diversity echoed by almost every future thrash metal, punk revival, rap metal, and nu-metal band.

Faith No More began as a San Francisco industrial culture band called Faith No Man. The band was centered around classically trained keyboardist Roddy Bottum, punk bassist Billy Gould, and drummer Mike Bordin, raised on hard rock, deep funk, and Third World rhythms.

The band's 1985 debut, *We Care a Lot*—released on Mordam Records, the label founded by *Maximum Rocknroll* writer Ruth Schwartz—contained the original version of the rock-rap classic "We Care a Lot," featuring then-vocalist Chuck Moseley. A highlight of the early rock/rap explosion was Halloween night, 1987, at The Ritz in New York, featuring the Red Hot Chili Peppers, Faith No More, and the funky Royal Crescent Mob. That concert foreshadowed the future of rock music, featuring tight rock grooves and an angry rap flow.

MARIA FERRERO: Faith No More, featuring Chuck Moseley on vocals, was one of the first great rap-metal crossover groups. That original version of "We Care a Lot" was the formula for so much of the music to come. It was a time when everyone was coming together: hardcore punk, thrash metal, and aggressive rap. Their music was the first to interconnect bands like the Dead Kennedys, Metallica, and Run-DMC. It was a fascinating time. (2024)

CHUCK MOSELEY: Our music reflects who I am, Black and white and all shades of grey. It's not a pre-planned thing. Funk and soul are in my roots. I grew up on California rock culture and spent years in the Hollywood punk scene. This band organically brings it all together. (1985)

Faith No More signed to *Slash* Magazine publisher Bob Biggs' Slash Records in 1987. *Introduce Yourself*, with an updated "We Care a Lot" (released as a dance 12" remix), resulted in hipster inroads and UK fame. The band achieved American success on their late 1989 album *The Real Thing*, which featured the 1990s' first rap-rock hit, "Epic." The song introduced their dynamic new singer, Mike Patton, of the FNM-like band Mr. Bungle. For a while, FNM was bigger than RHCP, especially in Europe.

MIKE BORDIN: Our old singer was more of a personality. He could have been a great singer but never lived up to it. He developed into a spectacle, which was cool, but that's what he was. I think people understand what we're about now more than ever. But that probably has a lot to do with the fact that we do it better. (1989)

Released in 1992, *Angel Dust* was a sonic coup d'état featuring impressive songs, such as "Midlife Crisis" and their instrumental cover of the theme from *Midnight Cowboy*. The classic album also marked the beginning of the band's eventual demise.

JIM MARTIN: We still rap on records. Sometimes, it is appropriate for the song. If it fits, we use it. We are not a rap band, although people pick up on that aspect of our music. It's an obvious thing to pick up on. People always pick up on the surface shit. It's easier to grasp. (1989)

FNM's decline and fall was ultimately self-inflicted. Patton was behind the firing of metal guitarist Jim Martin to replace him with his Mr. Bungle mate Trey Spruance, which did not pan out. Martin was tight with James Hetfield (the band received a massive boost in popularity when James wore an FNM shirt on the cover of Metallica's *Garage Days Re-Revisited* EP), so Patton's move killed FNM's relationship with Metallica. Nasty onstage comments about Axl Rose, Bret Michaels, and Anthony Kiedis burned more bridges. Patton quit the band at several key moments to pursue Mr. Bungle. Once, he canceled a tour, blaming long-standing mental health issues, only to reunite weeks later with Bungle. While Patton's departure from Faith No More was inevitable, he had operated with divided loyalties for decades.

GREG GUTFELD: We live in a binary universe. You're either a Faith No More fan or a Red Hot Chili Peppers fan. You cannot love Mike Patton and Anthony Kiedis because they are two different people. You have to love Mike Patton; you cannot love Anthony Kiedis. That is why the Red Hot Chili Peppers are the worst band in the universe—because Faith No More is the greatest band in the universe. (2016)

> *Television, the drug of the Nation*
> *Breeding ignorance and feeding radiation*
> —The Disposable Heroes of Hiphoprisy,
> "Television: The Drug of the Nation"

The Disposable Heroes of Hiphoprisy consisted of Michael Franti, a light-skinned Black kid adopted by a white couple in Oakland, and Hong Kong-born Rono Tse. They emerged from the late 1980s Bay Area punk band the Beatnigs, which released one fiery album on the Dead Kennedys' Alternative Tentacles label. Their style was reminiscent of the late, great Gil Scott-Heron, with Franti's half-spoken vocals and upfront political messages in the music, forever changing hip-hop by tackling media bias, racial equality, and homophobia. The difference was that they used sampling and scratching as primary music recording tools, mixing heavy hip-hop, jazz, and industrial genres.

Their album *Hypocrisy is the Greatest Luxury* (Island Records) came out in 1992 but didn't receive much attention, despite a powerful rendition of the Kennedys' "California Uber Alles" and the thought-provoking dance hit "Television: The Drug of the Nation" (originally on 1991's debut EP). The album was deemed too funky for REM alt-rockers and too avant-garde for b-boys. Before achieving jazz fame, guitarist Charlie Hunter made his recording debut with Hiphoprisy. The duo disbanded after a 1994 tour with U2. Franti pursued a solo career as Michael Franti and Spearhead, intermingling rap, rock, funk, reggae, jazz, and folk. He reworked Steve Miller's "The Joker" on 1995's *Hempilation: Vol. 2: Free the Weed*, a benefit record produced by *High Times* for reforming marijuana laws.

MICHAEL FRANTI: One cool thing about hip-hop is that you have a groove; over that, you can say whatever you want. We've got a song where we say, "What will we do to become famous and dandy, just like Amos 'n Andy?" It's about to what extent we will go into creating the stereotypical racist images that have been presented through *The Amos 'n Andy Show* and television and music today. To what extent will we go into recreating those images to reach a modicum of success? Hiphoprisy is all about the hypocrisy of being a political hip-hop artist, an artist of conscience in an industry with no conscience. (1992)

> *Kick it like a steel toe, real slow hits from the bong*
> *Makes me feel like Cheech, and I'm kickin' it with Chong*
> —Cypress Hill, "Stoned is the Way of the Walk"

Cypress Hill took its name from a street in the South Gate area of East Los Angeles where the three teenagers spent time together. DJ Muggs, whose real name is Lawrence Muggerud, an Italian-American kid from Queens, NY, moved to LA when he was fourteen. He started DJing with rappers Brett and Sean Bouldin as The 7A3, whose 1988 album, *Coolin' in Cali*, sold enough for Muggs to purchase an SP-1200 drum machine, which helped create the Cypress sound. The 7A3's first independent 12" released in 1987, titled "The 7A3 Will Rock You," was an early-1980s mad scratch-off to "We Will Rock You." The Bouldin brothers had significant musical sway in the early days of Cypress.

Sen Dog (Senen Reyes) worked at physically demanding jobs in factories, warehouses, and department stores. He also performed with his younger brother, the Cuban-American rapper Mellow Man Ace (1989's "Mentirosa"). Muggs produced the first Mellow Man Ace album and rescued B-Real (Louis Freese) to write lyrics for the album. B-Real, who is also of Cuban heritage, sold drugs and was involved in gang activity, during which his lung got punctured by a hollow-point .22 caliber bullet in a Crips-Bloods shooting. In his spare time, B-Real wrote poetry.

The first recording by Cypress Hill was a disaster because B-Real's raps were lousy. Muggs advised him to listen to other records for inspiration. Mellow Man Ace introduced B-Real to the music of Rammellzee (Death Comet Crew, etc.), a colorful NYC rapper and artist who spoke strangely and used a high-pitched squeal when he performed. Rammellzee inspired B-Real's distinctive nasally rasp, which he delivered as if speaking through a lungful of marijuana smoke. It's equal parts Ad-Rock and *Pineapple Express*. Sen's gravelly baritone perfectly complemented B-Real's high-octane, ricocheting vocal twang.

Cypress Hill shaped their dynamic sound by incorporating heavy metal's rebel darkness within DJ Muggs' multicultural framework. As products of Southern California rock culture, there's a lot of Black Sabbath and Led Zeppelin buried in their samples and magnified in their sound. Sen Dog's first exposure to live music was seeing his high school friend, drummer Dave Lombardo's band, which became Slayer. Ozzy Osbourne inspired B-Real before he got into a thug lifestyle and Public Enemy-style hip-hop. "Rap Superstar" involved Everlast rapping and Chino Moreno (Deftones) on guitar. Cypress' rock-rap merger had a lasting impact on the genre.

SEN DOG: We listened to classic rock, punk rock, and even 1980s metal. I remember the first time a mosh pit broke out at one of our performances. It was at Drop in the Park with Pearl Jam in Seattle in 1992. We came on, and all this wild activity went on up front. The kids broke down the barricade and stopped our show four songs in! (1995)

B-REAL: In terms of the metal imagery and vibe, that's because the three of us listened to a lot of different things growing up: funk, punk, metal, reggae, and eventually hip-hop. You have these things that represent those influences in the dynamic, whether it's the artwork, certain sounds that might be added to a song, or our overall "We don't give a fuck" attitude, which is very punk rock. All those culminated in Cypress Hill. (2022)

Muggs sent the finished demo to a few record executives. Chris Schwartz and Joe "The Butcher" Nicolo, of the new Columbia-distributed Ruffhouse label, liked what they heard and signed the group in 1990. Cypress Hill had a brush with fame on their 1991 self-titled album. The lead single, "The Phuncky Feel One," flopped, but its B-side, "How I Could Just Kill a Man," became their first hit, receiving heavy rotation on MTV for a video starring Q-Tip and Ice Cube.

In February 1992, Cypress played an industry showcase at the hippie-rock venue Wetlands. Earlier that day, they held a press conference for their March 1992 *High Times* cover by editor Steve Bloom. This was when Cypress downplayed their Latino heritage, which later became a central part of their public image. Their music evolved from homicidal gangsta rap to a focus on weed worship. Muggs convinced B-Real and Sen Dog to become the Cheech & Chong of hip-hop.

B-REAL: We've played a lot to rock crowds. We connected on the subject of smoking weed legally. Lollapalooza was our first experience, like an alternative rock version of Woodstock. I don't like playing to all these old dirty Grateful Dead motherfuckers. I tell them, "I don't ask for a sip of your beer, you don't get a hit off my joint." (1995)

In 1993, *Black Sunday*, produced by Muggs and his Soul Assassins, debuted at #1. The album was a stroke of genius, a rap-rock crossover with blunted dub jams and a headbanger attitude—full of songs made with their middle finger up. The opening foghorn beckoned "I Wanna

Get High," based on "One Draw" by Rita Marley. The seventh track, "Interlude," featured a sample of this writer discussing marijuana at a 1992 New Music Seminar panel called "Pop Goes Pot." Cypress Hill took a break in 1995 after *Cypress Hill III: Temples of Boom*, with Muggs focused on his solo career and Sen Dog's brief departure due to feeling overshadowed by B-Real. Sen Dog also fronts the nu-metal band Powerflo.

SEN DOG: What stands out in my mind are the shows with Nirvana, Soundgarden, and Pearl Jam, the grunge-era rock that dominated back then. Here we were, LA kids, right in the middle of Kurt Cobain, Chris Cornell, and all those dudes. It felt like we made the big time; we'd arrived. Then we went on tour with Nirvana; it was the kind of thing that I thought we'd never do. I'm glad we were there to partake in it. It opened up our audience in a big way. (2023)

> *This is the House of Pain*
> *To come inside is insane*
> —House of Pain, "Put Your Head Out"

House of Pain began with Everlast (Erik Schrody), who was born in 1969, the day after the Woodstock Festival. He grew up in Hempstead, Long Island, before moving with his family to the San Fernando Valley as a child. As a teenager, he was deeply involved in b-boy culture and attended LA's Taft High School, where his friend Divine Styler (Mark Richardson) encouraged him to record a demo. The demo reached his classmate Ice-T (Tracy Marrow), who was impressed and signed Everlast to his Rhyme Syndicate Cartel, which had a deal with Warner Bros. The cover of the 1990 album *Forever Everlasting* showed Everlast in a robe in a boxing ring, suggesting him as hip-hop's Great White Hope. The single "I Got the Knack," based on a sample of "My

Sharona," received some MTV play but did not become a hit record, and the album flopped.

EVERLAST: In high school, you had to have a rap if you wanted to hang out. Ice-T said that he'd like to meet me. Then my friends told him I was white, and he said that he really wanted to meet me. (1992)

DANNY BOY: When I ran into Everlast after his record, his mother was kicking him out of his house because he had failed as a rapper, wasn't making any money, had no job, and was probably smoking weed in the house, so she was over that. His big dreams of becoming a famous rapper were over, and I picked him up, put him under my wing, and moved him in with us. Back then, I was doing credit card scams and selling drugs, so I put some clothes on him, got him a scooter, and adopted him. That's when we started talking about music and going through my records: We went through the old Madness and punk records to get samples of what we wanted to do. I had a massive record collection because I used to work at Wherehouse. We used to boost more shit out of that record store than we ever sold. (2024)

Everlast knew Danny Boy (O'Connor) from the Taft parking lot cutting classes. The two had a lot in common. Danny's family moved West from Staten Island when he was an infant after his father went to prison and later became one of the few white hardcore b-boys in the Valley. They shared an Irish heritage, so their punk-edged hip-hop duo projected an image of being Irish toughs, characterized by beer-guzzling, fist-pumping, slam dancing, and fighting. The two brought in their Taft classmate DJ Lethal (Leor DiMant), a mixologist not Irish but *litvak* (Latvian-Jewish). House of Pain represented the new post-Beasties, two-tone b-boy culture that darkened the hue and brought mad flava to the stratified suburbs.

WHEN ROCK MET HIP-HOP

DANNY BOY: House of Pain was a name I got from the Oingo Boingo song "No Spill Blood," which I thought sounded cool. I was doing four-track demos. One demo was called *House of Pain*. Erik [Everlast] was intrigued, so I told him my idea: that we should start a group my way, do it like Irish white boy tough-guy shit. And he was like, "Yeah, I'm Irish too." I'm like, "I know you are." So that's how House of Pain began. It was being drunk, talking shit, and never thinking in a million years that we would be an actual group. But Everlast was serious about making demos. He ran into Muggs from Cypress Hill, who had just signed his record deal and was looking for other people to sign a record deal as well. So when Muggs heard the concept, he loved it because, back then, you needed a concept; just rhyming would not cut it anymore. Everyone wanted a group, the whole package. (2024)

DJ MUGGS: Everlast's solo was coming off the Armani suits. So I said, "Why don't you come up with a group name?" A few days later, he came by with Danny Boy, like, "Yo, we got this group, House of Pain." And it was Danny Boy's concept. You know, Irish, straight razors, this and that. I was like, "That's fucking amazing!" So Danny Boy came up with the visuals and many ideas, and Everlast had the rhymes, which came together like that. (2013)

DANNY BOY: In 1992, when we came out, rap was on life support. The Beasties were MIA; then grunge started to happen. Cypress and House of Pain got people back into the fray; we went out with nothing but alt-rock acts. On our first headlining tour, we brought Rage Against the Machine on their first tour, and then we brought out Biohazard. People were losin' it at hip-hop gigs again. We were that disruptive force; we looked and sounded different. (2024)

House of Pain came together quickly. Muggs had a production deal to sign groups to Cypress' new label, the Epic-distributed Ruffhouse

Records. *Everyone* could tell "Jump Around" would be a hit. Monica Lynch, an Irish-American at Tommy Boy Records, related to the demo and signed the group.

MONICA LYNCH (Tommy Boy Records): When I got the package, I said, "What the fuck is this?" This shit reminds me of my brothers. After church, they'd go to bars and get in fights. (2012)

Joe "The Butcher" Nicolo of Ruffhouse Records got revenge by rush-releasing a pop hit based on "Jump Around" called "Jump" by Kris Kross (known for wearing their clothes inside out). So the album sat for three months until "Jump" fell off the charts and into oblivion.

DANNY BOY: That record took two months to make. Tommy Boy loved "Jump Around" and was ready to rush the album to market. Then Kris Kross' "Jump" almost killed our career before it started. On "Jump Around," at the end, we say "dedicated to Joe "The Biter" Nicolo." We dissed these fucking mobsters. Then we were off to the races, going gold and platinum albums, *Seconds* Magazine cover, all that. (2024)

"Jump Around," with its grungy punk energy and scratchy rock grooves, became an instant anthem, a celebratory song still heard everywhere. The smash "Jump Around" video, shot in Midtown Manhattan during the St. Patrick's Day parade, enshrined their white hip-hop gangster stereotype of the classic pugilist hoodlums of Irish-American lore.

DJ MUGGS: I made the beat. I had a song called "Jump Around" already. I was saving it for the second Cypress Hill album. We'd just finished the first album, and the other guys felt burned out on recording. I had Son Doobie from Funkdoobiest rap on the song—it was all right.

I played the beat for a few people like Ice Cube. In the process, I'd met up with Everlast. (2012)

EVERLAST: After I left Warner Brothers, Muggs and I were dating chicks that lived together, so we hung out a lot. He played me the "Jump Around" beat, but it didn't have the horn yet. He had a studio in his bedroom at his aunt's house, where he lived in Bell Gardens. I wrote "Jump Around" in his driveway—it wasn't yet a song but a bunch of lyrics. I went out to his driveway, and as I wrote it, he found the horn. And then we both got chills. We knew it was good. (2012)

DANNY BOY: I'd play it for kids that hung out with us. You'd play them other demos, and they'd nod their heads and say, "Yeah, cool." I swear everyone started going bananas when they heard "Jump Around." I knew this was different. (2012)

EVERLAST: Everybody dreams about writing one of those songs. I've had a lot of songs that I'm proud of. But I can go to the darkest depths of Africa and go into a bar, and if they have a jukebox and you play "Jump Around," people will react. (2012)

DANNY BOY: My ex-girlfriends, their boyfriends can't stand it. Every time they hear it, they can't not think about me. (2012)

Their shamrock-festooned 1992 *House of Pain* debut album, often called *House of Pain (Fine Malt Lyrics)*, went platinum. Muggs' loud loping beats—courtesy of the SP-1200 drum machine the DJ bought for his two years in The 7A3—defined House of Pain's shit-kicker sound. As per *The Source* (5/92): "The atmosphere is like a cross between a frat party and a barroom brawl."

In 1992, Sub Pop Records was the hot grunge label. A pivotal moment in the rock-rap union was their Sub Pop Singles Club 45. The DJ Muggs' version of "Shamrocks & Shenanigans" got turned on its head by *Nevermind* producer and Garbage guitarist Butch Vig, redefining the song with crunching guitar over hardcore raps. The green-vinyl 7" had two mixes, the "In The Dirt Mix" and the "Buds & Brew Mix." Neither Muggs, Everlast, nor Danny Boy remembers the backstory, which means that the remixes were an artificial construct of cross-marketing rather than a genuine musical collaboration.

DJ LETHAL: You have to be flexible. I take everything as a challenge— and being able to cross genres is a challenge. So naturally, I'll take on that challenge and smash it. (2014)

Despite not having a hit single like "Jump Around," their 1994 album *Same as it Ever Was* went gold. Danny once referred to "Jump Around" as hip-hop's "Louie Louie." But Everlast wrote an album with more serious imagery and fewer party tunes, so it wasn't as fun. The underrated single was "Who's The Man," which appeared on a remixed 12". During the recording, the band had to deal with Everlast's home arrest for gun charges and a fallout with Cypress, which ultimately led to the dissolution of the Soul Assassins posse, comprising House of Pain, Cypress Hill, and Funkdoobiest.

The third and final House of Pain album did not involve Muggs. However, DJ Lethal did his finest work on 1996's *Truth Crushed to Earth Shall Rise Again*, which sold only 250,000 copies. During the album's release party, Everlast announced that House of Pain was over, shocking the band and the rap world. He then surprised everyone with his 1997 conversion to Islam, which he later renounced.

DANNY BOY: I was the branding, conceptual, and style guy. Everlast was the pro rapper. On the second record, I wanted to stay true to our fanbase, and he was worried about spitting lyrics to his boys, trying to cater to the Five Percenter and Black Muslim rappers—and it sold half as much as the first album. On the third record, Erik avoided our fan base and the hardcore rappers, instead reconnecting with a few Rhyme Syndicate friends. However, DJ Lethal and I had almost no influence on the record. Then he left and quit the band. A few years later, I put together La Costa Nostra, and he practically begged to get involved, only to quit again, fucking up that group, too. It led to bad blood between us. I love him, but I don't have to like him. It hasn't been the best of friendships. (2024)

Fred Durst and DJ Lethal became friendly on a 1995 House of Pain-Limp Bizkit tour. So when House of Pain crashed and burned, Lethal became the rock-rap DJ in Limp Bizkit. Danny Boy blew up his career to open and operate The Outsiders Museum in Tulsa, the ultimate tribute to the S.E. Hinton book and Francis Ford Coppola film.

Everlast reinvented himself with an unheard blend of acoustic rock, metal, and hip-hop. 1998's *Whitey Ford Sings the Blues,* made with the Stimulated Dummies production team of Dante Ross, John Gamble, and Geeby Dajani, went triple Platinum. The hit single "What It's Like" was nominated for a Best Rap Performance Grammy. But on the day he finished recording, the 29-year-old suffered a massive heart attack; an ambulance took him to Cedar-Sinai in LA for emergency aortic surgery. Like many of his peers, he had no health insurance, and the hospital bills wiped him out.

DANTE ROSS: Everlast was hanging out at my house when he began strumming an acoustic guitar and singing a song he called "What It's Like." I loved it because it sounded like Johnny Cash reimagined as a b-boy troubadour. At first, he didn't want to record it, but I convinced him to do it, and it was easy—almost like doing a rap song. I programmed some drums, and he put his guitar down, which fit. It was natural, and it's a pattern we have continued to work on. Once we did that song and we nailed it, we were like, "This is what we need to do." (2001)

The maturing rhymer confronted his near-death experience in 2000's *Eat at Whitey's* with "Put Your Lights On." He rapped, sang, and strummed an acoustic guitar, further blending hip-hop, Southern rock, and folk/country on the Gold-certified recording. The following year, Clive Davis got Everlast to sing "Put Your Lights On" on *Supernatural*, Carlos Santana's mega-successful comeback that sold thirteen million copies. He played a monster set at Woodstock '99, and in 2000 guest-starred with Lords Of Brooklyn on an acoustic rave-up of Run-DMC's "Sucker MCs" for the *Take a Bite Out of Rhyme: A Rock Tribute to Rock* compilation. 2004's *White Trash Beautiful* for Def Jam/Island went unnoticed. Everlast and Eminem feuded in that era over the title of the new white king of hip-hop.

EVERLAST: Money and business get in the way of everything. Some cats have spiritual issues; some develop drug issues. The reason House of Pain broke up is that we were all unhappy. When I look back on it, I can't say, "This was the moment. That was the last straw." It was like, "Are y'all as unhappy as I am? Cause I can't do this anymore." (2010)

> *I got my stereo bumpin'*
> *I'm about to kill me somethin'*
> —Body Count, "Cop Killer"

Body Count originated in the late 1970s in South Central Los Angeles. Before Ice-T (Tracy Marrow) ventured into music, he used to hang out with heavy metal guitarist Ernie C (Ernest Cunnigan) and drummer Victor "Beatmaster V" Wilson. Ernie C's left-handed Stratocaster led jam sessions playing the music of Jimi Hendrix, Led Zeppelin, and the Isley Brothers. Ice-T was part of a small Black rock posse with bassist Lloyd "Mooseman" Roberts III and rhythm guitarist Dennis "D-Roc" Miles. After high school, they pursued their paths. Ice's tragic early life as an orphan involved homelessness and a stint in the army before he became one of the defining voices of 1980s West Coast hip-hop. Ernie C continued to play the guitar, so when the two reunited, his skills were exceptional.

Body Count started when Ice-T reunited with Ernie C and the rest of their high school crew to play on his rap records. The band got named for the song "Body Count" on T's 1991 album *O.G. Original Gangster*. Before Body Count entered the studio to make rock music, Jane's Addiction singer Perry Farrell invited them to play at his 1991 debut Lollapalooza tour. The rave reaction led to their self-titled debut in 1992 for Sire/Warner Bros., featuring songs like "Cop Killer" and "KKK Bitch." Their articulate antisocial messaging and diverse styles—hip-hop, thrash metal, hardcore punk, classic rock, and R&B—made them a perfect band for the 1990s alt-rock revolution.

ICE-T: Body Count wasn't trying to do rap-metal. We were trying to do metal. We based it off of Suicidal Tendencies, the LA punk band that had that gangbanger style. But we wanted to make it real from a Black perspective. I get messages from Black kids telling us they were outcasts and didn't have anyone who shared that love with them. We were trying to blend the energy of Suicidal Tendencies with the impending doom of Black Sabbath and the speed and precision of Slayer, so we combined those three bands to create our sound. We brought that mentality into the music. White kids were scared of the devil; we were scared of the streets. I think that's why we caught on; we brought the realism of the streets. It was almost like what rap was doing, but we put it in metal form. And it was sincere. It wasn't a novelty like Run-DMC and Aerosmith. It was a real rock band. (2022)

BODY COUNT: Rap legend Ice-T (center) and crew unleashed the ultimate in "ghetto metal" ¾ Virgin Records, 1994. Virgin Records/Photofest ¾ Virgin Records.

"Ghetto Metal" was an articulated concept that never materialized. It originated from in-depth discussions between NWA's Eazy-E and his manager Jerry Heller, who envisioned NWA as "The Black Beatles."

The idea involved brown-skinned Californians playing aggressive heavy metal in the vein of Metallica, Slayer, and Suicidal Tendencies. It was going to be a great new music movement. Heller signed NWA to Priority Records because no other record label was interested, and the label was open to exploring this new musical direction. Eazy-E continued to push for a rock direction before his untimely demise. Dr. Dre said they'd talked about doing some heavy metal, but nothing ever became of it for concerns about impacting NWA's street cred. "Ghetto Metal" manifested in the sound of Body Count, although the two camps had no affiliation. Insiders attributed Heller's negative portrayal in the movie *Straight Outta Compton* as a factor in his demise at age seventy-five, labeling him as the white devil of rap music.

DOCTOR DRE: Growing up in LA, you can't be ignorant about rock music. It's everywhere you go and everything you see. What I've been trying to do is Black rock and roll. I'm playing rock and roll, and my audience is getting into it. I call it "ghetto metal." You have to experiment. You can't do rock like how Aerosmith and Guns N' Roses do it. Do some shit niggas wanna hear. (1996)

JERRY HELLER: Ice-T was the original gangsta rapper in Los Angeles. He was a lot older than the guys in NWA. He was a friend, but Eazy didn't feel he was making the same magnitude of political statement that *Straight Outta Compton* made. "Cop Killer" was more of a rock and roll record than a rap one. We thought about it more from an economic point of view than we did from a groundbreaking, sociological-political point of view. (2015)

> *The rage is relentless*
> *We need a movement with a quickness*
> —Rage Against the Machine, "Take The Power Back"

BOMB TRACK: Rage Against the Machine changed the face of rock and rap, 1996. Photofest.

Rage Against the Machine was the evolutionary pinnacle of the rap-rock crossover. The band did for rock-rap what Run-DMC did for rap and the Clash did for punk. With an earth-shaking rap-metal-funk attack, they brought back radical social commentary to popular music.

Rage redefined rap, thanks to fiery frontman Zack de la Rocha, with pedigrees in hardcore punk and hip-hop culture. Tom Morello replaced typical rap sampling with his post-Hendrix agit-metal guitar interplay, merging the heaviest rock riffs with unheard rhythms mimicking DJ turntable scratches and electronic noise. The group—held together by the machinated rhythm section of bassist Tim Commerford and drummer Brad Wilk—inspired zillions of bands to adopt a similar formula, but none came close.

ZACK DE LA ROCHA: I don't particularly care for Black Sabbath, and Tom [Morello] doesn't particularly care for the hip-hop riffs I come up with. But the two, when fused, make something unique and powerful. (1996)

WHEN ROCK MET HIP-HOP

The band started in early 1991 in a San Fernando Valley rehearsal space. Tom Morello and Adam Jones, guitarist of the popular LA band Tool, were high school friends from Libertyville, Illinois. So Rage played to packed houses from Day One. They created such a stir around LA that Epic Records signed them after their second show. Their anticipated self-titled debut album—with a "no samples, keyboards or synthesizers" warning—was one of the most intense major label recordings since the 1960s. The album contained ten militant originals with shifting moods and tempos. By the 1990s, America was ready for an explosive mix of hardcore punk, heavy metal, and hip-hop, with a volatile "burn it down" energy not seen since the MC5.

TOM MORELLO: When you choose to be a political rock band, the road's steeper for you. Some bands are overtly political at any given time but may not be artistically viable. Fortunately, we have nosebleed seats in the arena built by the MC5, Bob Marley, and Public Enemy (2000)

KILLING IN THE NAME: Rage Against the Machine frontman Zack de la Rocha defined the heavy metal rapper, 1993. Fabio Diena / Alamy Stock Photo.

Zack de la Rocha grew up as an outsider, a Chicano breakdancer from a white high school in the town of Irving in the heart of "Reagan Country." He later fronted Inside Out, a straight-edge hardcore band in the style of Minor Threat. The group broke up while working on their second album, *Rage Against the Machine*. The title was Zack's metaphor for the inhumane treatment of oppressed races within capitalist America.

Zack's powerful performances with Rage Against the Machine were highlighted by his rap-singing calls to action and howls of alienation, with his fists clenched, middle fingers extended, and obscenities spewed. Harvard-educated Tom Morello punctuated the sound with his reinvention of the Sunset Strip guitar shredder. Morello had played in a great, underrated Hollywood band called Lock Up, with a can't-miss deal with Geffen. Oregon native drummer Brad Wilk was in a pre-Pearl Jam group with Eddie Vedder. Morello and de la Rocha shared socialist backgrounds. Morello's wealthy father partook in Kenya's late independence struggle, and his mother was a white civil rights activist. Zack's father, Roberto, was a member of the radical East LA arts collective, Los Four.

TOM MORELLO: I was excited about the prospect of playing hip-hop within the context of a punk band. And I won't make any excuses for not being a DJ. At that time, my chief influences were Terminator X and Jam Master Jay, and I was determined to re-create the record-scratching and the DJing—those rich, bizarre textures—on my guitar. (2001)

The band released many iconic albums, notably 1991's *Rage Against the Machine*, 1996's *Evil Empire*, and 1999's *The Battle of Los Angeles*. An interesting addition to their discography is the 2000 album "Renegades," a collection of cover songs. One standout from this album is their rap-metal version of Cypress Hill's "How I Could Just Kill

A Man," which paid homage to the original while giving it a unique twist. Another notable joint effort was the 2014 recording of the song "Close Your Eyes (And Count to Fuck)" with the hip-hop duo Run the Jewels working with Zack de la Rocha.

TRICKY: I've got this funny thing about Rage Against the Machine. I think, "Who do they represent?" They don't represent my feelings. I grew up with no money. You don't know how I survived. You're talking about everyone's pain. I'm very suspicious, and you can never represent my tension because you don't know my tension. So it doesn't matter how much you jump around on stage or how complex your lyrics are; you can't represent me. (1997)

Despite their crossover success and earning the respect of pioneers like Chuck D and B-Real, Zack is still not seen as an elite rapper, and Rage is barely considered part of the hip-hop scene. They cater to a disgruntled white audience and have never been considered viable for rap radio airplay. The major criticism is that they're seen as cultural appropriators, channeling the Black rage undercurrent of rap and riding that wave to mainstream success. It's similar to Elvis, who gained more fame and fortune than the Black artists he covered. The band's only limitations were self-imposed, stemming from ego explosions and Zack's struggles with handling success. It's a concern bordering on hypocrisy, as all four members became wildly wealthy (the band has a nine-figure valuation) and used their platform to cultivate themselves as Top 40 revolutionaries selling civil war and social chaos. Yet their historical impact remains undeniable, with a legendary following and induction into the Rock and Roll Hall of Fame.

MIKE SCHNAPP: Rage Against the Machine was the highest-quality band playing rock-rap. They were the best because they were so real.

There was nothing cheesy about them; it was intelligent, very musical, and on every level, they pressed every button correctly. Those gigantic riffs and incredible drum beats with Zack's rap delivery of intelligent, socially conscious lyrics, badass motherfuckin' rockin' out like nobody did before the first Rage album. It's like the cops kicking down your doors. Things would never be the same again. (2024)

> *I am not your rolling wheels, I am the highway*
> *I am not your carpet ride, I am the sky*
> —Audioslave, "I Am the Highway"

Audioslave was Rage Against the Machine, with Soundgarden legend Chris Cornell replacing de la Rocha. The short-lived project, organized by producer Rick Rubin in 2002, exuded a jumble of badass twenty-first-century Led Zeppelin boogie-metal with Morello's mind-boggling guitar volatility and an intense Commerford/Wilk update of the 1970s hard rock rhythm section thump. But some critics felt that the superstar heartthrob's trademark howl lacked Zack's tenacity. Cornell quit the group after completing the album and rejoined two months before its release—which raised doubts about the band's longevity. Cornell later teamed with hip-hop producer Timbaland for *Scream*, Chris's third solo album. *Scream* was a radical shift in style that confused fans and foes alike. This most surprising recording—Cornell's first *Billboard* Top 10 solo hit—favored sleek electro-pop tones over the bombast of the grunge king's sound.

CHRIS CORNELL: Hip-hop groups don't spend a lot of time making records, but they make a lot of records. They don't tour as much, but they do tour. They keep things going, and I think it's something that rock bands can relearn. You can take it from hip-hop, or you can take it from rock bands from the 1960s and 1970s. You've got to go for it. (2005)

WHEN ROCK MET HIP-HOP

> *I roll with the punches, so I survive*
> *Try to rock because it keeps the crowd alive*
> —Prophets of Rage, "Prophets of Rage"

Prophets of Rage was a politically charged supergroup featuring Chuck D and B-Real, rather than Zack de la Rocha, alongside Tom Morello, bassist Tim Commerford, and drummer Brad Wilk. Their purpose extended beyond music, with a strong emphasis on spreading a message. The powerful impact of Morello's music felt like the beginning of a revolution. B-Real said that his work on the *Judgment Night* soundtrack prepared him to join Prophets of Rage. Chuck D's connection came from Public Enemy being among the first bands to tour with Rage, alongside Cypress Hill and House of Pain. Prophets of Rage promoted their message "Make America Rage Again" at two significant shows: outside the prison walls of Norco, CA, and at the 2016 Republican National Convention in Cleveland. Their set list combined forceful Rage material such as "Guerrilla Radio," "Bulls on Parade," and "Testify" with Public Enemy's "My Uzi Weighs a Ton" and "Shut Em Down," Cypress Hill's "Insane in the Membrane," and the Beastie Boys' "No Sleep Till Brooklyn," interspersed with verses from "Bring the Noise"—without Zack's raspy vocals and California whine. Producer Brendan O'Brien (Bruce Springsteen, Pearl Jam) captured the group's urgent sound on the *Prophets of Rage* EP.

BRAD WILK: The idea of this band was born organically in a room, and it all had to do with chemistry. It concerned the political climate and the hip-hop/rock chemistry between us all. (2016)

> *You were raised to hate me*
> *I was raised to hate you*
> —Downset, "My American Prayer"

Downset delivered one of the first examples of joining hardcore punk with hip-hop. The original five-piece—former members of the LAHC band Social Justice (known for 1989's *Unity is Strength*)—combined insurrectionist politics, hardcore beatdown, and hip-hop rhythms, with lyrics interspersed between angry rants and artsy, spoken lulls. The group from Richie Valens' *barrio* hometown of Sylmar, CA, exploded on the scene with two albums for Mercury Records: 1994's *Downset* and 1996's *Do We Speak a Dead Language?* Downset frontman Rey Anthony Oropeza arose from hip-hop crews, art circles, and graffiti culture.

REY OROPEZA: I was a pissed-off kid who didn't want to end up like everyone else in the neighborhood and the family. Your whole world starts to crumble around you, so you grab onto anything you can before you die along with it. So I just hung on to what I could, which is my expression: graffiti, art, and music. (1994)

The band gained a following for its sociopolitical live shows, with aggressive, profane Black Flag-style vocals, brutal screams and unintelligible lyrics. The snarling guitars and relentless riffage were reminiscent of early Metallica or Pantera, with tribal tempo changes and blunt, heavy-duty repetition. Their powerful music, message, and energetic stage presence incited pandemonium, all part of their mission to revolutionize music and the world.

REY OROPEZA: I was inspired by people like Run-DMC using rock in their music. Public Enemy, on *It Takes A Nation of Millions*, sampled a Slayer riff on fucking "Channel Zero!?" We were fucking around with guitars and busting flows over beats, thinking it sounded sick, and then we heard Public Enemy and knew that was the sound. Slayer, damn! I saw them all the time in South LA at the Balboa Theater. (2012)

Their unique style stemmed from Rey's ability to transition seamlessly from a hip-hop flow to rebel yells. While Zack de la Rocha's powerful lyrics focused on national and global issues, Oropeza, also known as "The Messenger," channeled his passion into songs about spiritual devotion and unattainable redemption. His inspiration stemmed from a desire to break free from the cycle of Latin-Black gang violence in his Chicano community, leading him to express his social conscience on topics such as injustice, inhumanity, oppression, objectification, racism, and apathy. The band's innovative blend of rap, punk, and metal had a significant impact on the "nu-metal" genre of the late 1990s and early 2000s.

REY OROPEZA: I realize the need to vent. But if you bring an ill to the table, sooner or later, you have to start talking about solutions. (1994)

> *How would life be if the world smoked weed?*
> *Guaranteed there'd be peace not greed*
> —Kottonmouth Kings, "Peace Not Greed"

Kottonmouth Kings was an intense punk-metal b-boy crew of stoned-out beach town bad boys from the Orange County subcultural epicenter of Placentia, CA. Lead rapper Brad Xavier, also known as Daddy X, gained experience in Doggy Style, his brother Spike Xavier's late-1980s straight-edge hardcore band. Suburban Noize Records producer Spike and founder Brad, helped start the band before Eminem and Kid Rock gained mainstream success. Onstage, KK presented punk-rap mayhem, with six members—rappers, musicians, two DJs, and a 6'8" masked dancer doing unusual "hydro-mechanic" choreography. Live, they'd do rap renditions of TSOL, Agent Orange, Social Distortion, and Black Flag.

WEST COAST

BRAD XAVIER: For some reason, this band affects people. We see people from all walks of life who like punk rock, hip-hop, reggae, and old-school hippie music. It's a great collection of individuals who come together at a Kottonmouth Kings show to celebrate music and personal freedom. We've played shows with Cypress Hill for five or six years. They are legends. As far as what we do, they paved the way for bands like us to do our thing. (2005)

Their 2000 album, *High Society*, was their best work, highlighted by a mighty amalgam of heavy guitars, scratching, and rap samples inspired by Dr. Dre's Cali studio style and the Beastie Boys' encyclopedic vibe. The album showcased a bold "rip-hop" attitude, allying with punk singer Jack Grisham on a reimagining of TSOL's "Peace Through Power" called "Peace Not Greed," with hardcore scene vets Spike Xavier (Mind Over Four) and Pat Dubar (Uniform Choice). In 2000, they also made an impact with a compelling rendition of the Geto Boys' "My Mind's Playing Tricks On Me" on the compilation *Take a Bite Outta Rhyme: A Rock Tribute to Rap*. The group's unique rock-rap hybrid sound and DIY music production approach set them apart from the corporate framework. Their fan-friendly music focused on marijuana, with tracks such as "Where's the Weed At?," "Bong Toke," "Ganja Daze," and "Fire It Up." The self-sufficient Kings made it clear that they were serious smokers, not jokers, about their cannabis use.

The group went on a break in 2017 and reunited in 2018 without Daddy X. It was just Dustin "D-Loc" Miller and original member Steven "Saint Dog" Thronson. Unfortunately, everything fell apart in 2020 when Steve passed away at age 44. Daddy X fell out with the band's manager and partner in Suburban Noize and the SRH clothing line. Daddy X sold the label's catalog for an undisclosed sum and left, never to be heard from again. Rumors suggest he moved to Florida to work as an Uber driver. The other members said that they didn't enjoy doing business with Daddy X or D-Lo.

SPIKE XAVIER: When hip-hop started, rappers had to do it themselves. Nobody wanted to put their records out. Once they proved it was a viable form that would sell, everyone stepped in, bringing it to the rest of the world. (2000)

> *I take what I want, get whatever I need*
> *There ain't a soul who'll stop me*
> —Vince Neil, "Breakin' in the Gun"

Vince Neil made two solo albums after his mid-1990s resignation/dismissal from Motley Crue. The second one, 1995's *Carved in Stone*, was produced by the Dust Brothers, creators of the Beastie Boys' sonic pastiche *Paul's Boutique*. The intention was to blend the classic rock bombast for which Neil was known with hip-hop and industrial rhythms, utilizing recordings and sampling techniques for which the Dust Brothers were renowned. Warner Bros. executives made the head-scratching decision to pair a hair metal superstar in search of a fresh direction with the lo-fi hip-hop sampling tag team.

VINCE NEIL: Warner Brothers thought it would be a good idea for the Dust Brothers to do some rock, and I wanted to experiment a little bit, so we got together. We experimented a lot and went into recording a whole different way, using a lot of computer gear. (1994)

Neil attempted to expand his vocal range by incorporating funky beats and grungy harmonies into his music, moving away from his traditional metal grooves. While not all Motley Crue fans were pleased with the final result, Neil's energetic guitar rock and rhythmic pace remained central to the music. The opening track, "Breakin' in the Gun," was a killer song injected with shards of Public Enemy, elements of air-raid sirens, Alice in Chains riffs, and hip-hop breakbeats.

VINCE NEIL: That album was before Kid Rock, so no one was ready for it then. If it came out today, it would sell fifty million copies. (2000)

The record starred guitarist Brent Woods from the hair band Wildside and later as the guitarist for Warrant. Bassist Robbie Crane jammed in a reformed Ratt. Vik Foxx was the original Enuff Z'Nuff drummer. Vince put his recording on hold during his four-year-old daughter Skylar's four-month struggle, enduring six surgeries for stomach cancer at Children's Hospital in Los Angeles before her death; she inspired the album's touching ballad single, "Skylar's Song."

MIKE SIMPSON: I would describe the production experience as a crazy 1980s rock porno session, with Barbie Doll chicks coming by with Sasquatch titties. (1996)

Vince has often said that his Dust Brothers record killed his solo career. The album was too ahead of its time, showcasing futuristic production and musical adventure. Vince is correct in saying that the combination of rock and hip-hop failed to connect with his fanbase. His solo debut, *Exposed*, peaked at #13 on the *Billboard* charts, while *Carved in Stone* stalled at #139. In 1995, Neil rejoined the Crue and never again pursued hip-hop—or anything beyond metal.

VINCE NEIL: The Dust Brothers are a piece of crap. They had no clue about vocal harmonies, and they had no clue what a rock and roll song is. Rock and roll is not their element. They were a pain in the ass. (1997)

JUDGMENT NIGHT

> *Judgment Night, got gun, got badge*
> *Judgment Night, in the echo of a gun blast*
> —Biohazard and Onyx, "Judgment Night"

Judgment Night was the memorable soundtrack album of an unmemorable Hollywood "urban suspense drama" of the same name. There had never been an all-star album that combined rock and rap music, the dominant genres of the era. The 1993 compilation paired ten rappers with eleven rock bands (Cypress Hill contributed two tracks) and encouraged them to create original material. More collaborative than crossover, *Judgment Night* was the shining moment of the early 1990s rap-rock explosion. The music from these different worlds came together cohesively, creating an aural oasis of beats, riffs, and rhymes. The soundtrack went Gold during *Nevermind*-mania and inspired the rise of rap-metal, nu-metal, and alt-rock-rap. *Judgment Night* proved that these distinct genres had more in common than anyone imagined.

DMC: *Judgment Night* was a prophetic record. Right after that exploded, these groups, like Limp Bizkit, were doing what had been done on that *Judgment Night* record. Even when you listen to Fall Out Boy or P.O.D., those guys are rap-rockin'. (2022)

WHEN ROCK MET HIP-HOP

Happy Walters managed Cypress Hill and House of Pain. As a sports agent, Happy negotiated major deals for NBA stars like Jimmy Butler and Dwight Howard, and he inspired the Adam Sandler film *Happy Gilmore*. Everlast of House of Pain and DJ Muggs of Cypress Hill had been discussing with Happy the possibility of their bands collaborating with rock bands. Both groups performed on the second stage of Lollapalooza in 1992, so they experienced the alt-rock explosion firsthand. That hype led to another critical recording, the Seattle grunge label Sub Pop's release of Nirvana producer Butch Vig's metallic meltdown of House of Pain's "Shamrocks & Shenanigans." Walters launched his successful Immortal Records (distributed by Epic) with the *Judgment Night* soundtrack.

The film's director, Stephen Hopkins, hated everything about the soundtrack. However, his crime/action film starring Emilio Estevez, Cuba Gooding Jr., and Dennis Leary was a box office flop. Everlast from House of Pain, who had a small role in the film, was initially excited about the movie's gritty take on the gangster genre. After spending time on the set, he described the film as "a piece of shit" and "the most ridiculous movie ever."

The interracial collaborators had to figure out how to make music together. They aimed to unleash the potential of combining heavy rock with hip-hop. Most hip-hop artists had never worked with a live band before, and most alt-rockers were new to looped beats and syncopated rhymes. So, they had to find a way to merge their musical styles, work ethic, recording habits, and cultural differences. Each artistic team took different approaches to the project. Some worked in person, while others completed their parts separately and let the producers handle the rest.

HAPPY WALTERS: We came up with the idea of pairing edgy hip-hop and rock groups and getting them in the studio together—which doesn't happen nowadays because everything's digital. I used my relationships at the time to call other managers, sell them on the idea, and try to get hip-hop artists who didn't know the rock scene to consider it. Ice Cube at the time was "What!?" But it also was not easy to get Pearl Jam on board. Pearl Jam's manager, Kelly Curtis, was not into it, but Stone Gossard pushed it within the band. Most of the collaborations worked because they had members who were really into it and pushed it. (2018)

Only some ideas worked. Walters and film supervisor Karen Rachtman reached out to Kurt Cobain, Ministry, Metallica, Biggie Smalls, and Ice Cube, but they all rejected the offer for various reasons. Tool and Rage Against the Machine cut a demo for the album ("Can't Kill the Revolution") but never submitted it.

The album initially received negative reviews, with *Spin* editor Mark Blackwell giving it a "red light" rating. However, the recording became widely acknowledged for changing the course of popular music. It demonstrated the potential of combining rock and hip-hop, paving the way for the nu-metal explosion of the late 1990s and early 2000s. Immortal made a similar attempt with the 1997 soundtrack to *Spawn*, featuring collaborations between metal and punk artists, including Metallica, Korn, Incubus, Tom Morello, and Henry Rollins, alongside EDM stars such as Moby, the Crystal Method, Prodigy, Orbital, and Goldie. Yet, the project had a minor cultural and musical impact.

The *Judgment Night* soundtrack's heavy alt-rock presence reflected the era's musical climate. Its pairing of artists from different genres was said to have revolutionized film soundtracks. It was a perfectly executed release, as these collaborations were artificial constructs that came across as authentic.

D.X. FERRIS: The *Judgment Night* soundtrack started a genre. It came to fruition as a way to bring rock and rap groups together. Of course, no top rock critics took it seriously. Every great album has at least three or four great tracks, and *Judgment Night* has so many great songs from start to finish, be it Helmet and House of Pain, Teenage Fanclub and De La Soul, and Pearl Jam and Cypress Hill. It made for something new and unique. (2024)

JUMP AROUND: House of Pain (DJ Lethal, Everlast, Danny Boy) rose to fame for b-boy hip-hop with grunge production, 1994. Photofest.

HELMET AND HOUSE OF PAIN
"Just Another Victim"

Holy diver, I'm a survivor
Feeling like DeNiro in Taxi Driver

"Just Another Victim" was a Helmet song written by Page Hamilton, featuring his typically detuned, repetitive guitars. Producer T-Roy sampled the riff, and House of Pain rapped over it. Helmet and House of Pain alternated verses like heavyweight tag-team champions on the album's leadoff track. When Page stopped by House of Pain's studio in LA to record some vocals, he noted the group kept adult movies playing and centerfolds on the walls while they worked.

PAGE HAMILTON: We were in the studio together twice. I had a great riff I was saving for a Helmet song, but it became apparent that it was time to use it. The song came together quickly. The chorus in the Helmet part of the song increased the song's rhythm. Everlast and I talked about lyrics. I'd been mulling over the idea of people feeling victimized and not assuming responsibility, and he liked that idea. I did the vocals in their studio in California. Once we finished half of the song, we gave it to them, and they slowed the riff down. Then DJ Lethal did his thing. (2018)

DANNY BOY: We all grew up listening to AC/DC, Led Zeppelin, and Rush. Being a normal white kid in the 1970s, that's what you were listening to. There was no hip-hop at the time; when I hear "Black In Black" with the drums, I hear a hip-hop beat; when I listen to Led Zep, I hear a rhyming pattern. That's what we were getting back to with Helmet in *Judgment Night*. (2011)

TEENAGE FANCLUB AND DE LA SOUL
"Fallin'"

I lost touch with reality, now, my personality
Is an unwanted commodity

"Fallin'" was one of the best rock-rap tunes on the CD, melodic and radio-friendly. In 1993, the Scottish shoegazers were finishing their third album called *Thirteen* when Happy Walters approached Geffen about the two groups writing a slow, melodic, chill-out track with New York alt-rap icons De La Soul based on a sample of Tom Petty's "Free

Fallin'." The song was a pillowy, hypnotic, cathartic, feel-good jam that put *Judgment Night* on the mainstream map.

GERARD LOVE: The initially proposed pairing was between P.M. Dawn and us, which interested us. But, about a week or so later, word came through that P.M. Dawn was off, and would we be interested in working with De La Soul. I won't say it was like being asked if we would like to work with the Beatles. But De La Soul was such a unique group and made such a profound impact across the spectrum that the offer was like a dream come true. *Three Feet High and Rising* was a masterpiece. In the circumstances, considering the possibilities, a collaboration with De La Soul was the best possible outcome for us. We felt as if we'd won the lottery. We were delighted. (2018)

POSDNUOS: We could tell they were initially awed by us. But when they saw that we were regular dudes, they calmed down. We're both musicians, so we just started vibing. When we did the song with them, we were in Scotland and had no idea what we would do. We happened to be sitting in a little reception area outside the studio, and Tom Petty's "Free Fallin'" video came on. So that's how we flowed. (2009)

LIVING COLOUR AND RUN-DMC
"Me, Myself & My Microphone"
Like Al Capone, I am a dog, I foam
At the mouth, shout it out when I groan in tone

"Me, Myself & My Microphone" was inspired by a lyric from the Run-DMC song "Sucker MCs." The soundtrack's underrated cut was Living Color, with Run-DMC recording their parts independently and Jam Master Jay putting it all together. Run and DMC brought the energy to the track, while the metallic Living Color delivered their finest work since "Cult of Personality." The skilled guitar work of Vernon Reid perfectly complemented their partnership with Run-DMC.

VERNON REID: We came up with our part of it and then came up with the groove. It's funny because we did our parts separately, although we all lived apart. We had one or two very cool meet-ups. We each did our thing separately; we found our groove and adopted a particular mode, then sent it out. They made it work—a lot of it was Jam Master Jay. When we heard it, we were blown away! (2018)

BIOHAZARD AND ONYX
"Judgment Night"

It takes the death of me to make history
The whole world will remember my misery

"Judgment Night" came together because of the success of "Slam," the 1991 hit collaboration between Biohazard and Onyx. The rock band and rap group became friendly, so their reunion on the "Judgment Night" theme song was a natural development. Biohazard were the kings of the 1990s punch-in-the-mouth era of hardcore/metal, while hip-hop didn't get any more grimy and angry than Onyx. It was an incredible recording—one of the most intense mixes of rock and rap artistry, characterized by manic energy, rapid rhythms, and massive riffs. Hip-hop and metal never sounded so awesome.

BILLY BIO: We got to work with Jam Master Jay through the *Judgment Night* film, which was so cool. We had grown up with bands like Iron Maiden, Agnostic Front, and The Sugar Hill Gang. Everything seemed natural to us. Where we were coming from was very similar. We never sat down and said, "Hey, let's mix what you do with what we do." We were friends and put some tracks together. After doing other tracks with

Cypress Hill and House of Pain, we stepped aside and let Limp Bizkit collect all the money off that style! (2011)

SLAYER AND ICE-T
"Disorder"

Injustice drives you crazy, it drives LA insane
In this generation, hatred is the name

"Disorder" brought together the most intense rapper and metal band in Los Angeles. Ice-T, the rapper, had put out his first Body Count record, so it was no surprise that he sang on this unrelenting recording, too. Besides being fans of the LA Raiders, Slayer and Ice-T had more in common. Their medley of "War," "UK 82," and "Disorder," originally by the Exploited, showcased the bands' ability to incorporate different musical styles and create something groundbreaking. Slayer, known for their tight musical performances, took these three angry punk songs to a new level by playing and singing in unison with Ice-T. This 1993 alliance has left a significant impact on the music scene today.

TOM ARAYA: When we got asked to do the soundtrack for *Judgment Night*, they told us that they would match each band with a rap artist and that we would work with Ice-T. When we found out, we said, "Yeah, we'll do that!" So we started working on an arrangement and developed a punk medley of the Exploited. The LA riots, the civil unrest of the time, and the movie's title were the reasons we chose that route. (2018)

ICE-T: I knew what the fuck was up, and I knew Slayer was the baddest motherfuckers at the time. I had no idea what song we were doing until I showed up in the studio, and they were already laying down the drums. They were mashing us into the Exploited. That was a big moment for me. Later on, we covered Slayer's "Raining Blood." It all validated me. If you're gonna go out, and base your music off of a group, and that group thinks you suck, it doesn't work. (2022)

FAITH NO MORE AND BOO-YAA T.R.I.B.E.
"Another Body Murdered"

It ain't all about servin' time
It's about breakin' down the verdict and servin' mine

"Another Body Murdered" brought together Boo-Yaa T.R.I.B.E., a group of Samoan-American gangster rappers who played rock instruments, and eclectic Bay Area rock-rap legends Faith No More. The collaboration resulted in an ominous yet funky tune on *Judgment Night*. The first take was fantastic, but unfortunately, the engineer forgot to turn on the mixing board, and subsequent takes couldn't capture the same energy. Despite the troubling lyrics, Faith No More worked hard as the backing band, allowing singer Mike Patton to explore his uniquely surreal performance.

BILL GOULD: It was an unreal experience: we all walked in, not having met each other in person, picked up our instruments, and clicked. We immediately got caught up in an outrageous jam that was truly amazing and lasted around thirty minutes. I felt very close to these guys. It was an excellent experience for me. (2018)

GODFATHER: We'd been into heavy metal strong for years; it used to be an element in our show. We did the first Lollapalooza in 1992 when the Chili Peppers were headlining. It was great when we teamed up with Faith No More on the soundtrack to *Judgment Night*. That was different worlds colliding. (2003)

SONIC YOUTH AND CYPRESS HILL
"I Love You Mary Jane"

I love you, Mary Jane
Sugar, come by and get me high

"I Love You Mary Jane" was another track from music industry insider connections; surprisingly, it was a success. It was a collaboration in which Sonic Youth contributed some stray shoegazer clings and clangs, but Muggs took possession of it and chopped it into unrecognizable fragments in a way that he heard in his head. Kim Gordon's breathy chorus left enough space for B-Real to step in with some of his certified nasal stoner flow.

KIM GORDON: They wanted us to come in and do this rock thing. And we didn't think that worked so well. We tried to approach it sideways and feel our way into it. I don't know how they thought it worked, quite frankly. (2018)

DJ MUGGS: With Sonic Youth, it was my first time with a band in the studio. I was like, "Yo, this shit ain't gonna work man. I can't do this shit." I called my manager, and he said, "Please, can you just try?" The band was looking at me; they didn't know what the fuck I was doing; I don't think they'd been in a studio with a hip-hop artist. My style was unorthodox, so they'd play, and I'd let them play one or two takes, and I'd stop and go, "Thanks, that's all I need." Then, I'd sample the sounds and put them all together on a drum machine. (2018)

MUDHONEY AND SIR MIX-A-LOT
"Freak Momma"

I wanna put you in the mud, honey
Spittin' out of them guts like it ain't funny

"**Freak Momma**" was a Seattle thing. The first records by Mudhoney on Sub Pop Records, such as the "Touch Me I'm Sick" single and the *Superfuzz Bigmuff* EP, portended the gritty, high-distortion sound that defined grunge. Sir Mix-A-Lot, the first prominent rapper from Seattle, gained fame with "Baby Got Back." This one-time collaboration marked Mix's first time working with a live band. Afterward, he enjoyed being a rock frontman, reminiscent of bands like Primus or Red Hot Chili Peppers. Similar to his other songs, the lyrics of "Freak Momma" centered on his admiration for butts.

SIR MIX-A-LOT: I love music. I love hip-hop. The only thing I'm not crazy about is straight pop music. It's also always about rock music. Rock music with an edge—metal, grunge, and stuff like Metallica. (2017)

MARK ARM: Other than me playing in punk rock bands, the most punk rock thing Mudhoney ever did was our song "Freak Momma" with Sir Mix-A-Lot on the *Judgment Night* soundtrack. We'd met him once in a hotel after a gig, but he had no memory. But when we got together to record, it was spontaneous and exciting. Mix had an intense rock edge that he brought to the project. That album got made fun of at the time, but it turned out to be one of the most influential records of its time. It redefined the direction of music. (2006)

DINOSAUR JR. AND DEL THA FUNKEE HOMOSAPIEN
"Missing Link"

For the mind, and for the soul
That's how I roll

"**Missing Link**" is one of the compilation's most unique tracks. It paired top-tier lyricist Del Tha Funkee Homosapien, rapping over a Jimi-style shredder groove by J Mascis of Dinosaur Jr., along with layers of loops. Interestingly, the alt-rock bands on *Judgment Night* had minimal interaction with Black culture, and most bands took a backseat to the mixologists and producers. That was also the case with Dinosaur and Del.

J MASCIS: That project was fantastic. I even played live with him. The last thing I heard from Del was a song from Gorillaz. He was also rapping with Blur. It's a nice video, by the way. I checked it at a gas station that sold CDs, and it had "Del" in it. I haven't seen him since our collaboration for *Judgment Night*, but it was fun. We've even been on the same TV show together. (2001)

DEL THA FUNKEE HOMOSAPIEN: Dinosaur Jr. was there, but they didn't do anything. They were playing pool in the other room the whole time. J. Mascis did everything except for the 808 shit that I had running through the production. That sparked my interest in learning more about music and music theory. We were in the studio talking the whole time. He was a cool dude. I enjoyed working with them. (2018)

THERAPY? AND FATAL
"Come and Die"

Come and die with me, feel the helter skelter
Baby, come on, get help; you'd better run and shelter

"Come and Die" was the least-known song on the soundtrack, mainly because the artists weren't well-known. Therapy? was a top alt-rock band from Belfast, Northern Ireland. Their fifth album, with the incredible title *Suicide Pact—You First*, was released in the United States on A&M Records, which wanted to promote the group in America. Happy Walters paired the band with his client, Fatal, a member of DJ Muggs' Soul Assassins production posse. The track was over-the-top, with the raging testosterone of Fatal's screaming vocals that predated all nu-metal to come.

MICHAEL McKEEGAN: It was a cool collaboration to be involved with. We made some cool riffs for these guys, who were no joke and were all part of the Cypress Hill crew. We liked hip-hop, but we'd never done anything with a rapper before, so it was a great experience. Fatal and T-Roy were terrific to work with. There was quite a lot of piss-taking in the studio and general larking about. (2018)

PEARL JAM AND CYPRESS HILL

HITS FROM THE BONG: Cypress Hill (Sen Dog, Muggs, B-Real) made hardcore rap with hippie weed appeal, 1991. Columbia/Photofest ¾ Columbia.

"Real Thing"
It's time, I came to get mine
Runnin' through the hoods with a hand on the nine

"Real Thing," the soundtrack's final tune, earned the most hype, with Cypress Hill unleashing heavy raps over slinky Pearl Jam grooves. Both groups were huge in 1993: Cypress' *Black Sunday* came out earlier that year, and Pearl Jam's *Vs.* had just come out. The problem was that Eddie Vedder had no interest and bailed to go surfing. So, you got Pearl Jam as the backing band for B-Real and Sen Dog. Pearl Jam and Cypress had bonded on the 1992 Lollapalooza tour. So, Pearl Jam invited them to play the "Drop in the Park" show in Seattle. Members of Pearl Jam joined Cypress on stage, and that experience got everyone thinking about working together. The rest is history.

SEN DOG: We put heavy b-boy rhymes on top of some heavy metal-sounding shit. We were talking real street shit like we always do. (2017)

DETROIT

The Big Three and the finest cars, George Clinton's
P-Funk All-Stars
We spend our days on the line and our nights in the bars
—Kid Rock, "Detroit, Michigan"

Detroit hip-hop was never a significant force, but it did give rise to some of the most essential white rappers. Eminem, Kid Rock, and Insane Clown Posse emerged from the same harrowing Motor City hip-hop scene, white kids trying to fit into a tougher Black culture, so they had to be the toughest of them all to earn respect. Sociologically speaking, most interesting was that most of the verbal battles, violent confrontations, and shit-talking were not urban Black-on-Black or Black-on-white degradation, but rather white kids from greater Detroit trying to take each other down in purity tests for hip-hop supremacy and legitimacy. These Detroit artists ranged in various degrees of rock-rap crossover: Eminem was a straight-up white b-boy who had hits with deconstructions of Billy Squier songs. ICP rocked to a heavy, raunchy beat, dressed like Kiss or Alice Cooper; Kid Rock defined rock-rap (and post-Mötley Crüe stripper music) as one of the most successful hip-hop artists ever.

EMINEM
"Shady XV" (2014)

*I know you're really tired of me sampling Billy Squier
But classic rock acid-rap is the genre*

Eminem (Marshall Mathers), rose to fame under the guidance of his mentor, Dr. Dre, of NWA. Under Dre, the young white b-boy from Detroit immediately made a significant impact on the hip-hop scene. Eminem ventured into rock crossover with tracks like 2002's "Sing for the Moment," where he combined a metallic guitar riff throughout the song. But it wasn't until Rick Rubin produced his 2013 multi-platinum album, *Marshall Mathers LP 2*, with "Berzerk," that he achieved a true rap-rock crossover, with a bold reworking of "The Stroke" by heavy metal breakbeat legend Billy Squier. The album contained "Rhyme or Reason," which juxtaposed Eminem's hard-hitting riffs with the classic rock melody of The Zombies' "Time of the Season." This success led to 2014's *Shady XV*, with the opening title track "Shady XV" reworking "My Kinda Lover," another hit from Billy's 1981 album *Don't Say No*. Billy Squier praised Eminem's use of "My Kinda Lover" on Facebook, saying, "Eminem drops 'My Kinda Lover' on the acid-rap community!" Eminem had a history of taking shots at his white rap rivals, with one of the most notable instances being a diss against Insane Clown Posse on his 2000 album, *The Marshall Mathers LP*. In the song, he claimed to have chased the duo out of a club and sprayed them with paintballs.

RICK RUBIN: "Berzerk" is unlike any current hip-hop song. If you listen to what's going on in hip-hop, this song is not what that is. We wanted to do a throwback to some of the early records we made in the 1980s. It reflects the energy of the early days of hip-hop. (2013)

DETROIT

INSANE CLOWN POSSE
"The Juggla" (1992)
Violent J ain't even one to fake it
I've seen some folded-up skank bitches naked

Insane Clown Posse's Violent J (Joseph Bruce) and Shaggy 2 Dope (Joseph Utsler), in macabre clown makeup, are hard-ass lower-middle-class white outlaws making dirty Motor City street sounds since 1991. Equal parts end-of-the-century hip-hop hooliganism like NWA, Cypress Hill, and House of Pain, 1960s anti-hippie radicals like the Stooges and the MC5, brutal hardcore bands like Negative Approach and Necros, and local house music legends like Juan Atkins and Kevin Sanderson, ICP's work is the musical equivalent off a horror flick. The self-professed "most hated band in the world" create slow, rhythmic beats, spewing wildly profane lyrics and laughing over phat tracks supplied by producer Mike E. Clark. On tour, the Farmington, MI natives go through truckloads of the Motown soda pop Faygo, used by ICP as unholy water to ritually anoint "Juggalos"—their community of violent young nerd fans who paint their faces and buy all their records, tickets and merch—into their twisted church of pain. Every year, ICP hosts an annual summer festival, The Gathering Of The Juggalos.

DRAKE: My mom's friend's son was a huge ICP fan, so I used to listen to their shit at his crib. *Halls of Illusion!* I always respected the merch, the graphics, and the branding. It's like they took that shit to another level. Whoever was cooking that shit up is insanely talented. (2024)

To many people, this sick circus sucked. Critics, hipsters, and suits alike dismissed ICP as some lame-ass joke band. Disney's Hollywood label soured on ICP's unprintable song titles and dropped the band on the date of their debut album's 1997 release (Island Records scooped up their contract). However, the joke was on Disney because ICP excelled as a self-contained, independent recording and touring machine, gaining popularity through word of mouth, with no MTV or radio play and no mainstream press. In the 1999 song "Fucking The World," they drop f-bombs ninety-three times. Kid Rock was already three years into his heavy-handed rock shtick when ICP joined the bombastic MC during the early grunge era, and he later started a war with ICP that he could not win.

VIOLENT J: Detroit rock is famous for shit like Alice Cooper and Kiss. But I gotta be honest with you and cut straight to the fucking chase: I never listen to that shit. What Kiss is doing is fresh—blowing fire and bleeding all over. But they don't sing about being a demon or an alien; you listen to the music, which doesn't match. (1997)

KID ROCK
"Bawitdaba" (1999)

All the crackheads, the critics, the cynics
And all my heroes at the methadone clinics

Kid Rock is the original Detroit white-boy rapper coming from a rock-rap angle. The entertainer, born Bob Ritchie from the uber-white village of Romeo, Michigan, established himself in the Detroit hip-hop scene in the late 1980s as part of the Beast Crew. At seventeen, he signed his first record deal with the New York hip-hop label Jive Records—which issued his 1990 debut, *Grits Sandwiches for Breakfast*. He'd spent his teen years playing east side house parties and making connections on Detroit's fledgling hip-hop scene, and *Grits* was his Beasties-inspired record of bawdy, boasting rap.

But fame didn't last long, and the young rapper was back in Detroit plotting his next move in a scene with Insane Clown Posse, Esham, and Eminem. Mike E. Clark produced Kid's first demos; he said the rapper got dropped when Vanilla Ice came on the scene, giving all white rappers a bad name in 1990. That's when Kid decided not to count on any record company to make him a star.

Kid Rock was the only artist to break through during the peak of rock-rap and nu-metal, finding further success by changing things up—in his case, with a rap-infused country rock. After a decade of recording in relative obscurity (independent labels released his second and third albums), Kid developed an undeniable sound. He signed with Atlantic Records in 1997 after executives saw him perform live, resulting in the breakthrough album *Devil Without a Cause* in 1998. This album achieved incredible mainstream rap-metal stardom with hits such as "Bawitaba" and "Cowboy." Then came the 2000s smash *American Badass*. The onstage staple of Kid's classic concerts was Joseph (Joe C) Calleja, a 21-year-old Taylor, MI kid who stood three feet, nine inches, with a dynamic, dirty-mouthed presence. Kid Rock normalized the rap-metal phenomenon and has been a household name ever since.

KID ROCK: I came up in the rap scene and grew up around Johnny Cash and the Beatles and Hank Williams records, so it was natural to mix genres. I got on the turntables and learned how to play guitars, and so I was like, 'Screw it! Let's give 'em some corn-fed Lynyrd Skynyrd/Run-DMC stuff and mix it all together so it has a little bit of melody and it's a bit different. (1998)

TRIP-HOP

When there's trust, there'll be treats
When we funk, we'll hear beats
—Tricky, "Overcome"

Trip-hop played a crucial role in the global fusion of rock and rap. It was a blend of New York hip-hop flavor, punk DIY ethic, and sound-system DJ culture that began to thrive in the southwest of England. Along with turntablism, breakdancing, graffiti, and rap, Jamaican music helped hone the sound. It was a British response to hip-hop, characterized by cinematic ambiance, dub riddims, and a blend of hip-hop and soul. The genre defied classification, making it challenging to market in America. Unlike American rap, UK trip-hop artists created polished, surreal grooves, and it wasn't purely dance music but a mix of instrumental, down-tempo beats, jazz, and hip-hop best enjoyed through headphones. Massive Attack, Portishead, and Tricky were the primary pioneers of this distinctive Bristol-born sound, sharing closely connected backgrounds. The pioneering success of the Bristol scene launched a movement that spread throughout the UK, changing Britain's sonic landscape with a bohemian presence that befitted a musical blueprint for a new multicultural UK.

WHEN ROCK MET HIP-HOP

DADDY G: British journalist Jonathan Taylor bestowed the trip-hop label on our group to describe the trippy music that was simultaneously street and psychedelic. Trip-hop was a tag that, like jazz, was often rejected by the practitioners, but it fit perfectly. (1998)

> *I'm just practicing posing, face is shaded in black*
> *Is dominating as my color, the massive attack*
> —Massive Attack, "Five Man Army"

Massive Attack established themselves with brooding melodies, cultural intellect, and forward-thinking that helped them refine their sound across the boundaries of hip-hop and post-punk. They imbued modern technology without sounding robotic, using minimal studio trickery and actual singing. The band's spacey, mutant hip-hop grooves, filtered through a ganja haze, were designed for psychedelic introspection, not as dance floor fodder. Aside from their signature rap style in Bristolian accents, the vocals of Horace Andy and Shara Nelson became foundational to the sound of Massive Attack.

In 1991, the Bristol collective released their debut album, *Blue Lines*, marking the emergence of trip-hop. The seminal release incorporated elements of hip-hop, dub, reggae, and funk, blending them with soulful pop melodies and vocals; the songs were personal, harmonious, and soulful. While 1994's *Protection* failed to reach the same heights, it was still a significant album. Additionally, 1995's Mad Professor dub remix *No Protection* might be the essential modern dub album.

Massive Attack failed to achieve stardom despite inventing a new dance sound. Early member Tricky rapped on both albums but gained more fame than the founders, Barbados immigrant Grant "Daddy G" Marshall, half-NYC Dominican Andrew "Mushroom" Vowles, and teen delinquent Robert "3-D" Del Naja. Call it smooth, postmodern industrial funk.

TRIP-HOP

DADDY G: When we formed Massive Attack, we were DJs who entered the studio with our favorite records and created tracks. At the time, we tried to rip off the entire style of American hip-hop performers, but we realized, as artists, it's important to be yourself. We realized it made no sense for us to talk about the South Bronx. Slowly but surely, we had to reclaim our identities as British artists who wanted to do something different with our music. (1998)

> *The bitter taste of innocence, descent, or race*
> *scattered seeds, buried lives*
> *Mysteries of our disguise revolve, circumstances will decide*
> —Portishead, "Sour Times"

Portishead are rare innovators. The Bristol ensemble absorbed goth, jazz, and dub elements with a vague hip-hop feel from another dimension—fuzzy, sullen, and tinged with industrial nuance. The three members came together in 1991 from three different backgrounds representing three distinct styles at three different stages of life. Geoff Barrow was a 19-year-old hip-hop obsessive; Adrian Utley was a 30-something jazz/R&B session guitarist; Beth Gibbons was a mid-20s veteran singer-songwriter of the pub circuit. Barrow named the group after his hometown.

UK experts debated whether 1994's daring debut, *Dummy*, recorded where Massive Attack cut *Blue Lines*, was the record that invented trip-hop. The beloved hit album blended brooding, off-kilter, soulful sounds crafted from droning synthesizers, hip-hop beats, vibrating loops, bluesy guitar, and occasional abstract samples. Beth Gibbons' icily detached delivery matched the spacey sound, making them critical darlings and selling over two million records.

1997's self-titled second album continued the maudlin trip-hop with even more cavernous grooves. The recording was a scratchy byproduct of the sampling process, creating intriguing, otherworldly music. (*Cypress Hill IV* starts with a track evocative of the second Portishead record). Portishead returned on 2008's *Third*, which deviated musically from previous work, but they continued to invent new frequencies out of thin air, further solidifying their cult-like status.

GEOFF BARROW: We are people who feel they need to do something, rather than just the apathy of doing nothing—that alone is magical. Anger is crucial for me, and music has always been an outlet for that. We want to get some fucking distortion into your brain. It gives us a rush of achievement and self-worth. That's why we didn't do anything for a long time; we didn't feel like we had the ability to do it. And there's no point saying anything if you haven't got anything to say. (2011)

> *Insight, foresight, more sight*
> *The clock on the wall is a quarter past midnight*
> —DJ Shadow, "Midnight In A Perfect World"

DJ Shadow (Josh Davis) is a Bay Area producer who became famous on the London-based Mo' Wax label, started by UNKLE member James Lavelle, who claimed to have coined the term "trip-hop." Shadow, a confessed vinyl junkie, is a modern composer who creates through decomposition; he took vinyl and, with his turntables and Akai MPC60 sampler at a tiny in-home studio, combined bits of voices and phrases with obscure fragments of notes, riffs, strings, tones, and beats to create new music.

"What Does Your Soul Look Like," 1995's experimental, thirty-minute instrumental hip-hop single, topped the UK dance charts despite being unknown back home. The pioneering crate-digger, sampler, mixmaster, and producer Josh Davis' revolutionary white suburban hip-hop groove, *In/Flux*, became a surprise club hit of 1996. He didn't employ any musicians or play any music himself. But with samplers and sequencers, he created a series of startling sonic montages that resulted in a hip-hop album mostly devoid of lyrics, emphasizing old-school beats and audio snippets.

The near-religious zeal of 1996's *Entroducing*, his Gold-selling opus, opened with a flurry of scratching that took a year and a half to create. The ultimate sample record borrowed from almost every known musical genre. *Endtroducing* felt like an ethereal sound painting—a seventy-minute archaeological dig of head-trip beats, absurdist sampling, and block-party rocking transformed turntablism. The result was a rump-shaking journey to the center of your mind.

1998's *Preemptive Strike* integrated 1993–97 tuneage that read like one cohesive statement. Shadow's economy of words worked like titles on abstract paintings, leading the listener to unique perspectives. Radiohead said that *Endtroducing* had a huge influence on their smash hit, *OK Computer*.

DJ SHADOW: Hip-hop, for me, was never about fashion or hanging out with a gang. When I got a piece of vinyl, it was all about studying the label, where it came from, who produced it, where it got recorded, and who they thanked. It has to be hard to buy records as a pilgrimage. (1997)

Hell is around the corner where I shelter
Isms and schisms, we're living helter-skelter

Tricky (Adrian Thawes) became the primary exponent of the Bristol sound. He pushed pop culture's boundaries to create something striking, ambitious, meticulously thought-out, and labor-intensive. Tricky became famous as part of Massive Attack, penning and performing three songs on their 1991 smash *Blue Lines*. However, he strongly disagreed with his bandmates' stoner work ethic and jumped ship after contributing to 1994's *Protection*. He moved to London and signed with Island Records because he'd have more autonomy than the artistic control for which most artists clamor.

When Tricky released his 1995 masterpiece *Maxinquaye* (Island), named after his mother, it was a hallucinatory tapestry of orchestral soul, dub echo, industrial clang, sage lovers rock, and pointed punky vocals by his then-paramour Martina Topley-Bird that was so incredible that some critics said he defined a new subgenre: trip-hop. Tricky hated the tag and the media's self-proclaimed understanding of his work.

He responded with the *Nearly God* compilation, featuring guest appearances by some of his favorite singers, including Alison Moyet (Yaz), Terry Hall (The Specials), Björk, and Neneh Cherry. Then came *Pre-Millennium Tension*, striking an unsettling nerve. Tricky sets a pace antithetical to the world's lightning-speed information overload, with compulsive creativity, unique methodology, and an aura of sexual tension. Its angst-ridden, time-lapsed cyber-ghetto rhymes and diffusive presence presented something intuitive, abstract, and beyond genre definitions. During this time, Tricky teamed up with Debbie Harry to deconstruct "Heart of Glass," taking the pop song in a more rap-oriented direction. In the late 2000s, he launched a label called Brown Punk with legendary Island Records founder Chris Blackwell.

TRICKY: Beck had been after me for years. He wanted some friendly breakouts with a baseline, some so-called trip-hop remix. But by then, my music had gone in a different direction, and I gave him ten minutes of noise and irritation. And he turned it down. I like fucking around and pissing people off. I'm sometimes self-destructive. (1997)

ALTERNATIVE RAP

Step off stage, you scream for more
Native Tongues got rhymes galore
—De La Soul, "Buddy"

Native Tongues Posse was a short-lived but distinguished rap scene that crossed over to white kids on the rock side with its laidback anti-hardcore hip-hop. It was more hip-hop hippie-ness than rock, but it was a significant era that saw rock and rap cross into the mainstream. Rap diversified in new directions, with the *Judgment Night* soundtrack alt-rock dalliances making waves, opening musical doors, and confronting the grunge generation. Native Tongues Posse, an Afrocentric collective of like-minded artists focused on social commentary and artistic expression, was comprised of De La Soul, A Tribe Called Quest, Jungle Brothers, and Queen Latifah—one of the few successful women in the world of hip-hop, with DJ Mark The 45 King and later joined by Latifah's UK friend Monie Love on "Ladies First." Native Tongues dates back to Murry Bergtraum High School For Business Careers in Lower Manhattan with Afrika Baby Bam of the Jungle Brothers and Q-Tip of A Tribe Called Quest. P.M. Dawn, from New

Jersey, the first openly queer rap crew, played a role in this new consciousness. This new vibe opened doors for the Fugees, Mos Def, and the Roots.

ALI SHAHEED MUHAMMAD: The core of the Native Tongues Posse was Jungle Brothers, De La Soul, and A Tribe Called Quest. We're doing our own thing, De La's doin' their own thing, as are the Jungle Brothers. Outside of the business level, the friendship is still there. But as far as doing records and tours together, we quickly moved on to making our music. (1994)

Answering any other service, prerogative praised
positively, I'm acquitted
Enemies publicly shame my utility, after the battle, they
admit that I'm with it
—De La Soul, "Plug Tunin'"

De La Soul was a young Long Island rap trio, the core of the Native Tongues posse built on quirky samples from rock, funk, folk, country, and soul and using wordplay that ranged from psychedelic musings to nonsensical gibberish. The group got hailed as "the future of hip-hop." The 1989 album *Three Feet High and Rising*, with "Plug Tunin'," on which they introduced the concept of "The D.A.I.S.Y Age" (for "da inner sound y'all"), and the 1991 album *De La Soul is Dead*, with its album cover of a broken daisy flower pot, symbolizing the death of "The D.A.I.S.Y. Age," for Tommy Boy Records welcomed stoners, sinners, jocks, whites, Blacks, and women. It provided a much-needed invitation to check out their beats-to-the-rhyme riddims. This scene of NYC's outer boroughs and Long Island crews connected with other local groups, from Boogie Down Productions in the Bronx to P.M. Dawn from New Jersey.

TRUGOY (De La Soul): We've always dealt with the alternative rap tag. It's because of the level of what we're putting into our music that it appeals to Blacks, whites, Africans, and Asians. When we came out, we were different from what had happened in rap at the time. It's not even that we sampled punk, new wave, and 1970s rock. The media saw us as an alternative to what the haters were used to hearing. (1996)

> *Rock and roll to the beat of the funk fuzz*
> *Wipe your feet really good on the rhythm rug*
> —A Tribe Called Quest, "Can I Kick It?"

A Tribe Called Quest consisted of Q-Tip, Phife, and Ali Shaheed Muhammad in a never-ending quest for musical liberation. Verbose in their lyrics, minimalist in their beats, diligent in their work ethic, and committed to personal expression, their De La Soul-esque hippie-rap style was more than talk. "I Left My Wallet In El Segundo," the second single off their 1990 debut *People's Instinctive Travels And The Paths Of Rhythm* (Jive/RCA), became an instant MTV hit; the third single, "Can I Kick It?" was their most significant crossover, with Q-Tip rapping over Lou Reed's "Sweet Jane." 1992's *Low End Theory* was an early step into "jazz rap"—and like jazz musicians, Quest was recalcitrant, solemn, and suspicious of anyone not privy to their creative process. They were the first vegetarian rappers and the first rap crew to represent New York on the 1994 Lollapalooza Tour, where they trekked cross-country for nine weeks. Quest defined friendly hip-hop from their formation until their disbandment in 1998, when Q-Tip went solo.

WHEN ROCK MET HIP-HOP

Q-TIP: We're not trying to close any avenues. We may not sing, but we're the type of group that isn't afraid to try shit. A Tribe Called Quest is not confined to only one sect of hip-hop. We try to do everything as long as it is relevant to ourselves. We don't shy away from anything musically; we even rap over punk and rock records. (1994)

> *Many people tell me this style is terrific*
> *It is kinda different, but let's get specific*
> —Boogie Down Productions, "South Bronx"

KRS-One (Kris Parker), a former child delinquent-turned-rapper, met social worker DJ Scott La Rock (Scott Sterling) at a Bronx homeless shelter and decided to form a rap group called Boogie Down Productions. 1987's *Criminal Minded*, built on Run-DMC's hardcore, minimalist approach and focused on the realities of ghetto life, became an instant classic among hip-hop fans. As Boogie Down Productions began work on their second album, DJ Scott La Rock got gunned down following a petty altercation. Stunned by his partner's demise, KRS carried on, promoting an educated and socially conscious approach to hardcore rap music. In 1989, to quell the surge of Black-on-Black crime in New York (and as a tribute to Scott La Rock), KRS-One organized the Stop the Violence movement with several top New York rappers. In 1997, he reconstructed a mix of "Rapture" and "Rapper's Delight" as "Step Into A World (Rapture's Delight)" and collaborated with Michael Stipe on "Civilization vs. Technology." NYHC stars Sick of It All once teamed with KRS-One on one of the first rock-rap collaborations, with KRS' bold intro to the Queens, NY punkers on "Clobberin' Time."

KRS-ONE: Rock and roll was never part of our vocabulary when I first came on the scene with Scott LaRock and early BDP. In the South Bronx, where we come from, there's very little interest in that crazy white music. I got turned on to the New York Hardcore punk scene, but I didn't really get it at first; it was a little crazy to me. I loved what Rick Rubin did with heavy metal, but we never worked together. The alternative rock thing was different, but working with Michael Stipe was great. I think rock and rap together make for a higher degree of energy. (2019)

ALT-ROCK RAP

Take control, lose control, find your soul
Lose your soul, take it slow
—Luscious Jackson, "Let Yourself Get Down"

An attempt was made to blend alt-rock and rap, making for a powerful integration. The groovy, tripped out style incorporated smooth electronic loops and beats similar to the UK trip-hop movement. Beck's album *Odelay* was produced by the Dust Brothers, behind the seminal Beastie Boys album *Paul's Boutique*. Other artists, such as Luscious Jackson, Soul Coughing, and Cake, further expanded a postmodern multicultural movement of white alternative rock artists exploring Black hip-hop. Others dabbled, like Teenage Fanclub, Sonic Youth, and Dinosaur Jr.

BECK: Thinking of the "alternative" genre that I'm in, we're always looking to hip-hop culture and rap music to push things sonically. At least since I've been making music, that's always the one music constantly moving forward. So, I was trying to bring a hip-hop feel into my relatively homogeneous genre. (2017)

WHEN ROCK MET HIP-HOP

LOSER: Beck and the Dust Brothers created the alt-rock-rap fusion of *Odelay*, 1997. Pictorial Press Ltd / Alamy Stock Photo.

> *Pulling out jives and jamboree handouts*
> *Two turntables and a microphone*
> —Beck, "Where It's At"

Beck was a big fan of the Beastie Boys' *Paul's Boutique*. After his 1993 slacker hit "Loser," he was concerned about becoming a one-hit wonder. To avoid this fate, the real-life Beck Hanson recruited the producers of the Beasties' 1989 opus, Mike Simpson and John King of the Dust Brothers. The Dust Brothers had recently worked on the hit pop fluff of "MMM Bop" by Hanson (no relation) and tore it up with the illest b-boy breakdown of Motley Crue's singer Vince Neil's solo album, *Carved in Stone*. Their collaboration with Beck led to 1996's Grammy Award-winning *Odelay*, which sold over two million copies worldwide.

BECK: I thought *Odelay* might be the last time I got a chance to make a record. I was acutely aware that I was thought of as a one-hit wonder. (2007)

JOHN KING: Even though we had some cool stuff come out, we were a clever and insightful choice for him to make. (2016)

Beck and the Dust Brothers collaborated on *Odelay* at King and Simpson's Silver Lake home, creating a mix that blended Beck's vision with influences from Woody Guthrie to Africa Bambaataa. The album showcased diverse styles, including hip-hop, country, art/noise, lo-fi pop, and scratch-and-burn turntablism. Unlike Beck's debut album, *Mellow Gold*, which was recorded in a four-track home studio, *Odelay* took a year of editing and layering in a professional recording studio, weaving together Beck's music and samples. The incorporation of coffeehouse poetry and C&W redefined Beck as a post-modern hillbilly. The first single, "Where It's At," sampled the Mantronix b-boy classic "Needle to the Groove."

JOHN KING: *Odelay*, to me, is hip-hop. We applied the techniques that we learned to emulate Boogie Down Productions. The way we collaged it together was similar to how we would make rap music. Rap music had been sampling for years, but never in that dense, genre-bending way. (2016)

MIKE SIMPSON: It was the first time that we got to work with someone who could play every instrument, and so often we'd be playing records for Beck, and then he would grab an instrument, like a sitar or a French horn, and start playing that riff or riffing off that riff, and making something cool out of it. The album is a time capsule of all these different ideas and sounds. It's symbolic of a time when it felt like anything could go. (2016)

BECK: I'm a traditionalist in a lot of ways. A lot of what my generation is into, what it represents, I'm totally against. I find that I connect far more with older musicians. I think my generation has been fed such a disposable culture. (1997)

MIKE SIMPSON: Beck had just come off "Loser," and everyone wrote him off as a one-hit wonder. I think Geffen Records thought that and didn't expect him to have much of a future with them. So when we met Beck, it was like kids messing around in a playground, playing with popsicle sticks or whatever to create something cool with no agenda. We got to play and have fun, which is the key. That became a lightbulb moment for me. I learned that the records I had the most fun making were also the most successful. There's a direct correlation between your state of mind and your emotions while making a record and a final output. (2015)

In 1997, the Dust Brothers bought "The Boat" in Silverlake, a 1941-built radio studio converted into a state-of-the-art recording studio. They produced notable works for Korn, the Eels, Nitzer Ebb, and White Zombie at their studio. This experience led to opportunities like working on the *Fight Club* soundtrack and collaborating with the Rolling Stones and Carlos Santana.

JOHN KING: All kinds of people tried to get with Beck. When we finished *Odelay*, the rumor I heard was that Rick Rubin picked up Beck in his Rolls Royce, and they drove around listening to the record. Rick told him he shouldn't release it. He told him that they should start working together. (2016)

After *Odelay*, Beck overcame his one-hit-wonder status. In 2005, he reunited with the Dust Brothers on *Guero*.

BECK: Most people think that all of *Odelay* was sampled. It was not. Despite what you might have read, most of that is me playing. (1999)

> *Lifting me up like a garage door*
> *I need to feel it when the drug starts coming on*
> —Soul Coughing, "$300"

Soul Coughing took its name from a slang term for vomiting, taken from a poem by lead singer Mike Doughty about Neil Young throwing up in the back of his tour bus. Soul Coughing was an eclectic 1990s alt-rock outfit from Downtown New York that played a jaded "slacker jazz"—a mix of bebop, beatnik folk, keyboard samples, hip-hop beats, and spoken word. They were known for cutting through boundaries to create original music.

MIKE DOUGHTY: We were a product of Downtown New York at the time, the artists, poets, filmmakers, punks, squatters, the cafés, and the weirdos who worked there. There was a spirit of experimentation and unpredictability we fed off. There was a feeling that Manhattan was, as Spalding Gray said, "an island off the coast of America." (2020)

Doughty, a slam poet who worked at the Knitting Factory on Houston Street, formed Soul Coughing in 1993, blending his anti-folk background with his love of New York City hip-hop. Bassist Sebastian Steinberg, percussionist Yuval Gabay, and keyboardist/sampler Mark De Gil Antoni joined Doughty at avant-rock music nights at the Knit. The band signed with Bob Biggs at Slash Records and released their 1994 debut album, *Ruby Vroom* (named after the daughter of producer

Mitchell Froom)—the album incorporated various musical styles, such as alt-rock, trance, and hip-hop.

Their hip-hop-flavored song, "Super Bon Bon," from the album *Irresistible Bliss*, became a hit on alternative and modern rock radio, and the music video received airplay on MTV. In 1998, their album *El Oso* featured a distinct sound, incorporating techno-style jungle beats and shifting away from their previous hip-hop feel.

MIKE DOUGHTY: I listen to Soul Coughing, and it's still good. We all agreed that we had to have a dark, deep low-end and that we had to be as phat as hip-hop records. But I hear a lot of it and think, "Man, I wish those sounded like real hip-hop"—as opposed to this weird neither-nor kind of monster. (2013)

The band disbanded in 2000 due to conflicts that involved issues with publishing money, songwriting credit, Doughty's heroin use, and the other members' dislike of him. However, they reunited after twenty-five years of separation to the delight of their fans.

SEBASTIAN STEINBERG: Hip-hop showed Mike Doughty how to do that sort of slam poetry thing musically. The great thing about him is he never tried to be a little Black-white kid. He found his Caucasian self. (1999)

Original bone lovers straight from Manhattan
Keep your butt movin', keep your hands clappin'
—Luscious Jackson, "Keep on Rockin' It"

Luscious Jackson (named for a mispronunciation of former Philadelphia 76ers star Lucious Jackson) was an all-female, all-white, funked-up jazzy group with beats, loops, and hip-hop style. They came out of the Beasties' sphere of the NYHC and Downtown club scenes. Lead vocalist Jill Cunniff played in the pre-Beastie Boys punk group Young Aborigines and was friends with keyboardist Vivian Trimble. Kate Schellenbach drummed in the original Beastie Boys. They were friendly with guitarist Gabrielle "Gabby" Glaser (niece of graphic design icon Milton Glaser).

The "Jackson Four" from New York City grew up during the tail end of the early-1980s Danceteria-era nightclub scene and got deep into early hip-hop and post-punk dance funk, such as ESG, Y Pants, and Pulsallama. They were responsible for starting a new "alternative" rock-rap trend characterized by samples, hip-hop grooves, and rock instrumentation. In late 1991, they gave their demo to their Beastie Boys friend, Mike D. Their EP, *In Search Of Manny*, was the first release on the Beasties' Grand Royal label. After that, some people started calling them the Beastie Girls.

GABBY GLASER: Once you listen to one of our records, you see that whereas we might have similar influences as the Beastie Boys, we don't necessarily do the same music. I have no goals to be some gigantic success. I'm happy with where we are. (1997)

The band's first album, *Natural Ingredients*, released in 1994, had a distinct New York attitude, with sampled street sounds and car horns. It gained a devoted alt-rock following due to its bass-driven funk, heavy guitars, and Latin jazz piano, reminiscent of the Beasties' *Check Your Head*. Luscious made grooves that explored the streets from a female perspective but lacked a magnetic front person for pop appeal. Their song "Here" gained popularity in the film *Clueless*.

JILL CUNNIFF: Having a hit is scary in that *People* Magazine, Celine Dion way. That's not what we've aspired to be. We're kind of snobs. (1999)

Their follow-up album in 1996, *Fever In Fever Out*, produced by Daniel Lanois (known for his work with U2 and Peter Gabriel), showcased a softer, gentler girl group with a toned-down approach to man-bashing and a sultry, soulful, stylish, and sexy sound. The album featured their first hit, "Naked Eye," which led to tours with Lollapalooza and Lilith Fair, as well as a well-received performance on *Saturday Night Live*. In 1998, they appeared in a Christmas ad for the Gap, singing "Let It Snow! Let It Snow! Let It Snow!" However, the band faced challenges when Trimble "semi-retired" from full-time band status, and Luscious Jackson attempted to continue as a trio but faced difficulties.

GABBY GLASER: Sometimes people misunderstand and think the Beasties have more to do with our music than they do. They actually have nothing to do with our music. A writer at the *Village Voice* alluded to the fact that we were Mike Diamond's "little project," and that we were his pawns. He didn't say anything terrible, like Mike hit us in the face. It says we're just dummies. (1994)

> *I want a girl with a mind like a diamond*
> *I want a girl who knows what's best*
> *I want a girl with shoes that cut and eyes*
> *that burn like cigarettes*
> —Cake, "Short Skirt/Long Jacket"

Cake, the Sacramento alternative rock band, achieved a Top 10 *Billboard* chart hit in 2001 with "Short Skirt/Long Jacket." The song has a chord sequence similar to "Sweet Jane" by Lou Reed's Velvet Underground, sung in Cake crooner John McCrea's droll vocal style, reminiscent of Reed's spoken-word raps. Unlike Velvet Underground's dark themes, Cake's composition is funky in the tradition of

Beck, with lovelorn lyrics, Tijuana Brass-style trumpet squeals, chintzy keyboards, and sharp hip-hop breakbeats. Before his death, Lou Reed expressed sadness over Cake's "borrowing." The band, in turn, blamed Reed for working with "greedy corporate national advertisers like AmEx," implying that Reed didn't need the publishing money. There were three versions of the song's MTV music video, filmed in New York City, Los Angeles, and Mexico City. Nonetheless, "Short Skirt/Long Jacket," the lead single off 2001's acclaimed *Comfort Eagle*, sounded great on the car radio with the windows down. In Cake's music, one can feel that their rock-rap serves as fodder for McCrea's sarcastic examination of modern society.

JOHN McCREA: I feel like the way our songs are built, if you could look at them geometrically, you'd see they don't fit into an arena space the way AC/DC does with those slabs of guitar. Their gestures are more grandiose and extend over the heads of a huge audience. Our music is more dinky-sounding and economical. We play more 1/16 notes, but those don't work in large venues. (2001)

NU-METAL

We're to blame for shit I think is lame
It's time to stop the game
—Korn, "Y'All Want a Single"

In the late 1990s, mixing heavy metal with hip-hop was nothing new. Run-DMC and Aerosmith had successfully done it with "Walk This Way" over a decade prior, and Public Enemy and Anthrax had rocked "Bring the Noise" over the previous half-decade. Kid Rock was defining rap-metal every day. The next generation of "nu-metal" saw rap metal evolve from combining Pantera-style groove riffs and basic rap lingo to refining their rap skills and drawing upon extreme death metal and technical metal to shape their riffs.

MIKE SHINODA: In the late 1990s, rap and rock started to cross over into each other. Anthrax and Public Enemy, in particular, did a version of "Bring the Noise." I went to that concert, a crucial moment in my life. It was the first concert I'd ever been to, and it was the mixing of all kinds of music. I realized rap and rock were starting to merge, and it was groups like Rage Against the Machine and Red Hot Chili Peppers. The *Judgment Night* soundtrack, mixing rock and rap, was dope. Different artists were starting to experiment in one way or another. We attempted to study those styles and incorporate them into our work. (2023)

Nu-metal is a subgenre that merges extreme metal with hip-hop, hardcore punk, grunge rock, synth-pop, and funk, characterized by incessant syncopation, screaming vocals (often raging and misogynistic), and intense turntablism, featuring bragging and a rebellious attitude. The sonic stylings of the experimental Faith No More and rap-metal pioneers Anthrax largely inspired the sound. In serious music circles, nu-metal was derided and ridiculed: a cultural nadir of directionless rage and angst devoid of taste or meaning and particularly offensive to women. It was probably the most unfairly maligned genre in musical history; in 2013, *NME* named it "the worst genre of music ever." It was known to insiders as "rip-hop." But nu-metal was the nexus where metal and rap converged. The songs aren't particularly clever or well-structured, but live, it's what moshers' dreams are made of.

D.X. FERRIS: Nu-metal is the hip-hop influence on metal, delivered with that punk rock minimalism. It showed generations of fans that you didn't have to be technically proficient like Iron Maiden, Megadeth, or Metallica. It was a blend of hip-hop beats and metal riffs but without the Van Halen solos. Instead of working out complex sound structures, the scratching and sampling were about getting straight to the song's best part and playing that repetitively. Korn and Limp Bizkit were not trying to be Iron Maiden. Nobody was trying to sing perfectly anymore. Fred Durst had a hip-hop posture with a fierce delivery and rap lingo that boasted. It was about talking like homeboys. (2024)

JONATHAN DAVIS: The nu-metal scene was full of misogynistic, opportunistic dickhead jocks. They were the sort of people who'd be bullying me at school if they weren't supporting my band at shows. I'm about the art. We got lumped in with that stuff because of the way we dressed. We were kinda hip-hop, but there was nothing hip-hop about Korn other than the basslines. I didn't rap! In the beginning, nobody knew what we were. But I hate thinking that some people hear the name Korn and think we're some douchebag, misogynistic, fucking macho dickhead band. I think the fact that we're still here says a lot. (2019)

Woodstock '99—a corporate greed-fueled shitshow—was a lousy time for nu-metal. Limp Bizkit, Kid Rock, and others revved up a restless, intoxicated, predominantly white male crowd of 250,000 that eventually rioted, burned the concert site, and looted vendors. Police reported eight sexual assaults. Media condemnation, "woke" cultural shifts, and an uninspired run of contrived nu-metal albums delegitimized and stigmatized the entirety of the rap-rock scene. But it's laughable to suggest that some painfully average white dudes from Jacksonville singing about "doing it all for the nookie" caused the misogyny at a rock festival or in our broader culture. Nu-metal and rap-metal imploded due to some questionable results. But there were some solid exceptions.

DAVE MUSTAINE: Nowadays, nobody remembers nu-metal and all that shit that came out. It was painful. There were no guitar solos; everyone was playing with their pants down to the ankles, and most people in the music business know that these types of fashions are dead when something like this happens. They can't reinvent themselves, and if they reinvent themselves and it doesn't work, they don't have a music catalog to rely on to get ahead. It was a bleak period. But we got through it and regained our previous position at the top. (2024)

Most rock fans know "The Big Four" of 1980s thrash metal—Metallica, Megadeth, Slayer, and Anthrax. "The Big Four" of nu-metal are Limp Bizkit, Korn, System of a Down, and Linkin Park.

WHEN ROCK MET HIP-HOP

I did it all for the nookie
So you can take that cookie
—Limp Bizkit, "Nookie"

Limp Bizkit from Jacksonville became the world's most famous "rip-hop" act. They gained mainstream attention in 1997 with a shouty, trashy cover of George Michael's hit "Faith," which Michael abhorred. Notoriety came after they incited the Woodstock '99 crowds to "smash stuff" before fires began to break out, and for performing onstage with a colossal stage prop toilet. When asked by the festival's promoters to help calm the crowd down as they went batshit, Durst incited, "This is 1999, motherfuckers. Take your Birkenstocks and stick 'em up your ass." But to be fair, the organizers mismanaged the event, so blaming the night's negative turn on Durst's antics is incorrect.

FRED DURST: People call Limp Bizkit "jock rock." But I despise jocks because those were the guys beating my ass all the time. I was bullied and tortured my whole life. I was this peon kid in my city and at school. So, ultimately, the vehicle I put behind Limp Bizkit was, "I'll use this microphone to fight back against these guys!" But the irony was that the bullies that tortured me were now in the audience dressed like me. So, this massive art project became the most ironic thing. And here I am 25 years later going, "This is unbelievable!" (2023)

Fred Durst and Wu-Tang Clan rapper Method Man proved an unlikely but powerful hip-hop duo; Durst could more than trade verses with the big boys on the 1999 single "N 2 Gether Now." Gang Starr legend DJ Premier initially turned down Fred's offer to produce the track but changed his mind after the two met and Premier discovered that Durst owned a few of his old mixtapes.

DJ LETHAL: My DJing was sparked by Tom Morello; that's why my Limp Bizkit music was more guitar-oriented. My father was a guitar player. That's why I try to be innovative and run my stuff through a Marshall cabinet on stage, and using wah-wah and things like that. Like how Tom Morello wants to DJ and scratch, I was trying to be different and be like a second guitarist in the band. (2014)

Limp Bizkit became a formidable musical force once DJ Lethal of House of Pain joined them. The opening track on the 2000 compilation *Take a Bite Outta Rhyme: A Rock Tribute to Rap* contained their raw reworking of "Bring the Noise," credited as "Staind Featuring Fred Durst & DJ Lethal." Original guitarist Wes Borland fueled the band's energy to unforeseen levels before he quit the band in 2003 (and recently returned).

WES BORLAND: After all our success, I was trying to evaluate my life. I read an article where Maynard from Tool just completely shitcanned us in this article, and he compared us to McDonald's. He said something to the effect of, "Tool is like fine dining, Bizkit is like McDonald's." I was reading all these harsh things about us, and these major events were happening around the same time. We were like, "We're affecting people's lives negatively." So I went, "I'm fucking done, I don't want to do this. This has grown into something that is too much." (2021)

Despite all the middle-finger salutes and anti-pop posturing, it's critical to remember that Limp Bizkit was huge. *Significant Other*, with "Nookie" (starring Method Man), sold over three million copies by the late 1990s, knocking the Backstreet Boys off the charts. *Chocolate Starfish* set a record for the highest first-week rock album sales, with 400,000 sold on the release date. Limp Bizkit's "Rollin'" first came out in a rap version with Swizz Beatz, Method Man, Redman, and DMX.

The song showcased Fred Durst's uncelebrated strength as an executive producer. By the end, frontman Fred Durst became an executive at Interscope Records and a Hollywood film director.

DR. DRE: Limp Bizkit is my favorite. That guy knows how to market. I wanna go on tour with those guys: Korn, Limp Bizkit, and NWA playing stadiums. That's the cool thing about hip-hop music. Anyone can get involved in it. It gives me more motivation. We wanted to do something like that years ago. We called it ghetto metal. We all thought it would be interesting. (1999)

> *There's a place inside my mind, a place I like to hide*
> *You don't know the chances, what if I should die?*
> —Korn, "Blind"

Korn is notable for pioneering nu-metal and bringing it into the mainstream. Jonathan Davis and the band rose to fame at Woodstock '99, taking the stage to "Blind." When Korn arose in the mid-1990s, they were the "freaks of the freaks," unlike any other at the time, dressed in Adidas tracksuits with tattooed arm sleeves, twisted dreadlocks, and gold chains around their necks. Their dark, goth-flavored art involved lyrics working through personal travails: death, drug addiction, sexual abuse, and lapsed Christianity. The Bakersfield five-piece recorded music in Buck Owens' old studio, where they developed a malleable form of twenty-first-century riff-metal with hip-hop and synth-pop. Korn's self-titled 1994 debut album, produced by Ross Robinson, contributed to a cultural shift for a generation. It came out on Happy Walters' Immortal Records, who released the *Judgment Night* soundtrack. That led to a rap-metal triple-bill tour with House of Pain and Biohazard, as well as a 1995 road stint with NYHC stars Sick of It All.

JONATHAN DAVIS: I always felt weird in metal culture. I was always fighting the title of what a metal band should be. We were the ultimate black sheep. We destroyed what people thought the metal scene should be. Hip-hop inspired us. We'd subtly sprinkle it in. We weren't a rap-rock band like Limp Bizkit, but we were fans of it. It was incredible to work with all these hip-hop legends. They were all different. But the one that hit me the hardest was Ice Cube. (2016)

Korn touches upon all forms of music, from rock to hip-hop. But it's hard to call Korn a rap-metal band. They have engaged in powerful cross-cultural collaborations with rap stars such as Q-Tip, Xzibit, and Tha Dogg Pound. Most notable are 1998's "Children of the Korn" with Ice Cube and Nas's 2003 rapped verse on Korn's "Play Me" off their Top 10 album, *Take A Look In The Mirror*.

JONATHAN DAVIS: I called Nas and asked if he wanted to be on the album. He said he was a Korn fan and'd love to do it. It's very heavy—it has nothing to do with hip-hop. And he's such a great lyricist who has something to say. He's intense, and it comes across well. (2023)

Original drummer David Silveria left the band in 2006 to pursue a modeling career, temporarily replaced by Mike Bordin of Faith No More, whom Korn opened for at arenas throughout the 1990s. The most memorable thing about Korn on the road was their distressing VIP after-show parties with tanks of nitrous oxide.

JAMES "MUNKY" SHAFFER: We don't have to keep up with what's current. We can create something that holds its own lane in a timeless way. We're not looking for anything out of it except for enjoying the creative process. (2023)

> *In my self-righteous suicide*
> *I cry when angels deserve to die*
> —System of a Down, "Chop Suey!"

System of a Down is a four-piece band from Glendale, CA, consisting of singer Serj Tankian, guitarist Daron Malakian, bassist Shavo Odadjian, and drummer John Dolmayan. Their music defies categorization, with a nu-metal style that sets them apart from artists like Korn, Limp Bizkit, and Kid Rock. Tankian, who comes from a family of Armenian genocide survivors, initially worked in his uncle's jewelry business in downtown Los Angeles after college. However, he realized law school wasn't his calling and left to pursue music.

The band's big break came when legendary producer Rick Rubin heard their four-song demo and signed them to his American Recordings label in late 1997. *System of a Down*, the debut album produced by Rubin, was released in 1998. The band toured with Slayer and had a slot on Ozzfest, gaining attention for their distinctive mix of progressive and aggressive hip-hop, alt-metal riffs, punk angst, and Tankian's distinctive vocal style.

Their second album, *Toxicity*, released in 2001, was a defining moment for the band and the nu-metal genre. Despite reaching the top of the *Billboard* charts, Clear Channel radio banned the album for its perceived unpatriotic content in the wake of 9/11. *Steal This Album!* followed in 2002 with B-sides and outtakes from previous records, which showcased the band's songwriting strengths and sonic diversity. Their 2005 album, *Mezmerize*, received fame for its balance of aggressive and experimental elements, solidifying System of a Down's unique musical identity.

SERJ TANKIAN: It's a natural tendency for people to want to categorize. They train us that way in school, to put things into categories so that our minds can identify them. We're used to working with our minds rather than our hearts. Sometimes, it bothers me, but generally, I'm okay with it. We are metal in a way, and we are a new metal band—or a nu-metal band—although we can change and be non-metal if we want to be, depending on the song. But generally, we're a pretty heavy band, so I don't mind that definition. There are differences between all those bands, but people need to categorize, and I'm used to it by now. (1999)

Stacking up problems that are so unnecessary
wish that I could slow things down
—Linkin Park, "Heavy"

Linkin Park described itself as a six-member band with diverse personalities and styles. The final piece of the puzzle for the Agoura, CA rock-rap group was the 1999 addition of Chester Bennington, a powerful singer with a full-throttle rasp—volatile and laden with psychological baggage—to share tag-team vocals with rapper and producer Mike Shinoda. The band's music explored themes of emotional struggles and inner turmoil, focusing on self-doubt, betrayal, and heartbreak. Bennington's vocal style was a perfect foil for the Shinoda booms and squeals of Pro Tooled tech-metal bricolage that defined the band's sonic tsunami.

Their debut album, *Hybrid Theory*, captured their eclectic amalgam of electronic beats, death metal riffs, turntablist scratching, and melodic choruses, making it the top-selling record of 2000. A highlight was "With You," produced by Mike Simpson and John King of the Dust Brothers. Linkin Park collaborated with The X-Ecutioners and Jay-Z, further solidifying their place in the music industry. 2003's *Meteora* and 2007's *Minutes to Midnight* were also incredibly successful albums for the band.

Despite facing controversy over their unabashed commercial crossover pop—like Tool singer Maynard Keenan trashing them as

"Slipbizkit"—Linkin Park became one of the most successful rock bands ever, with over seventy million albums sold. However, Chester Bennington's untimely suicide in 2017 marked a tragic end to his career. He took his own life on what would have been his tragic friend Chris Cornell's fifty-third birthday. His replacement was Emily Armstrong.

CHESTER BENNINGTON: We grew up listening to a lot of hip-hop, rock, and electronic music, and it made sense to us to listen to all of it at the same time. If you combined our record collections, you'd have one huge, gnarly music store! (2002)

LOUD ROCKS

Loud Rocks on the Loud/Sony label was a hidden gem that starred dynamic collaborations between nu-metal and hip-hop artists. The 2000 CD involved pairings such as System of a Down with Wu-Tang Clan, Everlast with Mobb Deep, and Static-X with Dead Prez, blurring the lines between genres with explosive results. Loud Records, home to the Wu-Tang Clan, was a significant force in hip-hop at the time. *Loud Rocks* was the nu-metal answer to the *Judgment Night* soundtrack, marking the birth of modern rock-rap. The album was released in both clean and explicit versions, featuring stars from both genres reworking material written by the rappers, with crunching rock guitar replacing the fluid funk beats. The record delivered unrelenting blasts of rap-metal from start to finish, earning recognition for its raucous celebration of riff-rap.

Detractors who dismissed the album as rap transposed into Pro-Tools for rock bands missed the point. During Covid, *Kansas City Pitch* reflected on the compilation twenty years later in an article entitled, "What's Worse Than Coronavirus? The Rap-Rock Album *Loud Rocks* From 2000." But the album defined a new style and rates worthy of reappraisal.

SYSTEM OF A DOWN & WU-TANG CLAN
"Shame"

*I brought like 20 white boys in the back of a pickup truck
With hockey pucks and skateboards on
the way to Woodstock*

PRODUCER: Rick Rubin

BACKSTORY: *Loud Rocks* opens on a high note, with the two groups bringing the best of both worlds to the furious "Shame," produced by Rick Rubin, pioneer of the rock-rap hybrid. The sonic attack of Serj Tankian's unique vocal wail, alongside Wu-Tang's leader RZA, made for an instant classic. Wu-Tang's gritty beats meshed nicely with System's tasty instrumentation. The extreme music combined to pump you up and make you want to break things. Best of all, the song captures the irreverent intensity for which both groups became huge. The best part was when RZA rhymed about white boys in pickup trucks with hockey pucks. It's a record that should have sold millions of copies.

SHAVO ODADJIAN: System did a great song with Wu-Tang's "Shame," which we did with Rick Rubin. RZA and I clicked, and we started hanging out at his studio or my own. He wanted to learn how to play guitar, and I wanted to make beats and learn production. So he said he'd teach me what he knew if I gave him some guitar lessons. I was like, "Fuck, dude, whatever you need!" It was a true blend of rock and hip-hop. (2020)

•

SUGAR RAY & THA ALKAHOLIKS
"Make Room"

*You can call me sleazy 'cause my rhymes are kinda greasy
I used to have a curl now everybody wanna tease me*

PRODUCER: DJ Homicide

BACKSTORY: DJ Homicide, the producer for Sugar Ray, was briefly a member of Tha Alkaholiks before gaining fame with Sugar Ray, a multi-platinum crew known for Mark McGrath's smooth vocals. The Alkaholiks, a skilled and comical crew with solid production, elevated their game with lyrics like "I don't drink and drive 'cause I might spill my drink." Their collaboration with Sugar Ray—based on the 1993 LA jam from The Alkaholiks' classic *21 And Over* album—blurred the lines between genres and produced explosive results.

MARK McGRATH: We wanted to do this Alkaholiks song on our first record in 1994. So when the Loud people asked if we'd like to do a track for the compilation, I said, "Will we? We've already got one in mind . . . " (2000)

•

STATIC-X & DEAD PREZ
"Hip Hop"

One thing about music, when it hits, you feel no pain
White folks say it controls your brain

PRODUCERS: Wayne Static and Sean Canem

BACKSTORY: The Dead Prez song "Hip Hop" sampled Bob Marley And The Wailers' "Trenchtown Rock." The remix of "Hip Hop" featured techno-metal dance beats combined with Static-X's style, which suited the lyrics well. The breakbeat-driven sound of the band's late leader, Wayne Static, contained hyperspeed drums, overamplified guitars, muddied vocals, and layers of dense rhythmic fog, all of which perfectly complemented Dead Prez's rapid-fire delivery and skittish hip-hop rhythm.

WAYNE STATIC: I love the track. It's the definition of rock/rap. The guitars laid down take it to another level. There was this bullshit review in

NME that said all the original tracks were heavier without the guitars added and that rockers need rappers more than rappers need rockers. Sounds like some bullshit reverse racism to me. (2000)

●

ENDO & XZIBIT
"Los Angeles Times"

Where you can see the whole city burning
Because the cops got Uzis and the dealers keep serving

PRODUCERS: Amy Finnerty and Jose "Choco" Reynoso

BACKSTORY: One of the best rap-metal tracks on record documented Xzibit at his peak, delivering great rhymes over intense guitars and pounding drums, with the emotional and angsty sound of inner anger unleashed by the Miami band Endo. Endo guitarist Elijah Parker played amazing riffs; the song came together when Xzibit re-recorded his vocals in the studio to match the musical energy. After the powerful collaboration, Xzibit joined the crossover Anger Management Tour with Eminem, Korn, and Papa Roach.

GIL BITTON: We're not like the Miami we're from. We don't express what's around us; we express what's within us. What's around us is Ricky Martin and salsa and the pretentious South Beach vibe. But what we express is a deeper sense of reality. Having grown up on heavy metal, hardcore, and industrial, we live in our world. It's a world within. (2001)

●

EVERLAST & MOBB DEEP
"Shook Ones Part II"

For all of those who wanna profile and pose
Rock you in your face, stab your brain with your nose bone

PRODUCERS: Dante Ross and Stimulated Dummies

BACKSTORY: Everlast, known for his distinctive drunken rhyme style, displayed his natural talent for delivering intense vocals over hard-hitting, pounding basslines in a compilation highlight. The opening track of Mobb Deep's 1995 album *The Infamous*, "Shook Ones Part II," presented raw lyrics addressing the New York rap duo's tumultuous conflict with Tupac Shakur. They based the song on a Quincy Jones sample from the soundtrack of the 1971 movie *Dollars*, which starred Little Richard and Roberta Flack. Kejuan "Havoc" Muchita penned the contentious lyrics in his bedroom at Queensbridge Houses.

HAVOC: I made beats in my crib in the projects. We'd already put out "Shook Ones," and our confidence was up. At that time, I was into sampling jazz records, so I found this loop. I put it together. I tried to make it sound as crispy as possible while recording it in the studio. Then, five years later, Everlast from House of Pain came in with his white b-boy production team and kicked it up a notch on "Shook Ones Part II." That was pretty dope. (2011)

•

TOM MORELLO & CHAD SMITH & WU-TANG CLAN
"Wu-Tang Clan Ain't Nuthing Ta Fuck Wit"

Put the needle to the groove, I get rude
I'm forced to fuck it up, my style carries like a pick-up truck

PRODUCER: Rick Rubin

BACKSTORY: *Loud Rocks* featured a track where Rage Against the Machine's Morello played guitar, and Red Hot Chili Peppers drummer Smith contributed. Despite the skill of Morello and Smith, their collaboration felt somewhat unproductive. Fueled by the guitarist's virtuosity, the track exemplified the success of the rock-rap synthesis. Produced by Rick Rubin, the song sampled the theme to the 1960s TV cartoon *Underdog*. The original recording of *Enter the Wu-Tang: 36 Chambers* shed light on the Clansmen's hostilities and periods of incarceration.

METHOD MAN: That was one of the records when RZA was making the beats for my *Method Man* record. He made two beats that day: "Wu-Tang Clan Ain't Nuthing Ta Fuck Wit"—and everybody knows that's from *Underdog* because I remember he had the CD and it had all the children's songs on it. He just sat there and chopped that shit. He didn't do much to it; he just let it flow. (2011)

•

CRAZY TOWN & THA ALKAHOLIKS
"Only When I'm Drunk"

When I get drunk, I might act uncouth
But when I get drunk, I always tell the truth

PRODUCERS: Josh Abraham, Seth "Shifty Shellshock" Binzer, Bret "Epic" Mazur

BACKSTORY: Crazytown, the N-Sync of nu-metal, consisting of Seth "Shifty Shellshock" Binzer and former hip-hop producer Bret "Epic" Mazur. They combined hip-hop attitude with hard rock sound. Their most well-known song, "Butterfly," was a pop-rock-rap hit that reached #1 in 2000. In the same year, they joined Ozzfest with the help of Metallica's Q-Prime Management but were fired from the tour after Binzer was arrested for drunkenly throwing a chair through a glass window. Their intense raps and heavy metal hooks transformed Tha Alkaholiks' 1993 track by incorporating industrial new wave and electro-rap. Some critics believed that Crazytown's aggressive raps and loud volume took away the enjoyment of "Only When I'm Drunk."

SHIFTY SHELLSHOCK: We always loved that Alkoholics song, so when we had the chance to collaborate, it was an honor to do it our style and to bring in that rock flavor. It's one of the better things we've done. (2001)

•

SEVENDUST & XZIBIT
"What U See Is What U Get"

Start to shakin' you down, breakin' new ground, construction work
Heavy artillery, put your dick in the dirt

PRODUCERS: Sevendust with DJ Hurricane

BACKSTORY: The record's only track with a Black rapper and a Black nu-metal frontman combined Xzibit's smooth, rapid-fire hip-hop with brutal guitar riffs by the Atlanta band Sevendust. "What U See Is What You Get," from Xzibit's 1998 album *40 Dayz & 40 Nightz*, interestingly sampled Funkadelic's "Get Off Your Ass And Jam" and Arthur Prysock's rendition of "My Funny Valentine." Lajon Witherspoon's aggression and versatility encompassed the comp's concept.

LAJON WITHERSPOON: I don't think I'm a rapper, but it's easy because I write a chorus and sing it as usual. I brought the soul, and it blended nicely. I've worked with Xzibit, and "What U See Is What You Get" was one of our best collaborations. We've done stuff with LL Cool J. So we've done several things, and I'm not afraid to do it. I think it's a good mix, especially these days. (2017)

•

BUTCH VIG & M.O.P.
"How 'Bout Some Hardcore"

Me and mics, that's unlike niggas and dykes
So who wanna skate, cause I'm puttin' niggas on ice

PRODUCER: Butch Vig

BACKSTORY: M.O.P., which stands for Mash Out Posse, is an American hip-hop duo known for incorporating a rock sensibility into their music. The duo consists of Billy Danze and Lil' Fame, known for their aggressive delivery as emcees. The fierce underground hip-hop group gained mainstream success with their song "Ante Up," released on their 1993 album *Warriorz*. M.O.P. often collaborated with Gang Starr's DJ Premier, one of the most respected producers in the business. This union with grunge legend Butch Vig, as a guitarist and producer, features a club-ready rock-meets-electronica sound.

DANNY BOY: We didn't have much to do with the Sub Pop remix single. But I recall listening to Butch's mix, and that collaboration remains one of my favorites; he was one of the greats of that era. (2024)

•

OZZY OSBOURNE, TONY IOMMI & WU-TANG CLAN
"For Heaven's Sake (2000)"

We come from different worlds, don't you ever forget
I'm just a poor little white boy, showin' my respect

PRODUCER: Bob Marlette

BACKSTORY: The "doom rap" of Black Sabbath and Wu-Tang was an ideal union of rock and rap, seamlessly switching between two styles without missing a beat. Ozzy Osbourne and Tony Iommi collaborated with Wu-Tang on updating their Staten Island opus, "For Heaven's Sake," intermingling it with the trademark Black Sabbath heaviness. This collaboration affirmed Loud president Steve Rifkind's liner-note assertion that "rock and rap come from the same street, they just live on different blocks." Ozzy loved the song and put it on his 2005 album, *Prince of Darkness*.

TONY IOMMI: That was an exciting development. I couldn't have imagined Black Sabbath and the Wu-Tang Clan in the same sentence, let alone on the same track. But bringing a hard rock/heavy metal sound to a rap track takes the song to an intense level, which is only good. (2000)

•

SHOOTYZ GROOVE & BIG PUN
"Caribbean Connection"

Big Pun, count the stacks, make it fast
Illegal money turns legs now we runnin' a laundromat

PRODUCER: Gene "Machine" Freeman
BACKSTORY: Big Pun, aka The Big Punisher, was a Puerto Rican rapper from the Bronx and a part of Fat Joe's hip-hop empire. In 1998, he had a reggae-flavored hit called "Caribbean Connection," which portrayed the gritty thug life and spotlighted his friend Wyclef Jean of The Fugees. The song's title was a double entendre, a tribute to Caribbean pride, and a shout-out to their drug dealers. In 1999, Pun teamed with Bronx rap-rockers Shootyz Groove, who added aggressive riffs and hardcore raps to the melody, increasing its intensity. Additionally, *Loud Rocks* featured a track by the LA band Incubus, which included a remix by Big Pun of the rapper's song "Still Not A Player." Tragically, Big Pun, who weighed 698 pounds, died of a massive heart attack three weeks before the compilation's release. Shortly after his death, Fat Joe made controversial remarks, suggesting that Big Pun's legacy would soon be forgotten.

BIG PUN: The remix of "Caribbean Connection" is gonna be the biggest record to come out of the Bronx. It's me in the studio with my local boys Shootyz Groove, and we rocked that shit with loud guitars. We're taking rap and roll to another level. I can't wait to go out and tour this record for the world to hear. (1999)

SICK OF IT ALL & MOBB DEEP
"Survival of the Fittest"

My goal is to stay alive
Survival of the fittest, only the strong survive

PRODUCERS: Armand Majidi and John Seymour

BACKSTORY: NYHC punk band Sick of it All and NYC gangster rappers Mobb Deep collaborated on a track produced by SOIA drummer Armand Majidi. Havoc and Prodigy of Mobb Deep, known for their 1995 classic *The Infamous*, created a rugged rap track that tells dark tales of violent street life through dope beats and melodies. Years later, Sick of It All sued Mobb Deep (Havoc and the late Prodigy's estate) over the rappers' use of a dragon image that closely resembled SOIA's logo in a licensing deal with Supreme. The punk band's intellectual property lawyers stated, "This case arises out of the defendants' improper and illegal use of a nearly identical logo mark to the plaintiff's distinctive, incontestable logo. It is willful infringement and unfair competition."

LOU KOLLER: The hip-hop scene at the time shared many of the ideals of the hardcore scene. A conflict arose between us and Mobb Deep. They recorded *Hell on Earth* and promoted the album with a poster featuring the Sick of it All dragon tattoo. When we noticed this, we went to them to clarify it in a relaxed manner. After a bit of back and forth, we sorted things out. Afterward, they asked us if we could do a song with them to clear things up. This is how "Survival of the Fittest" came about. (2010)

CONCLUSION

Never lose your flow
In the end, it's just a rock show
—Run-DMC, "Rock Show"

When rock met hip-hop, it was an exciting time of fresh new sounds. Rock riffs got turned inside out by an infusion of young punk and metal musicians, rap's emerging technologies, and the burgeoning art of turntablism. The possibilities seemed endless. For 10–15 years, there was an explosion of Run-DMC, Beastie Boys, Public Enemy, Cypress Hill, House of Pain, and Rage Against the Machine, which artistically imploded in the late 1990s with the rise of nu-metal exemplified by Limp Bizkit and Korn.

The formula exploded because rock and rap weren't as different as they appeared. Rap-rock, and perhaps rock music itself, wasn't quite as lifeless as it sometimes seemed. When rock met hip-hop, rock sounded like it was supposed to sound: youthful, energetic, and utterly unpredictable.

EVAN SEINFELD: Rock and rap are different. But it's the same thing if you think about it because we both tap into this sound, which is the soundtrack to our angst. When rock met hip-hop, it was because this was the music of the underdog. This music was the sound of people from the underground who were either trying to escape the hood or make it from nothing, starting from the bottom. We were kids from the neighborhood; nobody would let us play music in their house, and nobody told me I could make it. Everyone told me, "You have no talent." When you're talking about hardcore or hip-hop, it has nothing to do with following the rules or how you pronounce the words properly in the studio. It became aspirational for many people to talk like rappers, hence the "wigger" expression. (2024)

CARLO McCORMICK: The most exciting art and music always come from the fringes and gray area. When it comes from one place, it can be harsh and uninteresting. But when it comes from different places, you'll come up with something unique and interesting that has probably never been tried before. When rock met hip-hop, it produced some high-quality music, at least for a while. (2024)

It's tough to determine why the merger of rap and metal didn't yield better-received results or why there wasn't more of this music. There's no clear explanation for why genres don't mesh. Maybe because the groups didn't do either style very well or because no one would argue that mediocre metal and lousy rap do not make great listening. Maybe people didn't despise rap-metal. Maybe groups like the Beastie Boys and Rage Against the Machine set the bar too high. Or maybe because the record labels didn't understand it, and most music critics dismissed it as another white fad.

MICHAEL HOLMAN: There was some crossover between rock and rap, which grew over the years. It started as breakbeats, and that mix of Black rap and white rock worked best, like MCs doing their thing to Billy Squier songs. Rappers like the Beastie Boys and Public Enemy created rock sounds, and West Coast groups like House of Pain and Rage Against The Machine were bands playing live hip-hop. If you asked me, it was all about the breakbeats, but the guitars in hip-hop never sounded right. They sounded like regular rock and roll. (2024)

EDDIE MARTINEZ: I don't think hip-hop has represented the guitar properly. There's still much more room for guitarists to make a statement with rap. That said, it must come from an authentic place and must be the artist's vision. I like what the Beastie Boys did on "Sabotage," but that was last century. (2023)

The niche audience may be small and shrinking. When you do a crossover, you won't necessarily get the bulk of folks who like each side individually to adopt it fully. There was a time in the 1990s when everyone was doing rap-rock, largely due to the popularity of a few great bands, and all the unimaginative and derivative rap-rock fell out of favor based on merit.

B-REAL: It's all destiny. Everything has a purpose, and we don't know what it is or why we do it, but shit happens. We take it as it comes. We and a few others crossed over rock and hip-hop early on. It's all good. Some of the shit is fucked up, and some of the shit is cool. (1995)

Interestingly, rap and metal crossed over to fans of all persuasions, but many of these fans didn't embrace rap-metal. There's a mercantile aspect because much rap-rock exists to combine two popular styles and maximize their monetization. There's also a deep-seated racial component to the rap-rock dilemma that requires little cultural explanation. Then again, nobody today would think twice about bustin' freestyle rap over power chords and guitar solos.

WHEN ROCK MET HIP-HOP

MIKE SCHNAPP: You couldn't find a metal record without rap influence after a while. I enjoyed some of it, and I shied away from others. But every style gets overdone. Anytime something good comes out of the music business, they beat it to death until it receives a negative reaction. But there were a lot of brilliant songs. Groups like Run-DMC and the Beastie Boys changed people's minds. They saved music from becoming stagnant and boring. (2024)

Rock and rap weren't finished with each other. Nu-metal emerged, and after years of massive popularity, it ultimately burned out among its audience.

The reintegration of American music continues, turning the integrationist dream into a brilliant marketing scheme. Today's rappers resurrect the spirit of punk rock and heavy metal, be it Lil Jon jamming with the Bad Brains, the Wu-Tang Clan collaborating with Ozzy Osbourne and Tony Iommi, or DMC performing Ram Jam's "Black Betty" alongside Sebastian Bach, Duff McKagan, and Mick Mars. The song remains the same.

BARRINGTON HENDRICKS: Back in the early 1980s, when rappers couldn't perform, the punk venues let them in to perform. Race was the big thing separating rap and punk in the general public eye, but they were both resilient genres that got frowned upon by the elites just for being what they were. They gave a home to outsiders. I have always felt that punk and rap are the same, but both are wrapped up differently. (2022)

BILL ADLER: Punk was the revolution that failed; rap is the revolution that succeeded. Of course, there were great punk bands like the Ramones at CBGB, but they never charted. The entire movement was

CONCLUSION

a critic's wet dream. Whereas "Rapper's Delight" charted in a dozen countries, and the song was fifteen minutes long. Rap came along at precisely the right time to reinvigorate rock and roll. Objectively, it was exciting in the way you want rock and roll to be. It was sexy and aggressive, and it occurred when rock music was at its lowest point. Punk understood that. They want to reinvent rock because too much Pink Floyd made them sick. They tried to bring it back to basics, and people, by and large, did not bite. Half a decade later, rap became the new rock, doing so on its own merits. On its own merits, rap won. (2014)

Actually, when rock met hip-hop, everybody won.

APPENDIX: LOST GEMS

•

THE JAGGERZ
"The Rapper"
(Kama Sutra, 1970)
Rap, rap, rap, they call him the rapper
Rap, rap, rap, you know what he's after

PRODUCER: Donnie Iris and Sixuvus Productions

BACKSTORY: Donnie Iris (Ierace) was the singer, guitarist, trumpeter, and songwriter/arranger of the Jaggerz, a rock and roll band from Pittsburgh that has been around since 1964. His self-composed hit song "The Rapper" was a funky mix of Eric Burdon & War and Creedence Clearwater Revival. It sold over one million copies, reaching the *Billboard* Top 10 and peaking at #2 in the spring of 1970, just below the Beatles' "Let it Be" and the Paul McCartney-penned Badfinger hit "Come and Get Your Love."

The song predated hip-hop, but it was significant as the first instance of the word being used in pop culture. The term "rapping"

APPENDIX

in the late 1960s and 1970s was similar to "laying a rap on a hot babe in a barroom pick-up move." The Jaggerz had a second single, "I Call My Baby Candy," which reached #47 on the Canadian charts. Radio legend Wolfman Jack had a minor hit cover version of "The Rapper." Iris joined the disco group Wild Cherry ("Play That Funky Music") in 1975. He then reinvented himself as a new wave star with the 1980 hit "Ah Leah." The Game sampled "The Rapper" in his 2008 hit, "Letter to the King."

DONNIE IRIS: We recorded "The Rapper" around the summer of 1969. It was released in late 1969 and reached the top of the charts by 1970. The song was just something I wrote watching people in nightclubs and all the bars we played in. I'd see these dudes go over and start rapping to all the chicks. In those days, we used to call trying to pick up chicks "rappin'." What they were doing, though, was hitting on them. That's how the song came about. Just watching these guys and all their moves. (2006)

•

MCA & BURZOOTIE
"Drum Machine"
(Def Jam, 1985)

Listen to the sound of MCA
I'm not a DJ, but I've got some records to play

PRODUCER: Jay Burnett

BACKSTORY: Adam "MCA" Yauch collaborated with Jay Burnett at Arthur Baker's Shakedown Sound Studios. Burnett provided the iconic vocoder voice on "Planet Rock" ("Rock, rock, the Planet Rock"). "Drum Machine" was the only original Def Jam 12" not produced by Rick Rubin and the first solo recording released by MCA. Jay Burnett, a film student at NYU, was nicknamed

Burzootie by his classmate Rubin. In 1982, Jay released a 12" called "Drum Machine" on his own Jayco imprint. Rick Rubin and the Beastie Boys loved the original version and sampled it in "Beastie Groove." They admired Jay's work as a recording engineer, and he went on to work on LL Cool J's "I Need a Beat" and the Beastie Boys' "Rock Hard." In late 1984, Jay and Adam remade "Drum Machine," but with MCA's enthusiastic lyrics expressing his love for the drum machine, which was controversial when many in the industry thought it was replacing real musicians (!!). The plan was to release the record on Arthur Baker's Streetwise label until Rubin gave Burnett $5,000 in cash. "Drum Machine" remains one of the rarest and most sought-after Def Jam releases.

ADAM YAUCH: "Drum Machine" is one of my favorite records I've made. All these years later, it still sounds great. I guess we were a bit ahead of our time. In retrospect, it was a highlight of the early glory days of the Beastie Boys with Rick Rubin. (1998)

•

THE LONE RAGER
"Metal Rap"
(Megaforce, 1984)

Chill out, brothers, don't get temperamental
There's just no stoppin' Heavy Metal!

PRODUCER: Jon Zazula

BACKSTORY: The first rap-metal song ever recorded was a novelty project by Jon Zazula, also known as Jonny Z, the founder of Megaforce Records, a New Jersey-based metal label notable for bands such as Metallica, Anthrax, and Manowar. The 1983 recording was one of the label's early releases. It attempted to combine rock and rap elements but didn't fully capture the power of either genre. Jon Zazula provided theatrical and cartoonish vocals backed by the Rods, the metal legends of Upstate New York. The song's lyrics recounted the history of heavy metal, from Cream to Deep Purple to Raven. The accompanying video showed Jon Zazula in front of a wall of encyclopedias and an American flag, wearing a bondage mask and whipping his heavy metal bullet belt. The 12" cover said "Metal Rap," but the A-Side track was titled "Metal RAPsody." The instrumental flipside, "Special Air-Guitar Headbanging Dub," was the most exciting track.

MIKE SCHNAPP: There was this heavy metal label called Megaforce Records run by Jonny Zazula, who signed Metallica, Overkill, and Anthrax. He put out records and even put out his own record, called The Lone Rager. Not The Lone Ranger. It was his story about what was happening in the heavy metal world. The Ragers were the really good bands; they were fucking raging. His line in the song was about the majors signing all the ragers. He was saying that the major labels were coming in and stealing all the independent label bands—which is about Jonny Z's experience of Elektra Records signing/stealing Metallica from his Megaforce label. It's a slow, plodding, heavy metal riff with this white guy telling a story in rap cadence. To me, that makes it the first heavy metal rap. (2024)

MARIA FERRERO: "Metal Rap" was driven by Johnny's ego. He grew up in the Bronx, where rap came from. He thought he'd become as famous as his band Metallica. It was a record made for fun. (2024)

•

FAT BOYS AND THE BEACH BOYS
"Wipeout!"
(Polydor, 1987)

PRODUCER: Albert Cabrera and Tony Moran
BACKSTORY: This unique collaboration between the Fat Boys and the Beach Boys in the 1980s resulted in a rock-flavored pop/rap

release. The Fat Boys, who had just starred in the movie *Disorderlies*, met the Beach Boys on set, which led to a new recording of the Surfaris' 1960s surf instrumental "Wipeout." The song, mixed by The Latin Rascals, became a Top 10 hit in the United States and six other countries; one version of the record featured metal guitar by Dweezil Zappa.

Combining two vocal groups to reimagine a primal surf instrumental over synth drums and a human beatbox resulted in a novel musical style. The video featured cameos by boxers Hector "Macho" Camacho and Ray "Boom Boom" Mancini. It showcased the acts in various settings, including the Fat Boys on an LA beach and the Beach Boys driving b-boy style through Little Italy and Chinatown. The video showed the Fat Boys performing a take on "The Watusi" while doing human beatboxing.

PRINCE MARKIE DEE: We recorded with many classic stars like Chubby Checkers. But the wildest, weirdest, and most successful thing we did was with the Beach Boys. We didn't surf, and they didn't get us at all. "Wipeout!" was hilarious and challenging to pull off. But it was amazing, and there was plenty of food, so we liked it! (1987)

•

CAVEMAN
"I'm Ready"
(Profile UK, 1990)

Bringin' the crosstown
Back in effect

PRODUCER: Robi Lasker

BACKSTORY: Caveman was a British biracial hip-hop crew consisting of rapper Mark "MCM" Layman, DJ Julian "Diamond J" Small, and producer Robi "The Principle" Lasker. Their name reflects their raw, hard-hitting, and back-to-basics sound. Hailing from rural Buckinghamshire, the group released two relatively unknown singles before gaining attention with "I'm Ready." This track, featuring a heavy sample of Jimi Hendrix's "Crosstown Traffic" and hints of a jazzy New Jack Swing beat, made its way onto the UK charts for two weeks and became an underground hit. "I'm Ready" emerged precisely two decades after Jimi Hendrix's passing. Following the single's success, Caveman released the album *Positive Reaction*. They became the first British rappers signed to an American label, Run-DMC's label, Profile Records. However, just as the album was released, they disbanded for personal reasons and faced copyright lawsuits from the Hendrix estate. Despite these challenges, "I'm Ready" remains a powerful example of rock and hip-hop fusion.

THE PRINCIPLE: To us, making it doesn't mean getting a Top 40 hit; it means gaining respect from the hip-hop crowds. With "I'm Ready," we also had to prove ourselves to the rock crowd. Respect to rock. (1991)

•

THE DON & TED NUGENT
"Big 12 Inch"
(Rush/Columbia, 1991)

You gotta go with the flow
of the almighty Gonzo

PRODUCER: Daniel Schulman

BACKSTORY: The Don (Don Saunders) emerged from the old-school NYC hip-hop scene as part of the Eric B & Rakim "Paid In Full"-era posse. The story goes that Russell Simmons had just lost The Fresh Prince as a client, so he steered the young gangster rapper in a pop direction. A new Young MC style featuring rock breakbeats led to a management deal with Russell and Rush (in their early post-Rick Rubin era), who had a label through Columbia. The Don's 1991

APPENDIX

album, *Wake up the Party*, remixed Kiss' "Calling Dr. Love" as the opening track and featured the closing track, "Prove it to Me," produced by Bret "Epic" Mazur (later of Crazy Town). The first single, "In There," was a pop party jam big on MTV.

Columbia believed The Don could achieve a Run-DMC/Beastie Boys-level hit with "Big 12 Inch"—a funky rendition of "Cat Scratch Fever" with lyrics about women loving his "big 12 inch (record)." The album's second single starred guitar legend Ted Nugent guest rapping and delivering a wild solo in a rock-rap blend that must be heard to be believed. "Big 12 Inch" came out on a 12", with an Extended Mix on the flipside starring Andreas Straub's syncopated guitar akin to what Straub did on Run-DMC's "Tougher Than Leather," co-engineered by Chuck Valle of Murphy's Law (RIP).

TOUGHER THAN LEATHER: Rick Rubin and Run-DMC in the *Tougher Than Leather* film, 1988. New Line Cinema/Photofest ¾ New Line Cinema.

But things did not go as planned. During a break in their large-scale video shoot in a Brooklyn industrial space, "The Nuge" spoke about his connection to the Detroit blues and jazz cats and roared for all to hear,

APPENDIX

"I am the ultimate nigger!" He said something similar that night to Russell. If you've never heard of this record, that's probably the reason.

TED NUGENT: When this guy The Don wanted to use the "Cat Scratch Fever" lick in his new rap song called "Big 12 Inch," I said, "Sure, Don, let's rock!" When I went in and met him, the guy was cool as hell, and his boys were rockers. I could puke when I hear most rap. I'm an adventurous son of a bitch, and I wanna find out about shit like that. So, I went to New York City and told those guys that when they grow up, they might be as big a nigger as I am—and they loved it. You're gonna dig it, too. (1992)

•

BRIDE AND THE D.O.C.
"God Gave Rock and Roll to You"
(Music For Nations, 1993)

And you're tired of wishin' on a falling star
You gotta put your faith in a loud guitar

PRODUCERS: Tedd Tjornhom and Rodney A. Gibson

BACKSTORY: "God Gave Rock and Roll to You" was originally a hit for Rod Argent in 1973 and was later popularized by Kiss in 1991. In 1993, the song was redone with a Christian theme, with D.O.C. (Disciples of Christ, no relationship to the N.W.A.-linked gangsta The D.O.C.), a devout Black Christian group rapping with a twist of soul, in a heavenly collaboration with the hard-rockin' Christian metal band Bride, who by then had transitioned from their 1980s hair metal look to a 1990s Pearl Jam style. Their frontman, Dale Thompson, was briefly rumored to be replacing Michael Sweet in Stryper. A year before this collaboration, D.O.C. member Alton Hood, Jr. had rapped on the song "Holy War" by their Christian label mates Whitecross. "God Gave Rock and Roll to You" was released by the noted UK heavy metal label Music For Nations and became one of the most requested songs at the Sioux Falls College radio station. This shockingly incredible recording—a Christian music business attempt to unite pious rock and rap forces—may be one of the Lord's hidden gems. Bride was known for playing a wide range of styles and remained popular in Brazil, but they never worked in hip-hop again, and D.O.C. did not return to rock.

DALE THOMPSON: The "God Gave Rock and Roll to You" video was shot in a cotton mill at about 3:00 a.m. when we returned home from a show. It was cold and exhausting, but it's my favorite video. The guys in D.O.C. were so cool, and our guitarist's riff, which I consider a lame rock song, added the spark to make it the best version of that song ever recorded. (2015)

•

BLOODHOUND GANG
"Fire Water Burn"
(Geffen Records, 1996)

This hardcore ghetto gangster image takes a lot of practice
I'm not black like Barry White, no, I am white like Frank Black is

PRODUCER: Jimmy Pop

BACKSTORY: The Bloodhound Gang was a comedic five-piece rock and rap band formed in 1991 in the Philadelphia suburb of Collegeville, PA. They became famous for their raunchy lyrics and ability to offend with infectious, sample-laden rap-rock. Their big breakthrough came with the song "Fire Water Burn," with the chorus "burn, motherfucker, burn," which resonated with audiences and received airplay on LA's KROQ. Geffen Records emerged victorious in a major label bidding war and re-released the band's 1996 album, *One Fierce Beer Coaster*.

Following this achievement, the group played over 300 shows, including appearances on *The Howard Stern Show* and *The Jenny*

APPENDIX

McCarthy Show, and recorded a cover of The Association's "Along Comes Mary" for the *Half Baked* soundtrack. Their cover of Run-DMC's "It's Tricky" on the 2000 compilation *Take a Bite Outta Rhyme* was a notable example of rock-rap. They became one of the first bands to achieve success through internet exposure. Bloodhound Gang, who have sold over six million records, are no longer recording new music, although frontman Jimmy Pop maintains that the band is still together.

JIMMY POP: I'm not in a band because I like music. If I weren't able to tell poop jokes over music, I wouldn't be in a band. It just helps that I know something about music. (2024)

D.X. FERRIS: Bloodhound Gang was undeniably juvenile and brilliant. They started as a white hip-hop group dressed like the Beastie Boys, with all the typical white rap tropes. They got dropped after their first album with Jenna Jameson on the cover—and reunited after a schism that resulted in a new lineup. The following year's 1996 album for Geffen included a cover of Run-DMC's "It's Tricky," and the song "Boom" with Vanilla Ice, back when nobody cared about him. The band developed a shtick of verbal acrobatics full of crude raps and sampling with live instruments. It's a great, successful band that people have forgotten about. (2024)

•

ILL BILL
"U.B.S. (Unauthorized Biography of Slayer),"
(Fat Beats, 2008)
They met Rick Rubin at Def Jam, struck a deal
The same year Rick produced Raising Hell and Licensed to Ill

PRODUCER: Necro
BACKSTORY: Ill Bill, aka William Braunstein, is known for making hardcore hip-hop with a heavy metal style. In 1994, MC Serch from

3rd Bass brought the Brooklyn native into Non Phixion, an underrated underground 1990s rap group that disbanded after a decade of creating a deep discography. Ill Bill's solo debut, *What's Wrong With Bill?*, came out in 2004 and was co-produced by his rapper brother Necro (Ron Braunstein). In 2005, Bill joined La Coka Nostra, a supergroup led by Danny Boy of House of Pain. Their first album featured all three House of Pain members before Everlast quit.

In 2008, Ill Bill released his epic rap-metal second album, *The Hour of Reprisal*. The album title came from the lyrics of the title track of Slayer's groundbreaking 1986 album, *Reign in Blood*, their first album with Rick Rubin. *The Hour of Reprisal* featured guest producers DJ Muggs, DJ Lethal, and DJ Premier, as well as rappers Everlast, B-Real, and Raekwon, alongside musicians Max Cavalera of Sepultura and H.R. and Darryl Jenifer of the Bad Brains. The album featured the most extreme rap-metal moment, "U.B.S. (Unauthorized Biography of Slayer)," a song about Slayer, and is considered by many to be the best song about the band—not that any others come to mind.

ILL BILL: Growing up, I was a rare breed of kid who was listening to both metal and rap and could understand that there were many more similarities than differences. That's why I always related to Rick Rubin, who was working on Run-DMC and Beastie Boys records at the same time he was working with Slayer and Danzig. He was an inspiration and a validation that I'm not weird for understanding both types of music. I was on both ends of the spectrum. (2013)

•

SAGE FRANCIS
(with Bad Religion)
"Let Them Eat War"
(Epitaph Records, 2010)

They're America's working corps
Can this be what they voted for?

PRODUCER: Brett Gurewitz and Greg Graffin

BACKSTORY: Paul "Sage" Francis is considered one of the great white rappers and one of our generation's great lyricists. He's recognized as a forefather of the indie hip-hop movement, known for his cerebral sampling, such as "She's Lost Control" by Joy Division. His career is based on gifted wordplay, creating vivid narratives. Sage's first demo tape, released in 1996, featured "Mullet," which combined rap with a live band, reacting against the white-boy b-boy stereotype.

His first album, 2002's *Personal Journeys*, gained popularity in the underground scene. The Providence, Rhode Island native's intense political manifestos and social activism led to three albums on Epitaph Records, breaking barriers as the first rapper on a hardcore punk label. The master lyricist (aka "Epic Beard Man") also ventured into rap-rock, making a guest appearance on the Bad Religion song "Let Them Eat War" (the opening track of the punk kings' thirteenth studio album, 2004's *The Empire Strikes First*). Unfortunately, that collaboration was not well promoted.

SAGE FRANCIS: Yes, sir. That's me on Bad Religion's "Let Them Eat War" song. I recorded that verse in Brett's house. It took a punk rock label to treat hip-hop with a little respect and dignity in the 2000s. Epitaph showed a genuine interest in what I talk about and how I make my music, whereas the hip-hop labels poked around to see what kind of mold they could fit me into. Hip-hop and punk rock have a lot of things in common—but don't tell the purists of each respective genre that. Irony is not dead. (2011)

•

EASTCIDE
"Nowhere's Child"
(S/R, 2001)

Yo, she's turning me on
I lean back my head and turn up the song

PRODUCER: Nuno Bettencourt

BACKSTORY: Eastcide was the first New England crew to merge hip-hop, industrial, nu-metal, and tough-guy hardcore punk. The band emerged in the mid-1990s from the blue-collar town of Taunton in Southern Massachusetts. With rapping vocals, mad turntablism, twin guitars, and a thumpin' rhythm section, Eastcide became a regional force. They self-released several tapes and made intense CDs for three local indie labels: 1996's "Look What You've Created" six-song tape and 1997's "Everybody's Walking Away" CD (both on Sektion 8 Records); the Eastcide EP (Fountainhead); and the Eastcide album (DRP), both issued in 2000. Their rap-core was mentioned in *Playboy* and portrayed on TV shows like *Farm Club*. In 2003, their final recording featured the quasi-power ballad "Nowhere's Child," produced by Nuno Bettencourt, guitarist of the Boston-based hair metal heroes Extreme. This record should have scored them a major label deal. It's yet another story of a band of misbehaved young adults decimated by big heads and bad drugs.

D.X. FERRIS: Eastcide was a fascinating coulda-woulda-shoulda band. They got in the game in the mid-1990s when punk and rap had comingled into one misleadingly labeled genre briefly called "hardcore." Limp Bizkit was the most successful refinement of that general formula: musicians with a punk past met a hip-hop present. Eastcide was a live band. Their rap and urban elements included the lingo and the look—with loose clothes, dreads, and whatnot. If it got released one day, it would still get big. (2024)

•

MARZ
"DeeBaby"
(Spotify, 2011)

We got this shit out of the mud
Really be slangin' them drugs

APPENDIX

PRODUCER: Bobby Marz

BACKSTORY: Zoltan "Bobby" Hukic, also known as Bobby Marz, is a Croatian-American who grew up in Chicago, surrounded by gangs and witchcraft. While working at Chicago Trax recording studio, he was credited as the engineer on Peter Gabriel's 1989 album *Passion for the Christ*. His spec work on an Al Jourgensen solo album led to his full-time hiring as a Ministry guitarist during their darkest, drug-riddled late-1990s days, on *Filth Pig* and *Dark Side of the Spoon*.

In 2000, Marz formed a band with Ministry mates, drummer Rey Washam and guitarist Louis Svitek. They gained popularity among fans of Insane Clown Posse, resulting in two national tours together. However, legal disputes led to a falling out between the two groups. Marz also collaborated with Jonathan Davis of Korn, and a Korn-Marz tour was initially successful. However, tensions arose due to a dispute between Davis and Violent J of Insane Clown Posse, as well as Marz's checkered past with ICP. Over time, Marz's music appealed more to the Chicago African American market than to crossover crowds. Now a Christian, he ministers in venues where he once toured with Ministry.

BOBBY MARZ: Smoking weed took me a while to stop. I kept quitting, and then one day, out of frustration, I prayed and told God to take it away. A month went by before I even noticed I didn't smoke. I never smoked again. I got delivered. (2017)

•

HESHER
(featuring Everlast and Biz Markie)
"Whose Generation"
(Warner Bros., 2000)

PRODUCERS: Dante Ross and John Gamble

APPENDIX

BACKSTORY: Chip Love (Wolfson) started as a teenager in the NYHC scene as a Bad Brains roadie. Inspired by his hero, Bad Brains bassist Darryl Jenifer, Chip and Danny Illchuck founded the great-forgotten rap-metal-punk crew Roguish Armament, which recorded killer homemade demos and a 1995 album for the Philly-based SFT label. Roguish was best known as the opening act at Woodstock '94. In 2000, Chip, also known as Hesher, teamed up with Grammy Award-winning producers Dante Ross and John Gamble behind Everlast's triple-platinum album, *Whitey Ford Sings the Blues*. On his self-titled album for Warner Bros., Chip seamlessly meshed thrash, hip-hop, Britpop, and heavy rock grooves. The album included instrumental contributions by Darryl Jenifer, Mackie Jayson (Cro-Mags), Charlie Garriga (CIV), Chino Moreno (Deftones), Warren Haynes (Gov't Mule), and Gabby Abularach (Cro-Mags). The album's notable track, "Whose Generation," parodied the Who's "My Generation" and featured "Human Beat Box" by Biz Markie, who traded vocals with Everlast. Chip's press photo shows him standing in front of the cube at Astor Place in Greenwich Village.

CHIP LOVE: I'm trying to be pretty diverse and hit a lot of angles—blurring the lines between genres. I wear my influences on my sleeve, just trying to do things my way. (2000)

BIBLIOGRAPHY

Aaron, Charles. "Rap-Rock: From 'Punk Rock Rap' to Mook Nation." *Spin*, February 11, 2014.
Ableton, C. "Money Mark: Constructing Creativity." *Ableton.com*, September 23, 2015.
Abrams, Howie, and Sacha Jenkins. *The Merciless Book of Rock Lists*. Abrams Books, 2013.
Adair, Don. "McLaren Offer Eclecticism." *Spokesman-Review* (WA), January 13, 1984.
Adams, Gregory. "James 'Munky' Shaffer Talks Venera, Korn's 'Party Mode' Years, Bucking Expectations." *Revolver*, December 14, 2023.
Adler, Bill. "Interview by Steven Blush." November 5, 2024.
Adler, Bill and Dan Charnas. *Def Jam: The First 25 Years of the Last Great Record Label*. Rizzoli Books, 2011.
Adrianson, Doug. "24-7 Spyz: A Hot, Hard and Creative Rock Band." *Miami Herald* (FL), September 21, 1989.
ADX23. "Art Police: Paul's Boutique." *Shreveport Journal* (LA), August 18, 1989.
AH. "Songs of Impossible Lust: Loud Rocks." *The Guardian* (UK), September 1, 2000.
Ahmed, Insanul. "Method Man Breaks Down His 25 Most Essential Songs." *Complex*, October 19, 2011.
Alexis, Jeremiah. "House of Pain: Danny Boy." *Hip Hop SH*, April 8, 2011.
Ali, Lorraine. "Downset: A Personal Take on Punk-Rap." *Los Angeles Times*, September 3, 1994.
Alvarez, James. "5 Metal-Rap Collaborations That Ruled." *Metal Injection*, August 28, 2015.
Amith, Dennis A. "The One About Time Zone (Lydon & Bambaataa)." *Detroit Free Press* (MI), August 29, 2022.
Amorosi, A.D. "Quick Spins: *Loud Rocks*." *Philadelphia Inquirer* (PA), September 24, 2000.

BIBLIOGRAPHY

Angle, Brad. "Body Count's Ice-T and Ernie C Look Back on the Making of Their Incendiary 1992 Debut Album." *Guitar World,* June 1, 2022.

AP. "Don't Call This a Comeback: Squier Says He's Content." *Santa Maria Times* (CA), September 12, 1993.

AP. "People Love to Hate These Clowns." *Fort Worth Star-Telegram* (TX), July 15, 1999.

AP. "Rock Band Anthrax Still Making Noise with Stomp." *Statesville Record Landmark* (GA), November 13, 1995.

Appleford, Steve. "Run the Jewels Talk Heavy Music, Heavy Rap, Heavy Everything." *Revolver,* June 11, 2018.

Armstrong, Gene. "Rockers from Bronx Play Hard, Fast Mean." *Arizona Republic* (AZ), June 23, 1989.

Armstrong, Stretch and Bobbito. "The Beastie Boys on Their Hip-Hop Journey and Missing Adam Yauch." *NPR,* October 24, 2018.

Baker, Arthur. "Key Tracks: Arthur Baker on 'Planet Rock'." *Red Bull Academy,* April 4, 2013.

Banks, Alec. "The Definitive Grandmaster Flash Interview." *Rock the Bells,* December 31, 2022.

Barshad, Amos. "Rude Boys." *New York,* April 22, 2011.

Barton, David. "Can't Beat the Rap." *Fresno Bee* (CA), February 1, 1986.

Barton, David. "Public Enemy's Rap Is Potent." *Sacramento Bee* (CA), July 31, 1988.

B&E. "Too Much Effing Perspective: Bill Stephney." *Breaking & Entering* (WI), November 8, 2022.

Became, Abe. "A Conversation with Director Charlie Ahearn About 'Wild Style'." *Okayplayer,* August 10, 2023.

Becker, Jordan. "Unusual Collaborations: Run-DMC and Aerosmith." *Star Maker Machine,* August 14, 2013.

Beckmann, Jim. "Inside Story of *Paul's Boutique*: Interview with Mike Simpson of the Dust Brothers." *KEXP,* July 25, 2015.

BeDan, Nick. "The Red Hot Chili Peppers' *Freaky Styley* Should Receive More Praise." *Union Street Journal,* May 24, 2023.

Bee News Services. "Record Capsules: Rage Against the Machine." *Modesto Bee* (CA), December 4, 1992.

Bell, Max. "A Posse of Comic Book Characters: Public Enemy and Anthrax at Brixton Academy." *Evening Standard* (UK), January 15, 1992.

Bell, Max. "Cypress Hill Spark Another One." *Spin,* March 17, 2022.

Bernard, Adam. "Boo-Yaa T.R.I.B.E Interview." *Dub CNN,* October 7, 2003.

Biese, Alex. "Party Crashers: Prophets of Rage Bring It to Jersey." *Asbury Park Press* (NJ), August 26, 2016.

Bloch, Richard. *Grandlife,* "Everybody's Fly: Fab 5 Freddy Talks." *Grandlife,* 2023.

Blomquist, Brian. "New Releases." *Star-Democrat* (PA), September 22, 1989.

Blueskye, Brian. "Still Mixing A Lot: Man of 'Baby Got Back.'" *Coachella Valley Independent* (CA), July 3, 2017.

BIBLIOGRAPHY

Blush, Steven. *American Hardcore: A Tribal History*. Feral House, 2001 (First Edition), 2010 (Second Edition).
Blush, Steven. "A Tribe Called Quest: A Tribe Grows." *Paper*, May 1990.
Blush, Steven. "Beastie Boys: Raisin Hell." *Seconds*, #1, 1986.
Blush, Steven. "Beastie Boys: What Do They Want?" *Seconds*, #19, 1992.
Blush, Steven. "Crazy Town." *Seconds*, #53, 2002.
Blush, Steven. "Cypress Hill." *Seconds*, #32, 1995.
Blush, Steven. "D.X. Ferris Interview." August 24, 2024.
Blush, Steven. "Drew Stone Interview." July 12, 2024.
Blush, Steven. "Faith No More: Hate Ashbury." *Seconds*, #2, 1987.
Blush, Steven. "Fun Lovin' Criminals." *Seconds*, #43, 1997.
Blush, Steven. "Gang Star: Just to Get a Rap." *Seconds*, #25, 1994.
Blush, Steven. "Get Into the Groove." *Paper*, February 1995.
Blush, Steven. "House of Pain: Feel the Pain." *Seconds*, #22, 1993.
Blush, Steven. "Insane Clown Posse." *Seconds*, #45, 1997.
Blush, Steven. "Kool Moe Dee." *Seconds*, #5, 1988.
Blush, Steven. "Loud Faith Rules." *Details*, June 1989.
Blush, Steven. "Maria Ferrero Interview." May 2, 2024.
Blush, Steven. "Motley Crue." *Seconds*, #45, 1997.
Blush, Steven. "Murphy's Law." *Seconds*, #5, 1988.
Blush, Steven. *New York Rock: From the Rise of the Velvet Underground to the Fall of CBGB*. St. Martin's Griffin, 2017.
Blush, Steven. "Public Enemy." *Seconds*, #5, 1988.
Blush, Steven. "Red Hot Chili Peppers: Get Them While They're Hot." *Paper*, October 1987.
Blush, Steven. "Run-DMC: Kings and Queens." *Seconds*, #22, 1993.
Blush, Steven. "Scarface: Face Is the Place." *Seconds*, #24, 1994.
Blush, Steven. *Seconds*, "Ice-T: Still Hustling." *Seconds*, #15, 1991.
Blush, Steven. "SuperSeconds: Sensational." *Seconds*, #51, 2000.
Blush, Steven. "Ted Nugent: Still Gonzo." *Seconds*, #16, 1991.
Blush, Steven. "The Disposable Heroes of Hiphoprisy: Language of Violence." *Seconds*, #17, 1992.
Blush, Steven and Paul Rachman. *American Hardcore: 1980–1986*, 2006.
Boggs, Sheri. "CD Review: Cake." *Inlander* (WA), November 1, 2001.
Boyd, Glen. "Overload of Funk: An Interview with Afrika Bambaataa." *Seattle Rocket* (WA), October 1, 1984.
Brannigan, Paul. "Shavo Odadjian: This Is What a Musician Should Be Doing." *Kerrang!* (UK), August 13, 2020.
Breihan, Tom. "*Judgment Night* Soundtrack Turns 20." *Stereogum*, September 16, 2013.
Britt, Bruce. "Album Reviews: Rage Against the Machine." *Leader-Telegram* (WI), November 22, 1992.
Britt, Bruce. "Beastie Boys Face Predicament." *Belleville News-Democrat* (IL), November 17, 1989.

BIBLIOGRAPHY

Broili, Susan. "Public Enemy's Chuck D Talks About Racism and Music at Duke." *Durham Herald-Sun* (NC), January 24, 1992.

Broughton, Frank. "Interview: Afrika Bambaataa." *Red Bull Academy,* April 7, 2017.

Brown, Mike. "Recordings: Shootyz Groove." *Hartford Courant* (CT), June 30, 1994.

Brunner, Jeryl. "Joe Perry Reveals the Juicy Story Behind Aerosmith and Run-DMC's Historic Video." *Parade,* July 24, 2019.

Bukkems, Tom. "Belgian Interview with J Mascis and Mike Watt." *Freak Scene*, September 23, 2001.

Buyanovsky, Dan. "Rick Rubin Reflects on His Contributions to Iconic Hip-Hop Albums." *XXL,* July 2, 2013.

Caffin, Carol. "A Conversation with Debbie Harry: The Complete Interview." *Westchester Magazine* (NY), September 27, 2012.

Callahan, Maureen. *New York Post,* "The Hip Hop Rebirth of Billy Squire." *New York Post,* November 16, 2013.

Callahan-Bever, Noah and Toshitaka Kondo. "The Mobb Deep's *the Infamous.*" *Complex*, April 25, 2011.

Capobianco, Ken. "Recordings: *Ill Communication.*" *Boston Globe* (MA), June 2, 1994.

Carey, Jean. "24-7 Spyz: Code Word for Fun." *Tampa Bay Times* (FL), March 15, 1991.

Carmel, Novena and Anthony Valadez. "DJ Shadow: Action Adventure' KCRW Interview." *KCRW.com,* October 12, 2023.

Carnwath, Ally. "Portishead: 'We Get Really Scared of Trying to Make Music.'" *Observer* (UK), July 16, 2011.

Carnwath, Ally. "Portishead: 'We Get Really Scared Trying to Make Music." *The Guardian* (UK), July 16, 2011.

Carr, Kevin. "One Step Closer: Linkin Park." *Lancaster Eagle-Gazette* (PA), January 22, 2004.

Carroll, Vincent. "Meet LL Cool J." *Hip Hop Hit List* (NJ), June 10, 1985.

Catalano, Jim. "24-7 Spyz Bring Heavy Metal Soul to Haunt." *Ithaca Journal* (NY), August 9, 2007.

Childers, Chad. "The 90s Metal and Rap Bands Drake Grew Up Listening to." *Loudwire*, March 13, 2024.

Christopher, Michael. "Interview: The Cult's Ian Astbury on Touring *Electric.*" *Vanyaland,* August 22, 2013.

Ciriza, Francisco. "Notas Musicales: Doownset." *Daily News* (NY), September 26, 2004.

Coleman, Bill. "Chris Stein Delivered the Rapture." *DJ History,* April 17, 2023.

Coleman, Brian. "Larry Smith Q&A: January 2006." *Medium,* January 21, 2015.

Comer, Tracy. "Interviews: The Sugarhill Gang." *Evening News* (UK), November 11, 1999.

BIBLIOGRAPHY

Condran, Ed. "Clowns Get Respect from No One." *Asbury Park Press* (NJ), May 3, 2001.
Condran, Ed. "Rock Group Spyz Comes in from the Cold." *Courier-Post* (NJ), December 12, 1991.
Conner, Thomas. "Hot and Not: Shootyz Groove." *Tulsa World* (OK), August 13, 1999.
Conner, Thomas. "They Look Normal, but Dog Eat Dog Delivers Tough, Urban Sounds." *Tulsa World* (OK), July 30, 1995.
Considine, J.D. "Anthrax's Musical Diversity Takes It Beyond Heavy Metal Stereotype." *Baltimore Sun* (MD), June 28, 1991.
Considine, J.D. "Blondie Bursts Back on Rock and Roll Road with Enthusiasm and Confidence." *Baltimore Sun* (MD), August 16, 1982.
Considine, J.D. "Polyester, Sequins Are Gone, but Disco's Stayin' Alive." *Baltimore Sun* (MD), August 14, 1983.
Considine, J.D. "Singer Becomes Just Part of Hip-Hop Sounds." *Baltimore Sun* (MD), February 26, 1984.
Considine, J.D. "Soundtracks Show How Well Hip-Hop Music Will Prosper in the Mainstream." *Baltimore Sun* (MD), June 10, 1984.
Cook-Wilson, Winston. "Kim Gordon on Sonic Youth Working with Cypress Hill." *Spin,* September 13, 2018.
Cornish, Audie. "Rick Rubin, Russell Simmons: Def Jam's First 25 Years." *NPR,* October 9, 2011.
Cosin, Elizabeth M. "Downset: Do We Speak a Dead Language." *Idaho Statesman* (ID), September 24, 1996.
Cotter, Robert. "Anthrax Discuss Public Enemy Collaboration." *BlabberMouth,* July 16, 2020.
Cotter, Robert. "Ice-T Says Working with Slayer on *Judgment Night* Soundtrack Was a Career Highlight." *BlabberMouth,* October 11, 2022.
Coval, Kevin. "Hip Hop's Planet Rocker." *In These Times,* October 3, 2008.
Cromelin, Richard. "Local Acts: Rage Against the Machine." *Los Angeles Times,* December 13, 1992.
Cube, Ice. "Ice Cube's Rock and Roll Hall of Fame Speech." *IceCube.com,* April 11, 2016.
Cullen, Kevin. "When Public Enemy Raps, Many Get the Message." *Boston Globe* (MA), May 30, 1990.
Cunningham, Joe. "The Best Bands You've Never Heard of: These New York Groups Are Headed for Success." *New York Post,* September 17, 2000.
Czaykowski, Bob "Nitebob" (soundman/producer). Interview by Tony Mann, February 5, 2024.
D., Davey. "Interview with Kool Herc, 1989 New Music Seminar." *DaveyD.com,* 1989.
D., Davy. "Chuck D Interview." *Props,* September 1996.
D'Souza, Miguel. "Run-DMC Interview." *Bomb Hip-Hop,* May 22, 1998.

BIBLIOGRAPHY

Daly, Andrew. *Guitar World,* "Session Guitar Legend Eddie Martinez Shares the Studio Secrets Behind Classic Records." *Guitar World,* March 9, 2023.

Danielson, Shane and John Casimir. "Metro Disclocation." *Sydney Morning Herald* (AUS), August 5, 1994.

Davidson, Neil. "Communicating Through Anger." *The Standard* (CAN), January 13, 1995.

Davies, Sam. "How Cypress Hill's 1991 Debut Turned the Trio into Hip-Hop Royalty." *DJ Magazine,* December 1, 2021.

"Def Jam at 30: MCA & Burzootie's Drum Machine." *Cornell University Hip Hop Library* (NY), 2014.

Deiterman, Corey. "Rap-Metal Is Back...and Its Good." *Houston Press* (TX), May 27, 2014.

Delmonico, Veronica. "Anthrax and Public Enemy Bring the Noise." *The National Student,* May 2013.

Denselow, Robin. "Cave's Gloomy View: Malcolm McLaren." *The Guardian* (UK), May 24, 1984.

DeRogatis, Jim. "Whitey Sings the Blues." *Penthouse,* March 2001.

Deters, Alexandria. "Wild Style 40 — An Interview with Curator Carlo McCormick." *Up Magazine,* Fall 2023.

Devenish, Colin. *Rage Against the Machine.* St. Martin's Griffin, 2001.

Diamond, Yaya. "Planet Rock and Beyond: A Conversation with Hip Hop Icon Afrika Bambaataa." *NewsBreak,* July 30, 2023.

Dibbell, Julian. "House of Pain Jump Around." *Details,* June 1992.

Dillon, Nancy and Kerry Burke. "Rest in Beast: MCA Dies at 47." *Daily News* (NY), May 5, 2012.

Dolan, Jon, ed. *Rolling Stone: The 500 Greatest Albums of All Time.* Abrams Books, 2022.

Dollar, Steve. "Hey, Hey We're the Beasties." *Pensacola News-Journal* (FL), May 4, 1987.

Doran, John. "Bill Laswell Interviewed: Bass. How Low Can You Go." *The Quietus,* July 15, 2009.

Downer, Sorrel. "Clubbing with Caveman." *Evening Standard* (UK), April 5, 1991.

Dubasik, Zac. "Interview: Run-DMC Talks Adidas." *Complex,* August 2, 2013.

Ducker, Jesse. "Examining Young Black Teenagers' Self-Titled Debut Album, 30 Years after its Release." *Medium,* February 20, 2021.

Du Lac, J. Freedom. "Meet the Song Doctor." *Washington Post,* February 5, 2006.

Du Lac, J. Freedom. "Nothing Beastie About Them." *Sacramento Bee* (CA), November 27, 1994.

Dunlevy, T'Cha. "Beastie Boys: Rolling Stones of Rap." *Montreal Gazette* (QUE), November 6, 2004.

Earls, John. "Blondie Interview: 'Innovation Is Probably our Greatest Strength.'" *Classic Pop* (UK), November 8, 2022.

BIBLIOGRAPHY

Edgers, Geoff. "Breaking Down the Wall." *Slate,* February 6, 2019.

Edgers, Geoff. "More Than 30 years After Their Split, Rick Rubin and the Beastie Boys (Almost) Open Up." *Washington Post,* June 22, 2020.

Edgers, Geoff. "The Collaboration That Altered Music and Popular Culture." *Washington Post,* May 18, 2016.

Edgers, Geoff. *Walk This Way: Run-DMC, Aerosmith, and the Song that Changed American Music Forever.* Blue Rider Press, 2019.

Edwards, Gavin. "Beck's *Odelay*: The Secret History." *Rolling Stone,* February 21, 2008.

Ehrlich, Dimitri. "Beastie Boys Career — One Long Punch Line." *Orlando Sentinel* (FL), August 12, 1994.

Eiserike, Josh. "Mike Doughty's New Album Delicious." *Manassas Journal Messenger* (VA), March 13, 2008.

Ellis, Bill. "Recordings." *Commercial Appeal* (TN), May 16, 1998.

Erskine, Evelyn. "Rock: Beastie Boys." *Ottawa Citizen* (CAN), August 11, 1989.

Ethington, Tommie and Matt Barnard. "Stay Gold, Danny Boy." *Rolling Stone,* November 5, 2021.

Ettelson, Robbie. "Interview: Tuff City's Aaron Fuchs." *Red Bull Academy,* November 26, 2015.

Ettelson, Robbie. "T La Rock Interview Pt 1: The Story of "It's Yours." *Unkut,* June 23, 2008.

Ettelson, Robbie. "The Triumphs and Tragedies of Larry Smith." *Medium,* October 15, 2014.

Ettelson, Robbie. "Tommy Silverman: The Unkut Interview." *Unkut,* August 24, 2015.

Eustice, Kyle. "Def Jam: More Than a Label (Part 1)." *Daily Double,* June 29, 2023.

Eustice, Kyle. "Onyx Talks 30 Years of "Slam." *Rock the Bells,* April 6, 2023.

Eustice, Kyle. "Run-DMC Is Over." *Rock the Bells,* January 21, 2023.

Eustice, Kyle. "Sex Pistols' John Lydon Speaks on Afrika Bambaataa Allegations and Rap-Rock Incarnation." *Hip Hop DX,* February 17, 2017.

Everingham, Henry. "Rock: Malcolm McLaren." *Sydney Morning Herald* (AUS), June 25, 1984.

Everson, John. "Vince Neil: Soulful Soundtracks." *Southtown Star* (IL), October 12, 1995.

Every, Dave. "Ten Rap-Metal Bands That Time Forgot." *Metal Hammer* (UK), August 23, 2021.

Fab 5 Freddy. "Futura with Fab 5 Freddy." *Art in the Streets,* 2020.

Farber, Jim. "Luscious Jackson Carries Beasties Burden." *Daily News* (NY), August 28, 1994.

Farber, Jim. "Wheels on A Bus: Loud Rocks." *Daily News* (NY), September 3, 2000.

BIBLIOGRAPHY

Farberman, Brad. "How Rick Rubin Connected Beastie Boys with the Heavy Metal Scene While Recording *Licensed to Ill.*" *Genius,* November 15, 2016.

Ferman, Dave. "A Parents Guide to Rip-Hop." *Fort Worth Star-Telegram* (TX), October 19, 1999.

Ferraro, Mat. "Beastie Boys Ad-Rock and Mike D Look Back on Their Once Misunderstood Classic Paul's Boutique." *Interview,* August 15, 2019.

Ferrero, Robert. "Darryl 'DMC' McDaniels Interview: A Rich Past and a Meaningful Present." *NJArts.net* (NJ), December 28, 2020.

Ferris, D.X. "Everlast: Emmy-nominated Rap-Rock Pioneer Discusses Getting His Groove Back." *Cleveland Scene* (OH), September 10, 2008.

Ferris, D.X. Slayer's *Reign in Blood 33 1/3 series.* Continuum/Bloomsbury Academic, 2008.

Ferrucci, Anthony. "Bosstones, Mercury Mates, Blast the Roof Off Marquee Theater." *Record-Journal* (CT), October 19, 1993.

Fielding, Julien R. "Downset: Changing Music, the World." *Daily Nonpareil* (IA), October 5, 2000.

Finney, Patricia. "Hip-Hop Hooray." *Evening Standard* (UK), June 29, 1984.

Fitsch, Chris. "Rap and Rock Have a Perfect Marriage on Loud Rocks." *Record-Journal* (CT), September 28, 2000.

Fitzgerald, Trent. "30 Years Later: Run-DMC's King of Rock Album Delivers a Bold Statement." *Boombox,* January 21, 2015.

Fletcher, Tony. "Hometown Boys Bring the Noise to the Ritz." *Newsday* (NY), September 28, 1991.

Fontaine, Dick. *Beat This: A Hip Hop History.* BBC, 1984.

Foster, Jason. "Express Yourself: Downset." *San Bernardino County Sun* (CA), February 28, 1997.

Fox, Katrina. *Official Blondie Website,* "Interview with Jimmy Destri." *Official Blondie Website,* August 2003.

Fraser, Kirk, director. *Kings from Queens: The Run-DMC Story.* Peacock, 2024.

Freydkin, Donna. "Everlast: Took a Licking, Kept on Ticking." *CNN.com,* August 3, 1999.

Fricke, David. "Immaterial Girl." *Melody Maker* (UK), June 22, 1985.

Fruchter, Alexander. "Dante Ross on His New Book: I Got Something That Will Preserve My Place in the Culture." *Rock The Bells,* May 22, 2023.

Futch, Michael. "The First Rap Record Came from Fayetteville's Bill Curtis and His Fatback Band." *Fayetteville Observer* (NC), March 7, 2020.

Futura, with Larry Warsh. *Futura-isms.* Princeton University Press, 2021.

G, Lucas. "Sevendust Frontman Lajon Witherspoon Talks Strange Visit & Recording Experience." *Strange Music,* February 22, 2017.

Gaudiosi, Jeff. "A Conversation with Darryl McDaniels of Run-DMC." *Misplaced Straws,* February 15, 2022.

Gee, Andre. "Legendary Producer Keith Shocklee on Being Part of Hip-Hop's Pre-History." *Rolling Stone,* May 14, 2023.

BIBLIOGRAPHY

GNS. "Album Review: Loud Rocks." *The Leaf-Chronicle* (TN), September 8, 2000.

Gold, Jonathan. "Record Rack: Rhyme the Beastie Way." *Los Angeles Times*, July 23, 1989.

Gorman, Paul. "Beat This: A Hip-Hop History: Malcolm McLaren Taken By Michael Holman to the Zulu Nation in August 1981." *PaulGorman.com*, 2024.

Graff, Gary. "Beastie Boys All Grown Up — Almost." *Akron Beacon Journal* (OH), June 2, 1992.

Graff, Gary. "Rah! Rah! Rock." *Detroit Free Press* (MI), January 12, 1992.

Graff, Gary. "Still Fighting the Power." *Salt Lake City Tribune* (UT), October 11, 1991.

Gray, W. Blake. "Beastly: Beastie Boys Take the Revolting Route." *Tampa Tribune* (FL), February 20, 1987.

Green, Amy and Jerry Granelli. "Sometimes You Just Gotta Shut Down." *Salon*, May 1995.

Grierson, Tim. "Rap-Rock and Its Hip-Hop Origins." *LiveAbout.com*, April 12, 2019.

Gross, Terry. "'Fresh Air' Celebrates 50 years of Hip-Hop: Run-DMC's Darryl McDaniels." *NPR*, August 29, 2023.

Grow, Kory. "Hear Ill Bill's Boom-Bap Tribute to Exodus Singer Paul Baloff." *Spin*, February 13, 2013.

Grow, Kory. "Rick Rubin: My Life in 21 Songs." *Rolling Stone*, February 11, 2016.

Gundersen, Edna. "Linkin Park's Music a Hybrid of Brains, Rap, Metal, Melody." *Asbury Park Press* (NJ), March 26, 2002.

Gutfeld, Greg. "The Five." *Fox News*, August 21, 2016.

Guzman, Isaac. "Beck's Odelay a Sweet Return." *Bellingham Herald* (WA), August 1, 1996.

Hafflon, Scott. "Bloodhound Gang." *Lollipop Magazine*, February 1, 1997.

Hagar, Steven. *Hip Hop: The Illustrated History of Break Dancing. Rap and Graffiti*. St. Martin's Press, 1984.

Haidari, Niloufar. "It's Been Over Two Decades and Everyone Is Still Wrong About Limp Bizkit." *Noisey/Vice*, August 6, 2021.

Halada, James. "Fight for Your Right to Party Again." *Seattle Rocket* (WA), May 11, 1994.

Ham, Robert. "Fred Durst Slams People Who Call Limp Bizkit 'Jock Rock'." *Revolver*, April 11, 2023.

Hamersly, Michael. "DMC McDaniels Looks Back Before Taking Stage." *Miami Herald* (FL), March 20, 2015.

Hanson, E. Scott. "Luscious Jackson Sweet As Honey." *Columbia Daily Tribune* (MO), July 18, 1999.

Haring, Bruce. "Bad Boys From New York Make Good." *Courier-News* (NJ), July 14, 1984.

BIBLIOGRAPHY

Hart, Ron. *Observer* (UK), "The Punk History Behind Beastie Boys' *Licensed to Ill.*" *Observer* (UK), November 11, 2016.

"Hate 'Em Or Love 'Em: Downset." *Burlington Free Press* (VT), January 19, 1995.

Hatfield, Amanda. "Sick of It All Suing Mobb Deep Over Supreme Collaboration." *Brooklyn Vegan* (NY), October 17, 2023.

Hay, Travis. "Interview Transcript: A Conversation with Chris Cornell." *Guerrilla Candy*, October 14, 2005.

Heath, Chris. "Pop: Public Enemy/Anthrax." *Sunday Telegraph* (UK), January 5, 1992.

Heller, Greg. "Cake's Head Baker." *Rolling Stone*, October 10, 2001.

Hempel, Paul. "Beastie Boys Act the Part." *St. Louis Post-Dispatch* (MO), February 18, 1987.

Henke, James. "Record Reviews: Time Zone." *Fort Lauderdale News* (FL), December 21, 1984.

Hermes, Will. *Spin*, "Storm Windows: Massive Attack See Through A Glass Darkly." *Spin*, March 2003.

Hernandez, William. "Sticky Finger of Onyx." *Who Mag*, 2004.

Hilburn, Robert. "Getting Beck to the Future." *Los Angeles Times*, February 12, 2008.

Hill, Stephen. "Ice-T on Metal." *Metal Hammer* (UK), May 19, 2023.

Hill, Stephen. "*Judgment Night*: The Story of the Greatest Rap-Rock Soundtrack Album of the 90s." *Metal Hammer* (UK), May 16, 2022.

Hillburn, Robert. "Arthur Baker Changes Music with Mixed Results." *Journal Herald* (OH), September 1, 1984.

Hillburn, Robert. "Rap: More Than Public Enemy's Future at Stake with New Album." *Minneapolis Star Tribune* (MN), February 18, 1990.

Hillburn, Robert. "Taking Stock of a Grim Period in Rock." *Salt Lake City Tribune* (UT), July 16, 1994.

Hilleary, Mike. "That's a Record." *MikeHilleary.com*, May 10, 2017.

Hinckley, David. "Afrika Bambaataa: The Force Is with Him." *Daily News* (NY), July 3, 1984.

Hinckley, David. "The Birth of a 'Nation'." *Daily News* (NY), February 25, 2005.

Hinckley, David. "To Be Young, Gifted, and, Well, Hip." *Daily News* (NY), January 15, 1991.

Hinson, Mark. "Rap Around the Clock: The Music for the 80s." *Tallahassee Democrat*, July 31, 1987.

Hirschberg, Lynn. "The Music Man: Rick Rubin." *New York Times Magazine*, September 2, 2007.

Hirst, Andrew. "Beyond The Beat: Paul's Boutique." *Hudderfield Daily Examiner* (UK), August 5, 1989.

Hobbs, Thomas. "How Today's Rappers Are Resurrecting the Spirit of Punk." *BBC*, October 16, 2019.

BIBLIOGRAPHY

Hochman, Steve. "Various Artists: Loud Rocks." *Los Angeles Times,* September 15, 2000.

Holden, Kameelah. "Jay-Z/Linkin Park CD Combines Unique Sounds." *Courier-Post* (NJ), February 22, 2005.

Holden, Stephen. "The Pop Life: Malcolm McLaren." *New York Times,* July 26, 1989.

Hoochman, Steve. "The Aftermath of Public Enemy's Collapse." *Los Angeles Times,* July 16, 1989.

Hope, Rachel. "Who Is Rick Rubin? Is He a Hip-Hop Renegade, Creativity Catalyst or Hindrance?" *Sound of Life,* March 4, 2023.

Horn, John. "NWA: Not for the Faint of Ears." *Sacramento Bee* (CA), June 21, 1991.

Horn, Trevor. "Key Tracks: Trevor Horn on "Buffalo Gals." *Red Bull Academy,* January 31, 2013.

Horne, Jerry. "Exclusive Charlie Benantte Interview." *Twin Peaks Archives,* April 2008.

Horvit, Mark. "Hack Job: Soul Coughing Cuts Through Pop Boundaries." *Columbia Daily Tribune* (MO), August 11, 1996.

Hsu, Hua. "Ad-Rock Just Wants to Be Friends." *New Yorker,* May 24, 2020.

Huffman, Eddie. "Pop Life." *Durham Herald-Sun* (NC), June 25, 1992.

Hunter, Asondra. "Dr. Dre." *Seconds,* #41, 1996.

"Interview with Doug Pomeroy." *Beastiemania.com,* March 2004.

"In Tune: Rage Against The Machine." *Daily Press* (VA), December 11, 1992.

Isenberg, Daniel. "DJ Muggs Tells All." *Complex,* January 26, 2013.

Itzkoff, Dave/NYT. "A Crisis for Insane Clown Posse." *Montreal Gazette* (QUE), December 10, 2013.

Ives, Brian. "Judgment Night: A Hip-Hop/Rock Hybrid That Still Resonates." *Loudwire,* September 14, 2018.

Jasmin, Ernest. "Kottonmouth Kings Get Ready to Play High Notes." *News Tribune* (WA), July 30, 2004.

Jenkins, Craig. "We Were Obsessed: Linkin Park's Mike Shinoda." *Vulture,* April 3, 2023.

Johnson, Eric. "24-7 Spyz: The Raw Bronx Sound." *The Missoulian* (MT), October 6, 1989.

Johnson, Tommy. "A Bit of Savoir-Faire: An Interview with Mike Doughty." *Ghettoblaster,* October 28, 2020.

Jones, Lucy. "12 Reasons Why Rick Rubin's An Almighty Badass." *New Musical Express* (UK), August 1, 2013.

Jones, Steve. "Loud Rocks Vy Various Artists." *Green Bay Press-Gazette* (WI), September 14, 2000.

Jonez, Johnny. "The Story Behind Anthrax and Public Enemy's 'Bring the Noise.'" *Rap Reviews,* January 31, 2021.

Jordan, Chris. "It All Started Here: Dog Eat Dog Sweeps Europe." *Hackensack Record* (NJ), August 16, 1996.

BIBLIOGRAPHY

Juon, Steve "Flash". "Rage Against the Machine: Evil Empire." *Rap Reviews,* July 4, 2023.

Kalu, Nnana. "Russell Simmons Produces Film on the Life of Legendary Rapper T La Rock." *The Source,* October 23, 2017.

Kangas, Chaz. "Hip-Hop at 50: The Pioneers." *The Current,* August 8, 2023.

Kaplan, C.J. and Match Blum. *"Beastie Boys, Licensed to Ill."* Exile on Newbury Street, August 23, 2023.

Karas, Matty. "24-7 Spyz' Punk Music Uncontainable." *Asbury Park Press* (NJ), August 24, 1990.

Kelp, Larry. "Records: *Paul's Boutique.*" *Oakland Tribune,* August 13, 1989.

Kemp, Mark. "Beck: Where It's at Now." *Rolling Stone,* April 17, 1997.

Kening, Dan. "Music: Concert Line: Shootyz Groove." *Chicago Tribune* (IL), August 5, 1994.

Kenney, Shawna. "Brooklyn's Biohazard: Exclusive Interview." *American University Eagle,* September 5, 1994.

Keyes, Bob. "Bloodhound Gang Has Fun with Pop." *Argus-Leader* (SD), December 4, 1997.

Keyes, Bob. "Bride Not Married to Its Heavy Past." *Argus-Leader* (SD), August 5, 1993.

Kielty, Martin. "Why Vince Neil's So Career Stalled with *Carved in Stone.*" *Ultimate Classic Rock,* September 12, 2018.

Kinghorn, Peter. "Pop Music: Caveman." *Evening Chronicle* (UK), March 9, 1991.

Klosterman, Chuck. "Reviews: Slaves to the Grind." *Spin,* December 2002.

Knight-Ridder Services "Music Reviews: *Loud Rocks.*" *Anderson Independent-Mail* (IN), September 24, 2000.

Knopper, Steve. "Beastie Brats." *Spokesman-Review* (WA), June 21, 1992.

Kootter, Kelly-Jane. "Rage Against the Machine: The Naked Truth." *Central New Jersey Home News* (NJ), November 26, 1993.

Kot, Greg. "Public Enemy: Popular Music's Most Feared Group." *Hamilton Spectator* (CAN), September 13, 1990.

Kot, Greg. "Rave Recordings." *Chicago Tribune* (IL), August 3, 1989.

Kramer, Bruce. "*Judgment Night* Soundtrack Merged Rock and Hip-Hop 30 Years Ago." *Pop Matters,* August 22, 2023.

Krewen, Nick. "Portishead Dummy." *Montreal Gazette* (QUE), December 23, 1995.

Lambert, Yon. "It Came from the Bronx." *The State* (SC), February 21, 1997.

Lane, Barnaby. "Here Are 10 Times Rap and Rock Have Crossed Over Before." *Business Insider,* February 28, 2023.

Lang, George. "Event Draws Hip-Hop Pioneers Run-DMC." *Daily Oklahoman* (OK), June 8, 2001.

Lanham, Tom. "Smug and Rude Are the Boys in the Nude." *San Francisco Examiner,* January 12, 1986.

BIBLIOGRAPHY

Lasher, Grant. "Raging Where Others Die." *Boca Raton News* (FL), March 19, 1993.

Lawrence, Tim. *Life and Death on the New York Dance Floor, 1980–1983*. Duke University Press, 2016.

Lawson, Dom. "Dave Mustaine Talks About the Nu-Metal Years." *Metal Hammer* (UK), July 14, 2024.

Lawton, Adam. "Interview with Biohazard's Billy Graziadei & Danny Schuler." *Media Mikes,* December 29, 2011.

Leach, Dan. "The Birth of a Culture: Wildstyle Director Charlie Ahearn Talks." *Ransom Note*, February 3, 2021.

Lecaro, Lina. "Linkin Park's Rap N Rock." *Los Angeles Times,* February 1, 2001.

Leininger, Merrie. "Kottonmouth Kings Are Smokers, but Not Jokers." *Reno Gazette-Journal* (NV).

Leland, John. "Armageddon in Effect." *Spin,* September 1988.

Leland, John. "Hell Raisin." *Spin,* August 1986.

LePage, Mark. "Pop Music: Rage Against the Machine." *Montreal Gazette* (QUE), December 5, 1992.

LeRoy, Dan. *The Beastie Boys' Paul's Boutique (33 1/3)*. Continuum Books, 2006.

Licht, Alan. "An Oral History of the Beastie Boys: The Story of Yo." *Spin,* September 1998.

Linn, Sarah. "Once Just a Man, Now a King." *The Tribune* (CA), April 7, 2011.

Louis, Steven. "I Just Want to Make Music with My Middle Finger Up: An Interview with DJ Muggs." *Passion of The Weiss,* August 14, 2018.

Ma, David. "The Making of T La Rock's It's Yours." *Passion of The Weiss,* November 6, 2020.

Ma, David. "When He Ruled the World: The Kurtis Blow Interview." January 17, 2018.

Macias, Chris. "Kings of Rock N Rap." *Sacramento Bee* (CA), October 17, 1999.

Macias, Chris and Steve Appleford. "The Sweet Sounds of Cake." *Sacramento Bee* (CA), August 12, 2001.

Mackie, John. "A Night of Loud Music and Insane Antics." *Vancouver Sun* (CAN), October 26, 1991.

MacQueen, Steve. "Believe the Hype: PE Has Powerful Rap." *Tallahassee Democrat*, October 13, 1989.

Malkin, Maya. "The Success & Controversy of Hip-Hop's Sylvia Robinson." *Record Arts Canada*, July 28, 2022.

Maness, Carter. "Local Boys Made It Big with Ill Skills." *Daily News* (NY), May 5, 2012.

Mao, Jeff. "Mario Caldao, Jr." *Red Bull Academy,* 2008.

Marker, Mark. "Biohazard Interview with Bobby Hambel." *Rank & Revue*, April 11, 2013.

BIBLIOGRAPHY

Martin, Dale. "Vince Neil Takes Different Route on Solo Effort." *Victoria Advocate* (TX), September 24, 1995.
Martinez, Anthony. "Videography: Bride." *Classic Christian Rock*, April 11, 2015.
Masuo, Sandy. "LA's Downset Shows It's Up to Meeting Hard-Core Task." *Los Angeles Times*, March 3, 1997.
Matami, Jo. "Glenn Danzig Explains How Things Got Weird Between Him and Rick Rubin." *Ultimate Guitar*, January 5, 2019.
Matami, Jo. "Wes Borland Speaks on Limp Bizkit Tragedy, How It Led Him to Say 'Fuck You' to Bandmates and Quit." *Ultimate Guitar*, June 29, 2021.
Mayfield, Ricardo. "UTFO Is Wow!" *Rap Explosion*, Spring 1989.
Mayhew, Don. "Good Reasons We Use Categories for Pop Music." *Fresno Bee* (CA), January 9, 1994.
McCartney, Kelly. "Five Questions: Michael Franti." *KellyMcCartney.com*, November 5, 2014.
McCollum, Brian. "Kid Rock Before the Fame: The Definitive Detroit Oral History." *Detroit Free Press* (MI), August 6, 2015.
McCormick, Carlo. "Dondi White." *Interview* March 1992.
McCormick, Carlo. "Schoolly D: Killin' Time." *Seconds*, #7, 1988.
McDonnell, Evelyn. "Endo's Emo-Metal Evokes A World of Intensity, Angst." *Miami Herald* (FL), April 22, 2001.
McIver, Joel. "The Story Behind the Song: Bring the Noise by Anthrax and Public Enemy." *Metal Hammer* (UK), November 19, 2020.
McKinnon, Matthew. "When We Were Ruthless: An Interview with Jerry Heller." February 17, 2015.
McLennan, Scott. "Mike Chapman, Aussie Production King of the 1970s." *I Like Your Old Stuff*, April 7, 2020.
McMahon, James. "Korn's Jonathan Davis: 'I Have the Remains of at Least Seven People in My House.'" *NME*, September 13, 2019.
McShane, Larry. "Rock, Rap Collide to Make 'Noise.'" *Glens Falls Post-Star* (NY), August 29, 1991.
Means, Andrew. "The Boys in the Band." *Arizona Republic* (AZ), February 10, 1987.
Meeker, Ward. "Billy Squier: Recollections, Guitar Collection." *Vintage Guitar*, August 2006.
Menking, Lauren. "KXT Interview: Beck." *KXT.com*, October 23, 2017.
Merrell, Heather. "Bloodhound Gang Leaves Fans Howling for More." *Scranton Tribune* (PA), May 2, 1997.
Mervis, Scott. "Soul Survivor: Mike Doughty." *Pittsburgh Post-Gazette* (PA), April 10, 2006.
MF, Eric. "Interview: Downset." *Modern Fix*, January 24, 2012.
Miller, Debby. "Run-DMC Album Review." *Rolling Stone*, August 30, 1984.
Miller, Michael. "New Releases: Massive Attack." *The State* (SC), November 1, 1991.

BIBLIOGRAPHY

Mize, Cole. "History of Rap: The True Origins of Hip-Hop." *Cole Mize Studios*, September 23, 2014.

Monroe Montana, Marilyn. "The Fat Boys Are Phat!" *Rap!*, #2, 1987.

Moody, Nekesa Mumbi. "Linkin Park Follows Up Debut Album." *Ithaca Journal* (NY), March 20, 2003.

Moon, Tom. "24-7 Spyz, Follow for Now at TLA." *Philadelphia Inquirer* (PA), December 16, 1991.

Moon, Tom. "Beck Goes Back to Vintage Soul and Funk." *Philadelphia Inquirer* (PA), November 21, 1999.

Moon, Tom. "New Recordings: Beastie Boys Ill Communication." *Philadelphia Inquirer* (PA), June 5, 1994.

Moon, Tom. "New Recordings: Rewarding Beastie Boys." *Philadelphia Inquirer* (PA), April 26, 1992.

Moorhouse, Don. "It Is All About Madness." *Record-Journal* (CT), March 5, 1998.

Morris, Keith. "Soul Coughing Springs Into Action." *Daily Progress* (VA), April 16, 1999.

Morrison, John. "Interview: Arthur Baker on 'Planet Rock' and Disco Remixes." *Reverb*, April 13, 2021.

Morse, Steve. "Anthrax, Public Enemy Deliver a Night of Rock, Rap & Rage." *Boston Globe* (MA), September 26, 1991.

Mosley, Tonya. "'Fresh Air' Celebrates 50 Years of Hip-Hop: Rapper Melle Mel." *NPR*, August 28, 2023.

MTV Staff. "Public Enemy Makes Noise with Anthrax: This Week in 1991." *MTV.com*, June 21, 2002.

Mugan, Chris. "Rebels Without a Pause." *Independent* (UK), August 5, 2005.

Muldoon, David. "Check This Out: Beasties Find New Beat." *Boca Raton News* (FL), May 1, 1992.

Mullinax, Gary. "Pop Music: Blondie Goes with Latest Trend, Part Way at Least." *Morning News* (DEL), December 7, 1980.

Munson, Kyle. "Beats, Rhymes Dominate Dot Com 3." *Des Moines Register* (IA), June 13, 1999.

Murray, Robin. "Explore the Clash Link with Graffiti Artist Futura." *ClashMusic.com*, May 19, 2022.

Murray, Robin. "Hip-Hop and Punk Rock Is Brother and Sister!." *ClashMusic.com*, October 12, 2022.

Myers, Marc. "The Rap in Blondie's 'Rapture'." *Wall Street Journal*, June 10, 2019.

Nash, Pete (3rd Bass). "Interview by Steven Blush." August 6, 2024.

Nelson, Havelock. "Immortal/Epic Ready to Pass 'Judgment.'" *Billboard*, August 14, 1993.

Nicholson, Rip. "Hurts So Good: House of Pain Are Back." *Street Press* (AUS), Issue #1057, April 8, 2011.

BIBLIOGRAPHY

Noise, Jeff. "Music Reviews: Cake – Comfort Eagle (Columbia)." *Hybrid Magazine*, November 17, 2001.

O'Brien, Glenn. "The Story of Glenn O'Brien." *Noisey/Vice*, November 14, 2014.

O'Hare, Kevin. "Simmering, Summering, Hammering." *St. Louis Post-Dispatch* (MO), July 28, 1994.

Oseran, Anna. "How the Dust Brothers Saved Beck from Becoming a One-Hit Wonder with *Odelay*." *Pitchfork*, June 17, 2016.

Owen, Frank. "Christmas with Attitude." *Newsday* (NY), April 26, 1993.

Oz, Diamond. "An Interview with Death-Rapper Necro." *Metal Underground*, September 27, 2007.

Oz, Diamond. "Legendary Rapper DMC Discusses His Love of Metal." *Metal Underground*, August 14, 2018.

Palmer, Robert. "Can't Stop Afrika Bambaataa." *Myrtle Beach Sun-News* (SC), January 27, 1984.

Paltrowitz, Darren. "Judgment Night: The Soundtrack That Blew Up Pop Music." *Please Kill Me*, September 25, 2018.

Paltrowitz, Darren. "Living Colour's Vernon Reid on the *Judgment Night* Soundtrack and Working with Run-DMC." *Hype Magazine*, August 22, 2018.

Paltrowitz, Darren. "Michael McKeegan of Therapy? on the *Judgment Night* Soundtrack." *Hype Magazine*, August 23, 2018.

Pareles, Jon. "Rock: The Beastie Boys, Rap-Metal Group." *New York Times*, December 29, 1986.

Parker, Lyndsey. "The Private Life of Public Image Ltd: John Lydon Talks Childhood Illness, Marriage, and 'Butter Wars'." *Yahoo*, September 8, 2015.

Pasinski, Jim. "Mohegan Sun Gets Political with Prophets of Rage." *Record-Journal* (CT), September 1, 2016.

Pavitt, Bruce. "Sub Pop: A Guide to US Independents: Lone Rager." *Seattle Rocket* (WA), November 1, 1984.

Peacock, Tim. "'Scream': It's Time to Shout About Chris Cornell's Timbaland Collaboration." *U Discover Music*, March 10, 2024.

Pearlman, Nina. "Luscious Jackson Interview." *Seattle Rocket* (WA), January 29, 1997.

Pelton, Tristan Michael. "Public Enemy." *Black Past*, June 16, 2007.

Perez, Gregory. "Ill Will." *Tampa Bay Times* (FL), July 22, 1994.

Pervert, Metal. "Weird Tales of Metal: Lone Rage "Metal Rap."" *Impenetrable Sphere of Power*, May 1, 2016.

Pessaro, Fred. "Let's Get Real with Cypress Hill's B-Real." *Riot Fest* (IL), September 15, 2018.

Phull, Hardeep. "Def Jam's Wild Early Days: An Oral History." *New York Post*, October 11, 2014.

Pick, Steve. "On the Singles Scene: Onyx." *St. Louis Post-Dispatch* (MO), July 9, 1993.

BIBLIOGRAPHY

Pollack, Scott. "De La Soul." *Seconds*, #41, 1996.
Pollack, Scott. "Raekwon." *Seconds*, #35, 1995.
Pond, Steve. "A Rap with the Kings of Rock." *Los Angeles Times*, September 30, 1985.
Powell, Ricky. "Dust Brothers." *Seconds*, #42, 1997.
Powell, Ricky. "Eazy-E: Chronic Killer." *Seconds*, #24, 1994.
Prato, Greg. "Anthrax Drummer Charlie Benante Discusses the Band's Most Underrated Song, Flavor Flav's Drumming Skills, and How He Feels About Making Music Videos." *EddieTrunk.com*, May 9, 2017.
Prato, Greg. "Run-DMC Thought "Walk This Way" Would Ruin Them; Instead It Saved Aerosmith." *Classic Rock,* January 19, 2023.
Pratt, Tim. "Definitive Electronic Albums." *Detroit Free Press* (MI), May 21, 2000.
"Public Enemy, Anthrax to Appear at SIU Arena." *Paducah Sun* (KY), October 2, 1991.
Quan, Jay. "How Planet Rock Gave Birth to a New Sub-Genre." *Rock the Bells*, April 17, 2023.
Quan, Jay. "Run-DMC: Four Songs That Changed the Game." *Rock The Bells*, July 18, 2023.
Quan, Jay. "Rev Run: LL Cool J Remembers Ad Rock Gave Him His Break." *Rock the Bells*, July 21, 2022.
Quan, Jay. "Rev Run: My Favorite Place to Record Was DMC's Basement." *Rock the Bells*, October 5, 2022.
Questlove. "LL Cool J Part 1." *iHeart.com*, November 22, 2023.
Questlove. "Questlove's Top 50 Hip-Hop Songs of All Time." *Rolling Stone*, December 17, 2012.
Quinn, Martha. "'No Sleep Til Brooklyn' News Report." *MTV,* 1986.
Rafaeli, J. S. "We Spoke to Afrika Bambaataa About Hip-Hop and Futurism." *Vice*, December 2, 2014.
Ramble, Paul. *The Face*, "Rogue's Progress: Malcolm McLaren at Large." *The Face*, June 1983.
"Rap, Thrash Combine for Evening of Noise." *Statesman Journal* (OR), October 18, 1991.
Rasen, Edward. "Rap N Roll." *Spin*, May 1985.
Raw, Son. "Black Sunday at 30: Interview with Sen Dog of Cypress Hill." *Passion of The Weiss*, July 10, 2023.
Ray, Ray. "Huey of the Fun Lovin' Criminals." *Guitarist* (UK), July 15, 2001.
Reid, Graham. "Afrika Bambaataa Interviewed: The Shape of Things Hip-Hop and Political to Come?" *Elsewhere* (NZ), 1988.
Reid, Graham. "Caveman: I'm Ready (1991)." *Elsewhere* (NZ), November 15, 2012.
Reiff, Corbin. "DMC on the Enduring Links Between Rock and Hip Hop." *Uproxx*, March 20, 2018.
Reiss, Randy. "Kid Rock Raps with the Devil." *MTV News*, August 18, 1998.

BIBLIOGRAPHY

Renolds, Simon. "Pop View: Another City, Another New Sound." *New York Times*, May 28, 1995.

Reynolds, Simon. "Chuck D: The Enemy Strikes Black." *Melody Maker* (UK), October 12, 1991.

Rice, Frazier. "Billy Squier: From MTV Damnation to Rap Rejuvenation." *FrazierRice.com*, November 20, 2013.

"Rick Rubin Describes Creative Process Behind Eminem's Berzerk." *Eminem.com*, October 6, 2013.

Rindels, Jeff. "New Beastie Boys Album Assaults Your Senses with Punk and Rap." *Waterloo Courier* (IA), October 19, 1994.

Rivers, Byron. "A Luscious Sound." *Palm Beach Post* (FL), September 26, 1997.

Rizzo, Frank. "Beastie Horovitz Says He's Tired of the Hassles." *Hartford Courant* (CT), April 25, 1987.

Robb, John. "Massive Attack: The John Robb Interview." *Louder Than A Bomb*, April 8, 2021.

Robb, John. "Massive Attack: Wild at Heart." *Sounds* (UK), April 6, 1991.

Robbins, Ira. "Inscribed in Rock: Jimi Hazel's Mt. Rushmore." *Trouser Press*, December 15, 2022.

Robins, Wayne. "Taking the Rap to America." *Newsday* (NY), October 20, 1985.

Robinson, Lisa. "Beasties Rap to a Metal Beat." *New York Post*, June 7, 1985.

Robinson, Mark. "Read on: Be Grateful Once More." *Reno Gazette-Journal* (NV), October 31, 2003.

Roland, Tom, Rick Yampert, and Jay Orr. "River Stages Transforms City." *The Tennessean* (TN), May 1, 1999.

Romano, Andrew. "Rick Rubin on Crashing Kanye's Album in 15 Days." *Newsweek*, June 27, 2013.

Rosario, Fernando (Smashed Gladys). "Interview by Tony Mann." February 6, 2024.

Roswell, Clint. "1980 Marks Rebirth of Rock but Death of Lennon." *Daily News* (NY), December 28, 1980.

Roth, Jason and Adrienne D'Amato. "Press Release: Inside the January Issue." *Spin*, January 2000.

Ryan, James. "Fat Boys: A 1,000-Pound Success Story." *Daily Republican-Register* (IL), September 4, 1987.

Saccone, Teri. "The Signat: Bobby Chouinard." *Modern Drummer*, November 1985.

Said, Amir. "John King and the Story of Chung King Studios." *Beat Tips*, November 27, 2017.

Sanders, Jonathan. "The Substance and the Light: An Interview with Mike Doughty." *Pop Matters*, February 18, 2013.

Sanneh, Kelefa. "Rappers Who Definitely Know How to Rock." *New York Times*, December 3, 2000.

BIBLIOGRAPHY

Sarachick, Justin. "A Dream of Jesus Planted the Seed to Cast Out Marz's Own Demons." *Rapzilla,* October 13, 2017.
Sauer, Patrick J. "The Worst & Most Captivating of Run-DMC, According to DMC." *Vulture,* Saturday 1, 2023.
Saunders, Jessica. "Beastie Boys, Run-DMC Fight to Party." *Florida Today* (FL), August 8, 1987.
Sawyer, Miranda. "Beastie Boys: Being in a Band Is An Absurd Comedy." *The Guardian* (UK), October 21, 2018.
Schelkopf, Eric. "Kottonmouth Kings: Kings of The Road." *Northwest Herald* (IL), October 28, 2005.
Schmidt, Torsten. "Hank Shocklee." *Red Bull Academy,* 2005.
Schultz, Bret. "Soul Coughing Thrilled to Play Lincoln." *Daily Nebraskan* (NE), February 22, 1999.
Sculley, Alan. "Provoking An Exchange." *Detroit Free Press* (MI), September 1, 2016.
Sculley, Alan. "Rappin' and Rockin' in Linkin Park." *Capital Times* (WI), January 31, 2002.
Seiler, Casey. "Beasties Toss Rap, Funk and Grunge Into New Mix." *Jackson Hole Guide* (WY), June 24, 1992.
Sent, Rob and Jonathan Palmer. "Tracks: Bulletins, Blasts, News." *Louisville Courier-Journal,* January 2, 1993.
Shaw, Ted. "Seger Back Home with All the Right Moves." *Windsor Star* (ONT), August 29, 1986.
Shaw, William. "Surprise Attack: Massive Attack." *Details,* February 1991.
Skinner, Ernest. "Kerry King Regrets Flat Fee for Beasties Collaboration." *Border City Rock Talk,* July 2024.
Slevin, Patrick. "Interview with Everlast of House of Pain: Aged Malt Lyrics, Still Fine." *Aquarian Weekly* (NJ), March 15, 2010.
Smith, Dorian. "It's About Time America Got Sick Says Anthrax Bassist." *News Tribune* (WA), June 26, 1987.
Smith, R.J. "Red, Hot, and Bothered." *Spin,* October 1996.
Smith, R.J. "Reviews: Rage Against the Machine, The Battle of Los Angeles." *Spin,* December 1999.
Smith, Ryan. "Interview: DJ Kamron of the All-White Young Black Teenagers." *Complex,* June 26, 2015.
Smntcs. "25 Years of *Ill Communication.*" *Smntcs,* November 10, 2021.
Smulnick, Michael. "Records: Danny Iris and Thee Cruisers." *Morning Call* (PA), October 17, 1981.
Snyder, Michael. "Middle-Class White Boys' Street-Punk Sounds." *San Francisco Examiner,* February 1, 1987.
Soeder, John. "They Opened Hip-Hop to the Suburbs." *Cleveland Plain Dealer* (OH), April 9, 2012.
SongFacts. "Cake: 'Short Skirt/Long Jacket.'" 2001.
SongFacts. "Run-DMC, King of Rock." 2006.

BIBLIOGRAPHY

"Sound Bites: Mobb Deep." *Marshfield News-Herald* (WI), December 16, 2001.

"Spyz Like Us." *Charlotte Observer* (NC), March 13, 1991.

Stannard, Joseph. "Ultraviolet Dreams: An Interview with DJ Muggs." *Wire* (UK), October 2018.

Stephens, Stephanie. "Blondie Drummer Clem Burke Goes Deep Into the Inspiration for 'Heart of Glass,' 'Rapture,' and More." *Parade,* July 3, 2018.

Stern, Adam Keane. "A Tribe Called Quest: Quest for Fire." *Seconds,* #27, 1994.

Stern, Adam Keane. "Africa Bambaataa." *Seconds,* #31, 1995.

Stern, Adam Keane. "Pete Rock and CL Smooth: Rock the House." *Seconds,* #29, 1994.

Stetler, Carrie. "The Beastie Boys Are Beasties but Entertaining." *Morning Call* (PA), April 9, 1987.

Stout, Alan K. "Downset Brings Anger to the Stage." *The Times Leader* (PA), January 24, 1995.

Stout, Alan K. "Solid Sounds from Concrete." *The Times Leader* (PA), April 29, 1994.

Sussman, Elisabeth. "Conversation with Fred Brathwaite." *Keith Haring Foundation,* January 1997.

Sutherland, Mark. "They Were True Originals: Scott Ian on Beastie Boys' Enduring Impact." *Kerrang!* (UK), May 3, 2021.

Swenson, John. "Pop: Run-DMC's Raps Expand Audience." *Kingsport Times-News* (TN), August 29, 1986.

Tannenbaum, Rob. "Once More Into the Vaults: Blondie on the Music That Defined Its Legacy." *New York Times,* August 22, 2022.

Tarradell, Mario. "Beastie Boys Not As Dumb As They Act." *News-Journal* (OH), June 2, 1994.

Tatlock, John. "The Noise and How to Ring It: Hank Shocklee Interviewed." *The Quietus,* February 4, 2015.

Taylor, Paul. "CD Reviews: Downset." *Manchester Evening News* (UK), April 14, 1995.

Taylor, Paul. "Close to the Edgy: Portishead." *Manchester Evening News* (UK), September 26, 1997.

Taysom, Joe. "The Story Behind the Song: Blondie's 'Rapture,' The First Rap Song to Ever Top the Charts." *Far Out Magazine* (UK), September 7, 2020.

Tedeschi, Claire. "Malcolm McLaren: the Happy Exploiter." *Sydney Morning Herald* (AUS), August 13, 1983.

Terrell, Tom. "Kool Keith." *Seconds,* #50, 1999.

Testa, Jim. "Pumpkins Are Only Promising." *Jersey Journal* (NJ), August 6, 1993.

"The Jaggeerz Receive a Gold Record." *New Castle News* (PA), April 4, 1970.

"The Jury: Downset," July 2, 1996.

BIBLIOGRAPHY

"The Real Thing 35: Exclusive Interview with Roddy Bottum." *Faith No More Followers*, June 19, 2024.

Thompson, Ben. "Triumph of the Ill." *Independent* (UK), June 19, 1994.

Thorpe, Richard. "Recordings: UTFO." *Boston Globe* (MA), November 12, 1987.

Tingen, Paul. "The Dust Brothers: Sampling, Remixing & the Boat Studio." *Sound on Sound*, May 2005.

Torres, Richard. "Having Big Fun with Big Pun." *Newsday* (NY), October 25, 1998.

Trainham, Emily. "Kid Rock Rallies Trump Supporters at RNC as Rocker Leans Into Politics." *New York Post*, July 20, 2024.

Trakin, Roy. "Blondie: An American Band." *Daily News* (NY), November 9, 1980.

Trapp, Philip. "Every Nu-Metal 'Big Four' Album, Ranked Worst to Best." *Loudwire*, January 31, 2024.

Tribune Wire Services. "Portishead *Dummy* Shows Originality." *South Bend Tribune* (IN), February 18, 1995.

Tucker, Ken. "Beastie Boys Are Raucous, Raunchy and Respectable." *Corpus Christi Caller-Times* (TX), February 15, 1987.

Tucker, Ken. "Beastie Boys Both Delightful and Disgusting." *Spokane Chronicle*, February 5, 1987.

Tucker, Ken. "Beasties Unleash an Hour of Brattiness, with Style." *Philadelphia Inquirer* (PA), April 8, 1987.

Tucker, Ken. "Disrespect The Entire Point of Beastie Boys." *Moline Dispatch* (IL), February 8, 1987.

Tucker, Ken. "When Rockers Sing of Politics." *Philadelphia Inquirer* (PA), December 9, 1984.

Tyler, Steven. "Steven Tyler Remembers Jam Master Jay." *Entertainment Tonight*, December 23, 2002.

Uitti, Jake. "The Origins of Breaking with Its Biggest Name, Crazy Legs." *Under The Radar*, July 20, 2020.

Uncredited. "50 Years of Hip-Hop." *Centennial Specials*, August 28, 2023.

Uncredited. "Check Out A New Interview with Sage Francis." *Epitaph.com*, May 18, 2005.

Uncredited. "Hip-Hop History: From the Streets to the Mainstream." *Icon Collective*, 2022.

Uncredited. *NME*, "Metal with Attitude." *NME*, November 23, 1999.

Uncredited. "System of a Down: Quirky Is As Quirky Does." *Metal Edge*, December 1999.

Van Horn, Teri. "Sugar Ray Team with the Alcoholiks on Loud Rocks." *MTV.com*, August 30, 2000.

Varga, George. "Beasties Mature, Grow Up Personally, Professionally." *The Times* (IN), September 29, 1998.

BIBLIOGRAPHY

Vas, Israel. "Bill Adler Interview: Def Jam's Iconic Era." *Medium*, March 28, 2015.

Wake, Matt. "Whodini: Seminal Rap Group Tells Stories of Their Rap Classics." *AL.com* (AL), June 19, 2013.

Wall, Mick. "Who's Funkin You." *Kerrang!* (UK), June 1990.

Weingarten, Christopher R. "An Oral History of House of Pain's 'Jump Around'." *Spin*, February 24, 2012.

Weingarten, Christopher R. "Oral History of the *Judgment Night* Soundtrack: 1993's Rap-Rock Utopia." *Rolling Stone*, September 13, 2018.

Weiss, Dan. "Chester Bennington Turned Nu-Metal Universal." *Billboard*, July 20, 2017.

Weiss, Jeff. "A Conversation with Posdnuos of De La Soul." *LA Weekly*, April 30, 2009.

Weizmann, Danny. "The Beastie Boys: The Boogie and the Beast." *LA Weekly*, July 20, 1989.

Wessel, Lauri. "Interview: Sick of It All." *Ox Fanzine* (GER), April/May 2010.

Whalen, Nancy. "Gathering Dust." *BAM (Bay Area Music)*, April 1994.

WHBI-FM. "An Interview with Se'Divine the Master Mind." *Old School Hip Hop*, December 6, 2010.

Whitall, Susan. "Bands Squeeze Genres Together for New Sound." *Palladium-Item* (IN), April 25, 1991.

Wielander, Eric. "Tricky." *Seconds*, #44, 1997.

Wilbur, Brock. "What's Worse Than Coronavirus? The Rap-Rock Album *Loud Rocks* from 2000." *Kansas City Pitch* (MO), 2020.

William. "Retrospective: DJ Lethal Interview." *Eclectic Electric*, June 8, 2014.

Williams, Chris. "Key Tracks: Run-DMC's 'Rock Box.'" *Red Bull Academy*, December 23, 2014.

Williams, Stereo. "Rap Hip-Hop Deadline 1970–1989." *Digital Dream Door*, September 11, 2005.

Wilson, Toni. "Bloodhouse Gang in for the Fun of It." *Moline Dispatch* (IL), May 29, 1997.

Winik, Marion. "A Producer's Creative Wisdom." *Newsday* (NY), March 5, 2023.

Wire Services. "Album Cuts: Downset." *Waco Tribune-Herald* (TX), September 28, 1996.

Wirt, John. "Beach Boys Are Survivors." *Richmond Times-Dispatch* (VA), August 10, 1989.

Wiser, Carl. "Donnie Iris: "Ah! Leah!," "The Rapper." *Song Facts*, September 10, 2006.

Withers, Murray. "The Big Beat: Billy Squier's 1980 Track Was Endlessly Sampled, Sliced and Diced." *Financial Times*, July 3, 2023.

Wolgamott, L. Kent. "Beastie Boys Mince No Words; Latest Album Should He Heard." *Lincoln Journal Star* (NE), August 8, 1989.

Wood, Michael. "Revolutionary." *Los Angeles Times*, June 2, 2016.

BIBLIOGRAPHY

Woodlief, Mark. "Kottonmouth Kings Pull Out Stash of Hits from Pot Parodies." *Orange County Register* (CA), September 13, 2000.

Wyeth, Stefan. "How Trip-Hop Went from Obscurity to Chart Domination." *Music Tech,* August 23, 2024.

Yates, Henry. "The Story Behind the Song: Anthrax and Public Enemy 'Bring the Noise.'" *Classic Rock,* April 21, 2020.

Yates, Robert. "Stop Press: Oil and Water Mix." *The Guardian* (UK), January 4, 1992.

Zaleski, Annie. "We've Got a File on You: Korn's Jonathan Davis." *Stereogum,* February 1, 2022.

Zelenda, Jon. "Jon's Jams: Loud Rocks." *Schuyler Sun* (NE), October 26, 2000.

Zemun, David. "Kerry King Reveals How Rick Rubin Reacted to Slayer Refusing His Advice." *Ultimate Guitar,* August 15, 2024.

Zlatopolsky, Ashley. "Korn: 'We Totally Destroyed What People Thought Metal Should Be.'" *The Guardian* (UK), October 21, 2016.

INDEX

24-7 Spyz   129
"99 Problems"   49
100% Columbian   137

A$AP Rocky   49
Abraham, Josh   230–1
Abrams, Leonard   14
AC/DC   3, 80, 84, 177, 213
Adler, Bill   10–11, 41, 53, 76, 80, 238–9
  on Def Jam   75, 85, 133
  on Run-DMC   52, 59, 132, 202, 247, 251
Ad-Rock   45, 72, 75, 78–9, 81, 84
Aerosmith   3, 37, 40, 43, 48, 53, 56, 59–67, 90, 116, 117, 159, 160, 215
Afrika Bambaataa (Lance Taylor)   8–9, 12, 15–16, 31–40, 77, 207
  Punk rockers   2, 39, 42
  and Soul Sonic Force   12, 32–4, 77
  Time Zone   35–7
Ahearn, Charlie   16–7, 25
Akai MPC60   196
Alicia Keys   49
All Boro Kings   129
alternative rap   136, 199–203
alt-rock-rap   173, 205–13
American Badass   191
American Double Dutch League   31
A&M Records   184
"Angel of Death"   86, 111

"Another Body Murdered"   181
Anthrax   4, 39, 43, 113–21, 135, 215–17
Apocalypse '91 . . . The Enemy Strikes Black   112, 119
Araya, Tom   180
Arm, Mark   183
Astbury, Ian   90
Attack of the Killer B's   119
Audioslave   165
Âutoamerican   27–8

"Baby Got Back"   183
Bacdafucup   125
Bachman Turner Overdrive   20
"Back in Black"   3, 80
"Back to School Jam"   8
Baker, Arthur   34, 35, 75, 77, 79
Balboa Theater   167
Barrow, Geoff   195, 196
Basquiat, Jean-Michel   17, 24, 27, 28
Battle of Los Angeles, The   163
"B-Boy Bouillabaisse"   32
Beach Boys   244–5
Beastie Boys   3, 4, 32, 39, 43, 61, 69–72, 74, 76–7, 79–80, 82–92, 94, 123, 205, 206
"Beastie Revolution"   32, 73
Beatnuts, The   129
Beat Street   16
Beck   205–13
Belafonte, Harry   16
Belladonna, Joey   120, 121, 130
Benante, Charlie   113, 118–20
Benitez, John "Jellybean"   34

INDEX

Bennington, Chester 223–4
Berry, John 70, 72
"Berzerk" 49, 188
Bettencourt, Nuno 253
"Big 12 Inch" 246–8
"The Big Beat" 40, 48–9
Big Daddy Kane 44, 49–50
"Big Four, The" 217
Big Pun 233
Billboard 58, 65, 165, 171, 212, 222, 241
"Billy, Don't Be a Hero" 72
Binzer, Seth "Shifty Shellshock" 230–1
Biohazard 43, 90, 124–6, 128, 152, 173, 179, 220
Bitton, Gil 228
Black Flames, The 89
Black hip-hop 205
Black Rock Coalition 123, 130
The Black Spades 33
Black Sunday 149, 186
Blackwell, Mark 175
Blondie 16, 23, 24, 26–9
Bloodhound Gang 249–50
Blood Sugar Sex Magik 141–2
Blue Lines 194–5, 198
Blow, Kurtis 2, 18–20, 55
  on Rev Run 19–20
Bomb Squad 95, 109–10, 133–4
Boo-Yaa T.R.I.B.E. 181
Bordin, Mike 143, 145, 221
Borland, Wes 219–20
Bowie, David 24
Braunstein, William 250–1
Breakfast at Tiffany's 87
breaking 15
"The Breaks" 18–9
B-Real 148–50, 164, 166, 182, 186, 237, 251
Bride 248–9
"Bring the Noise" 4, 113, 115–21, 166, 215, 219
  Charlie Benante 113, 118–20

Chuck D 117, 118, 120
Hank Shocklee 117–19
Joey Belladonna 121
Maria Ferrero 116–17
Scott Ian 116–18, 120–1
"Bring the Noise Tour" 119
Brit Hop and Amyl House 132
Brown, James 9, 12, 41, 47, 50, 54
"Buffalo Gals" 23, 31–2, 73
Burke, Clem 28–9
Burnett, Jay 80, 242–3
Butler, Jimmy 174
Byrd, Gary 13
Byrne, David 24
"By The Time I Get to Arizona" 112

Cabrera, Albert 244–5
Cactus Album, The 131–2
Cake 212–13
Caldato, Mario, Jr. 98–9, 102–4
Canem, Sean 227–8
Captain Rapp 139
"Caribbean Connection" 135, 233
Carved in Stone 170, 171, 206
Cat Scratch Fever 103, 247–8
Caveman 245–6
Celluloid Records 37
Cerrone 12
Check Your Head 101–3, 211
Chocolate Starfish 219
Chong, Rae Dawn 16
Chouinard, Bobby 48–9
"Christmas Rapping" 19–20
Chuck D 66, 83, 108, 110, 117, 118, 120, 164, 166
  on rock music 3
Chung King House of Metal (Chung King Studios) 89
Clark, Mike E. 189, 191
Clinton, George 24, 47, 104, 141, 187
Cold Crush Brothers 12, 13, 48
Collins, Tim 60
Colon, Richard "Crazy Legs" 15

INDEX

Columbia Records 82, 94
Combat Rock 28
"Come and Die" 184–5
Come Find Yourself 136, 137
Comfort Eagle 213
Commerford, Tim 161, 166
Connor, John 128, 129
"Cooky Puss" 32, 72–3, 81
Coolin' in Cali 147
Cooper, Barry Michael 12
Cornell, Chris 150, 165–6, 224
Crane, Robbie 171
Crazy Town 230–1, 247
Criminal Minded 202
Crocker, Frankie 13
"Cult of Personality" 179
Cunniff, Jill 211–12
Curtis, Kelly 175
Cypress Hill 1, 4, 139, 147–50, 152–3, 155, 163, 166, 169, 173–4, 176, 180, 182, 185–6, 189, 196, 235
Cypress Hill III: Temples of Boom 150
Cypress Hill IV 196
Czaykowski, Robert "Nitebob" 60

Daddy G 194, 195
Daddy X 168–70
"D.A.I.S.Y Age, The" 200
"Dance to the Music" 9
Danny Boy 42–3, 151–6, 176–7, 232, 251
Danzig III: How the Gods Kill 91
Davis, Jonathan 216–17, 220–1, 254
Dead End Kids Doin' Lifetime Bidz 134
Dead Prez 225, 227–8
"DeeBaby" 253–4
Def Jam
  Adam Dubin 87, 89
  Adam Yauch 71, 80–1, 84–5, 95–6

Ad-Rock 75, 78–9, 81, 84
Bill Stephney 94–6
Chuck D 83
Daryl Jenifer 84
DJ Muggs 83
Drew Stone 76, 86
Glenn Danzig 91–2
Hank Shocklee 83
Ian Astbury 90
Jimmy G 87, 92–3
John King 89, 97
Kerry King 85–8
Mike D 83–4
Mike Schnapp 88–9
Pete Nice 90–1, 132
Rick Rubin 88–90, 93–4
Russell Simmons 81, 93–6
Scott Ian 93–4
Scott Koenig 87–8, 90
Def Jam Recordings 3, 69–96
De La Rocha, Zack 161–6, 168
De La Soul 176–8, 199–201
De La Soul is Dead 200
Delicious Vinyl Records 97–8
Del Tha Funkee Homosapien 183–4
Destri, Jimmy 28
Detroit 187–91
Devil Without a Cause 191
DiFontaine Carting & Asbestos Removal Co. 137
Dinosaur Jr. 183–4, 205
Disco Daddy 139
"Disorder" 180
Disposable Heroes of Hiphoprisy 146
DJ Frankie Bones 43
DJ Homicide 227
DJ Hurricane 231
DJ Kool Herc 8, 16, 40, 77
DJ Lenny Dee 43
DJ Lethal 140, 151, 155–6, 176–7, 219, 251
DJ Mark The 45 King 199

INDEX

DJ Muggs 11, 83, 139, 147–50, 152–5, 174, 182, 184–5, 251
DJ Premier 218, 232, 251
DJ Shadow (Josh Davis) 196–7
DMC 2–3, 12, 14, 20, 39–41, 43–5, 47, 49, 51–67, 76, 81, 83–4, 87, 89, 91–3, 96, 108, 116–17, 123, 126–7, 129, 133, 144, 159, 161, 167, 173, 178–9, 191, 215, 235, 238, 247, 251
  on early days of hip-hop 2
  on rock records 14, 41, 57
D.O.C. (Disciples of Christ) 248–9
Dog Eat Dog 128–9
Dolmayan, John 222
Don, The 246–8
Dondi 17, 29
Done with Mirrors 60
Don't Be a Faggot 82
Don't Say No 48, 188
Do the Right Thing 111
"Double Dutch" 31
Doughty, Mike 209–10
Do We Speak a Dead Language? 167
Downset 166–7
Downtown Science 132
Drake 189
Dr. Dre 139, 160, 188, 220
"Dream Weaver" 40
"Drum Machine" 34–5, 56–7, 63, 73, 76, 80, 147, 154, 182, 242–3
Dubin, Adam 87, 89
Duck Rock 31
Dummy 195
Durst, Fred 216, 218–20
Dust Brothers 97–9, 170–1, 205–9, 223
D'Ya Like Scratchin 31

East Village Eye 14
Eat at Whitey's 157
Eat to the Beat 28
Eastcide 252
EAZY-E 100, 159, 160
Ego Trip's Book of Rap Lists 113
Electric 89, 90
Eminem 49, 65, 157, 168, 187, 191, 228
Eminem 188
Endo 228
Enter the Wu-Tang: 36 Chambers 230
Entroducing 197
Eric B. and Rakim 44
Espindle, Michael 74
Estevez, Emilio 174
Everlast 1, 52, 148, 150–2, 154–7, 174, 176–7, 228–30, 251, 254–5
  on hip-hop 1, 52, 148, 174, 225
Evil Empire 163
Exposed 171

Fab 5 Freddy (Fred Braithwaite) 17, 24–7, 29
Faith No More 139, 142–6, 181, 216, 221
"Fallin'" 177–8
Fast 136–8
Fatal 184–5
Fatback XII 11
Fat Boys 2, 244–5
Fear of a Black Planet 112
Ferrero, Maria 42–3, 116–17, 144, 244
Ferris, D. X. 138, 175–6, 216, 250, 253
Fever In Fever Out 212
Fight Club 208
"Fight For Your Right (To Party)" 86, 87, 93, 98
Finnerty, Amy 228
"Fire Water Burn" 249–50
Firstborn 134
Flea 141–2

INDEX

Fluid, Peter 130
Foghat 40
Ford, Robert "Rocky" 20
Forever Everlasting 150
"For Heaven's Sake (2000)" 232–3
Francis, Sage 251–2
Franti, Michael 140–1, 146–8
"Freak Momma" 182–3
Freaky Styley 141, 142
Freeman, Gene "Machine" 233
Fresh, Doug E. 16
"Fresh is the Word" 132
Fripp, Robert 24
Fuchs, Aaron 12
Fun Lovin' Criminals 136–8
The Furious Five 11, 13, 23, 42
Futura 2000 17, 28–9

Gamble, John 154, 254–5
Gang of Four 141
Generation of Hope 135
"Get Ready" 40
Gibbons, Beth 195
Gibson, Rodney A. 248
"Gigolo Rapp, The" 139
"Girl on Fire" 49
Glaser, Gabrielle "Gabby" 211–12
Glenn Danzig 91
Godfather 34, 47, 111, 181
"The Godfather of Hip-Hop" 34
"God Gave Rock and Roll to You" 248
Gooding, Cuba Jr. 174
Gordon, Kim 182
Gould, Bill 181
Graffin, Greg 252
Grandmaster Caz 10, 14, 16
Grandmaster Flash (Joseph Sadler) 9, 11, 13, 16, 23, 26–7, 134
Grand Poobah 44
Grand Wizzard Theodore 16
Graziadei, Billy 125, 127–8, 179–80

"Grease" 72
Grisham, Jack 169
Grits Sandwiches for Breakfast 190
Groove, Shootyz 135–6, 233
Guilty of Innocence 125
Gurewitz, Brett 252
Gutfeld, Greg 145

Hambel, Bobby 127
Hamilton, Page 176–7
Hamilton, Tom 59, 63
Happy Gilmore (film) 174
Happy Walters 174, 177, 184, 220
Harry, Allen 107–108
Harry, Deborah 24, 26–7
Havoc 229, 234
Hazel, Jimi 129–31
"Heart of Glass" 26, 198
Heller, Jerry 159–60
Helmet 4, 176–7
Hempilation: Vol. 2: Free the Weed 146
Hendricks, Barrington 238
Hendrix, Jimi 54, 80–1, 129, 158, 246
Hesher 254–5
High Society 169
High Times 16, 146, 149
hip-hop 174
"Hip Hop" 14, 227
"Hip Hop is Dead" 49
Hipnosis 135
Hoffert, Eric 75
Holman, Michael 8, 14–15, 17, 30, 236
 on disco and hip-hop 8
 New York City Breakers 15–16
Hopkins, Stephen 174
Horn, Trevor 31–2
Horovitz, Adam "Ad-Rock" 41, 72
 on Rick Rubin 75–6
Hose 74
House of Pain 4, 166, 174, 176–85, 219

INDEX

House of Pain 152, 154
Howard, Dwight 174
"How 'Bout Some Hardcore" 231–2
"How I Could Just Kill a Man" 149
Hypocrisy is the Greatest Luxury 146

I Against I 95
"I am the Law" 113
Ian, Scott 93–4, 105–6, 112–13, 116–18, 120–1
Ice-T 150, 157–60, 180
"If You Want Me to Stay" 141
Iggy Pop 24
Ill Bill 250–1
Ill Communication 103
"I Love You Mary Jane" 182
"I'm Ready" 245–6
"I Need Love" 96
In/Flux 197
Insane Clown Posse 189–90, 254
Interview 23–4
Introduce Yourself 144
Iommi, Tony 232–3, 238
Iris, Donnie 241–2
"It's a New Day" 9
It Takes A Nation of Millions to Hold Us Back 111, 116, 167

Jaggerz 241–2
Jalil 21
James, Bob 12
Jamie Reid 18
Jam Master Jay 4, 20, 52–4, 66, 125, 129, 163, 178–9
Jammin' In Vicious Environments (J.I.V.E.) 135
Jay-Z 49
Jazzy Jay 12
Jenifer, Daryl 45, 84, 129
Jimmy G 87, 92
"Jimmy James" 80
J Mascis 183–4

Judgment Night 4, 125, 127, 166, 173–86, 215, 220, 225
"Juggla, The" 189
"Jump Around" 155
Jungle Brothers 199, 200
"Just Another Victim" 176

Kamron 134
Kangol Kid 113–14
Kansas City Pitch 225
Kid Rock 168, 171, 187, 190–1, 215, 217, 222
Kiedis, Anthony 141–2, 145–6
King, John 89, 97, 99, 206–8, 223
King, Kerry 42, 84–6, 88
King, Martin Luther 108
King of Rock 58
"King of Rock" 55–8, 60
King Tim III 10
Koenig, Scott 61, 76, 87, 88, 90, 125
Koller, Lou 234
Kolodner, John 62
Kool Moe Dee 21–2
"Korean Bodega" 137
Korn 175, 208, 215–17, 220
Kottonmouth Kings 168–9
Kraftwerk 12, 34–6
Kramer, Joey 59, 63
KRS-One (Kris Parker) 202–3

Lasker, Robi 245–6
Laswell, Bill 35–7
Latin-Black gang violence 168
Lavelle, James 196
Leary, Dennis 174
Led Zeppelin 40, 48, 83, 90, 130, 148, 158, 165, 177
Less Than Zero 116
Lethal 113
Letterman, David 24
"Let Them Eat War" 251–2
Lewis, Bart 63
Licensed to Ill 82–6, 88, 91–3, 95, 97, 99, 101

INDEX

Limp Bizkit   156, 173, 180, 216–22
Linkin Park   4, 217, 223–4
Living Colour   42, 111, 123, 130, 178
LL Cool J   21, 44, 76, 78–9, 89, 93, 96, 231, 243
Lone Rager   113, 243–4
"Louder Than a Bomb"   78, 111
Loud Rocks   225–34
"Louie Louie"   155
Love, Chip   255
Love, Gerard   178
"Love Is Alive"   40
"Love Unlimited"   137
Luscious Jackson   205, 210–11
Lurie, John   24
Lydon, John   35–7
  on Afrika Bambaataa   36–7
Lynch, Monica   153

Macmillan, Keith   27
Madonna   57, 72, 81
"Magic Carpet Ride"   40
Majidi, Armand   234
"Make Room"   226–7
Malakian, Daron   222
Malcolm X   108
Mapplethorpe, Robert   24
Marclay, Christian   18
Marlette, Bob   232–3
Marley, Bob   162, 227
Martin, Jim   145
Martinez, Eddie   55–6, 58, 237
"Mary Mary"   40
Marz, Bobby   253–4
Mash Out Posse   231–2
Maxinquaye   198
Mazur, Bret "Epic"   230–1
McCormick, Carlo   14, 17–18, 236
McCrea, John   212–13
McGrath, Mark   227
McKeegan, Michael   185
McLaren, Malcolm   23, 30–1, 73

MC poppin   34
MC Serch   131–2, 250–1
"Me, Myself & My Microphone"   178–9
Mel, Melle   11–12
Mellow Gold   207
Melman, Larry "Bud"   58
Melody Maker   116
Mercury Records   20, 135, 167
Merv Griffin   16
"Metal Rap"   243–4
Method Man   218–19, 230
Michael, George   218
"Midlife Crisis"   145
Midnight Cowboy   145
Mike D   69–71, 73, 83–84, 100–1, 104–5
Milarepa Foundation   105
"Missing Link"   183–4
Mizell, Jason, *see* Jam Master Jay
"MMM Bop"   206
Mobb Deep   225, 228–30, 234
Mobo   74
Mondale, Walter   36
Money Mark   102–3
Monkees   12, 40, 81
Monsters of Rock festival   116
Moore, J.B.   20
Moran, Tony   244–5
Mordam Records   144
Morello, Tom   4–5, 139–40, 161–4, 166, 175, 219, 229–30
Morgan, Huey   136–138
Moseley, Chuck   144
Mother's Milk   141
Mucky Pup   128
Mudhoney   182–3
Muhammad, Ali Shaheed   200, 201
Mustaine, Dave   217

"N 2 Gether Now"   218
Nas   49, 78, 131
Native Tongues Posse   199–200

INDEX

Nearly God 198
Neil, Vince 170–1, 206, 209
Nevermind 155, 173
New York City
   Billy Graziadei 127–8
   Bobby Hambel 127
   Danny Schuler 127
   Dante Ross 132
   Donny Radeljic 136
   Drew Stone 126
   D.X. Ferris 138
   Evan Seinfeld 124–6, 128–9
   Fast 136–8
   Firstborn 134
   Fredro Starr 125, 127
   Huey Morgan 136–8
   Jimi Hazel 129–31
   John Connor 128, 129
   Kamron 134–6
   MC Serch 131–2
   Mike Schnapp 137
   Pete Nice 131–134
   Peter Fluid 130
   Sticky Fingaz 126
New York City Breakers 15–16
New York punk and hardcore
     (NYHC) 69–70, 72, 92, 102–4, 126, 128, 130, 202, 210, 234
New York Thrash 71
New York Times 91
Nice, Pete 40, 42, 52, 90–1, 132–3
   Run-DMC 52
Nitebob 60–62
No Fronts: The Remixes 129
"No Sleep Till Brooklyn" 85–8, 166
No Sleep Till Hammersmith 87
"Nowhere's Child" 252–3
Nugent, Ted 103, 246–8
Numan, Gary 34
nu-metal 4, 43, 120, 141, 143, 150, 168, 173, 175, 185, 191, 215–24
NWA 44, 159–60, 188–20

O'Brien, Glenn 24, 26, 166
"Ocean, The" 83
Odadjian, Shavo 222, 226
Odelay 205–209
O.G. Original Gangster 158
O'Jay, Eddie 13
OK Computer 197
"Only When I'm Drunk" 230–1
Onyx 123–128, 173, 179
Oropeza, Anthony 167
Oropeza, Rey 167–8
Osbourne, Ozzy 137, 148, 232–3
"Out of this World" 49

Pareles, Jon 91
Parsons, Dave 71
Paul's Boutique 97, 170, 205, 206
   Adam Yauch 101–2, 104–5
   Dante Ross 106
   EAZY-E 100
   John King 99
   Mario Caldato, Jr. 98–99, 102–4
   Mike D 100–1, 104
   Mike Simpson 98–100
   Money Mark 102, 103
   Q-Tip 103, 104
   Scott Ian 105–6
Peace Sells But Who's Buying? 117
Pearl Jam 4, 148, 150, 163, 166, 175, 176, 185–6, 248
Perry, Joe 60–65
Persistence of Time 115, 121
Petty, Tom 138, 177, 178
"Phil Spector of Noize, The" 109
"Phuncky Feel One, The" 149
Pineapple Express 148
"Planet Rock" 32–5, 242
Play Games 129
P.M. Dawn 178, 199, 201
Pollywog Stew 70–71
Pomeroy, Doug 72–3
Pop, Jimmy 249–50
"Pop Goes Pot" 149–150

INDEX

Portishead 129, 193, 195–6
Posdnuos 178
Preemptive Strike 197
Pre-Millennium Tension 198
Prince Markie Dee 2, 245
Prince of Darkness 232
Prophets of Rage 166
Protection 194, 198
Public Enemy 78, 107–14, 123, 162, 166–7, 171, 215, 235–6
   Chuck D 107–110
   Hank Shocklee 108, 109, 111–12
   Kangol Kid 113–114
   Rick Rubin 108–11
   Russell Siedmmons 109–10
   Scott Ian 112–13
Pulp Fiction 137
"Put Your Lights On" 157

Q-Tip 103–104, 149, 199, 201–2, 221
Queen Latifah 199, 200
Quest 49, 199–202
Quiñones, Lee 17, 27

Rachtman, Karen 175
Radeljic, Donny 136
Raekwon
   on rock and hip-hop 4
Rage Against the Machine 4, 43, 121, 139, 140, 152, 160–5, 175, 215, 229, 235, 236
Raising Hell 60, 132
Rammellzee 16, 148
rap music 2, 10, 13–14, 17, 21, 29, 31, 41, 53, 61, 66, 72, 78, 110, 119, 160
"Rapper's Delight" 7, 10–11, 19, 202
"Rapture" 23, 25–9, 202
Rare Earth 40
Rat Cage Records 71, 72

Real Men Don't Floss 72
Real Thing, The 144
"Real Thing" 185–6
Red Alert 12, 133
Red Hot Chili Peppers 139–41, 144–6, 183, 215, 229
Reid, Vernon 111, 123, 179
Reign in Blood 4, 85, 86, 88
Reservoir Dogs 137
Reynoso, Jose "Choco" 228
"Rhyme or Reason" 188
Robbins, Cory 12, 53, 57
Robie, John 34
Robin Byrd Show 24
Robinson, Sylvia 10
"Rock Box" 51, 52, 54–8, 60
Rock in a Hard Place 60
Rock & Roll Hall of Fame 65, 94, 164
Rock Steady Crew 15–16
Rodgers, Nile 24
Rollins, Henry 42, 131, 175
Rosario, Fernando 63–5
Ross, Dante 41, 106, 132, 133, 156–7, 228, 254
The Roxy 33
Rubin, Rick 3–4, 41, 49, 55, 60–2, 66, 73–81, 83–5, 88–90, 93, 94, 97, 99, 108–11, 141, 165, 187, 188, 203, 208, 222, 226, 229–30
   Hoffert on 75
   Licensed to Ill 4, 82–6, 88, 91–3, 95, 97, 99, 101
   Simmons on 76
   Stone on 76
   on T La Rock 77, 78
Run-DMC 2, 3, 12, 14, 20, 37, 39–41, 43–5, 49, 51–9, 61–4, 66, 76, 81, 83, 84, 87, 89, 91–3, 108, 116, 117, 123, 126, 127, 129, 132, 133, 144, 157, 159, 161, 167, 178–9, 191, 202, 215

INDEX

b-boy style   52–3
"King of Rock"   55–58, 60
Nice on   40, 42, 52
Raising Hell   3, 60, 132
Robbins   12, 54, 57
"Rock Box"   51, 52, 54–8, 60
using rock   167
Rush Management   76, 90, 93, 125, 131

Sakamoto, Ryuichi   35
Same as it Ever Was   155
Sandler, Adam   174
Saturday Night Live   212
Schellenbach, Kate   69, 70, 72, 73, 80–1, 211
on "Cooky Puss"   73
Schnapp, Mike   3, 88–9, 137, 164–5, 238, 244
Schuler, Danny   127
Schulman, Daniel   246–8
Scream   165
Se'Divine the Master Mind   32
segregation   1
Seinfeld, Evan   43–4, 124–6, 128–9, 235–6
Sen Dog   148–51, 185, 186
Sevendust   231
Seymour, John   234
"Shady XV"   188
Shaffer, James "Munky"   221
Shaft/Superfly rhythms   99
Shattuck, Jeremy   70
"She's Crafty"   82, 83
"She's on It"   69, 81
"She Watch Channel Zero?!"   86, 111
Shinoda, Mike   215–16, 223
Shocklee, Hank   4, 9, 83, 108, 109, 111–12, 117–19
on Grandmaster Flash   9
Shocklee, Keith   7, 40, 109, 133
punk rock bands   40, 183
on rise of hip-hop   7–8

"Shook Ones Part II"   228–29
"Shut Em Down"   112, 166
Sick of it All   202, 220, 234
Significant Other   219
Simmons, Bobby   55
Simmons, Danny   55
Simmons, Joseph "Run"   19–20, 52
"Rock Box"   51, 52, 54–8, 60
on Run-DMC   52
Simmons, Russell   19, 21, 54–5, 60, 75, 76, 78, 80, 81, 94–6, 109–10, 246
Beastie Boys   3, 4, 39, 43, 61, 69–72, 74, 76, 77, 79, 80, 82, 83, 85–8, 90
on Rick Rubin   76, 187, 188, 203, 208, 222, 226, 229, 242, 243, 246, 247, 250, 251
on T La Rock   77, 78
Simpson, Mike   97–100, 171, 206–8, 223
"Sing for the Moment"   188
Sir Mix-A-Lot   182–3
Sixuvus Productions   241–2
Skopelitis, Nicky   37
Slash Magazine   144
Slayer   4, 39, 42, 76, 84–6, 88–90, 96, 111, 132, 136, 148, 160, 167, 180–1, 217, 222, 250, 251
"Slow and Low"   81
Sly and the Family Stone   9, 141
Sly Stone   12, 103
Smith, Chad   229–30
Smith, James Todd, *see* LL Cool J
Smith, Larry   55–6, 58
Smooth, CL
on rock and hip-hop   5
Sonic Youth   182, 205
"Sophisticated Bitch"   111
Soul Assassins   149, 155, 184
Soul Coughing   205, 209, 210
Soul Sonic Force   12, 32–4, 77

INDEX

Squier, Billy   12, 40, 47–50, 57, 113, 187, 188, 236
  "The Big Beat"   40, 48–50, 57
  career   48
  DMC on   47
  "The Stroke"   49
Starr, Fredro   125, 127
Static, Wayne   227–8
Static-X   225, 227–8
Stein, Chris   14, 16, 24, 26–8
Steinberg, Sebastian   209–10
Stephney, Bill   94–6, 108, 109, 133
Steppenwolf   40
Sticky Fingaz   125, 126, 128
Stone, Drew   44, 66–7, 76, 86, 126
  on Rick Rubin   76
Straight Outta Compton   139, 160
"Stroke, The"   47, 48, 49, 188
Strummer, Joe   28
"Sucker MCs"   53, 57, 157, 178
Sugarhill Gang   7, 10, 11, 34
Sugar Hill Records   10–12
Sugar Ray   226–7
Suicide Pact-You First   184
Sulmers, Georges   90
Superfuzz Bigmuff   183
System of a Down   4, 217, 222, 225, 226

Take a Bite out of Rhyme: A Rock Tribute yo Rap   137, 157, 169, 219
"Takin' Care of Business"   20
Tale of the Tape   48
Talking Heads   34
Tankian, Serj   222–3, 226
Teenage Fanclub   176–8, 205
"Television: The Drug of the Nation"   146
Terminator X   4, 109, 134, 163
Tha Alkaholiks   226–7, 230–1
Therapy?   184–5
The 7A3   147, 154
Third   196

Thirteen   177
Three Feet High and Rising   178, 200
Tibet Freedom Concert series   105
"The Tide is High"   26, 28
"Time of the Season"   188
Time Zone   35–7
Tjornhom, Tedd   248–9
T La Rock (Terry Keaton)
  background   77
  on Rick Rubin   78
  Simmons on   78
Tommy Boy Records   12, 153, 200
"Touch Me I'm Sick"   183
Tougher Than Leather   87, 247
Tower Records   84
Toys in the Attic   40, 62
Tribe Called Quest, A   49, 199–202
Tricky (Adrian Thawes)   164, 197–8
trip-hop   193–8, 205
Trugoy (De La Soul)   201
Truth Crushed to Earth Shall Rise Again   155
Tuff City Records   12
TV Party   24, 26, 28
Tyler, Steven   48, 59–4

"U.B.S. (Unauthorized Biography of Slayer)"   250–1
Uplift Mojo Party Plan, The   141
UTFO   49, 113
Utley, Adrian   195

Valens, Richie   167
Vedder, Eddie   163, 186
Vig, Butch   155, 174, 231–2
Village Voice   12, 212
Violent J   189, 190
"Voodoo Chile (Slight Return)"   80

Walker, Curtis   19
"Walk This Way"   3, 4, 37, 55, 56, 59–67, 116, 215

INDEX

The Wall 22
Warhol, Andy 23
Washington, Jerry 55
Washington, Tim 10
"We Can Get Down" 49
We Care a Lot 142, 144
West Coast hip-hop
  Anthony Kiedis 141–6
  B-Real 147–50
  Chuck Moseley 144
  Danny Boy 151–6
  Dante Ross 156–7
  DJ Lethal 151, 155
  DJ Muggs 147, 148, 152–4
  Dr. Dre 139, 160, 169
  Everlast 148, 150–2, 154–8
  FLEA 141, 142
  Greg Gutfeld 145–6
  Ice-T 150, 151, 158–60
  Jerry Heller 159–60
  Jim Martin 145
  Maria Ferrero 144
  Michael Franti 140–1, 146–8
  Mike Bordin 143, 145
  Monica Lynch 153
  Sen Dog 147, 150–1
  Tom Morello 140, 161–4, 166
  Zack De La Rocha 161–4, 166, 168
"We Will Rock You" 147
"What U See Is What U Get" 231
"When The Levee Breaks" 40
Whitey Ford Sings the Blues 156, 255
Whitford, Brad 59, 63

Whodini 21, 55, 113
"Who's the King?" 129
Wild Style 16, 17, 25, 29
Wilk, Brad 161, 163, 166–7
will.i.am 49
Williams, Alyson 89
Williams, Jerry 71, 72, 105
Williams, Jerry "J-Dub" 70
"Wipeout!" 244–5
Witherspoon, Lajon 231
Wonder Mike 11
Woods, Brent 171
Woodstock '99 157, 217–18, 220
"World Destruction" 35–7
"The World is Yours" 78
Worrell, Bernie 37
Wu-Tang Clan 129, 218, 225, 226, 229–30, 232–3
WWRL 13

Xavier, Brad 168–70
Xavier, Spike 170
Xzibit 221, 228, 231

Yauch, Adam "MCA" 70–2, 80–2, 84, 85, 95–6, 101–2, 104–6, 242–3
Yellow Magic Orchestra 34–5
"Yertle the Turtle" 141
Yo! Bum Rush the Show 111
Yo! MTV Raps 27, 118
"(You Gotta) Fight For Your Right (To Party)" 84, 86–7, 93
Young, Neil 2, 209

Zazula, Jon 113, 243–4

ABOUT THE AUTHOR

STEVEN BLUSH got his start in the 1980s promoting hardcore punk rock shows in Washington, DC. He published the award-winning *Seconds* Magazine and served as music editor for the late great *Paper* Magazine, where he became the first writer to cover both rock and hip-hop music. His journalism has appeared in over twenty-five publications, like *Spin, Details, Interview, The Village Voice,* and *The Times of London*. He is the author of ten books about rock culture and sports, including *American Hardcore* (2001), *American Hair Metal* (2005), *.45 Dangerous Minds* (2006), *Lost Rockers* (2016), *New York Rock* (2017), *Bustin' Balls* (2020), *American Hair Metal: Can't Get Enough* (2022), and the trilogy of *When Rock Met Disco* (2023), *When Rock Met Reggae* (2024) and the new *When Rock Met Hip-Hop* (2026). He wrote and produced the theatrically released, Sundance Film Festival-premiered documentary film *American Hardcore* (Sony Pictures Classics, 2006), and released an expanded Second Edition of *American Hardcore* in 2011. The *American Hardcore* book is now available in five languages.